Following Michigan's Ink Trails

FOLLOWING MICHIGAN'S INK TRAILS

Writing Michigan, Reading Michigan

DAVE DEMPSEY, JACK DEMPSEY, *and* PATRICK DEMPSEY

MICHIGAN STATE UNIVERSITY PRESS | *East Lansing*

Michigan State University Press
East Lansing, Michigan 48823-5245

Library of Congress Cataloging-in-Publication Data
Names: Dempsey, Dave, 1957– author | Dempsey, Jack, 1952– author | Dempsey, Patrick, 1960– author
Title: Following Michigan's ink trails : writing Michigan, reading Michigan / Dave Dempsey, Jack Dempsey, Patrick Dempsey.
Description: East Lansing : Michigan State University Press, 2026. | Includes bibliographic references and index.
Identifiers: LCCN 2026010413 | ISBN 9781611865882 cloth | ISBN 9781611865875 paperback | ISBN 9781609178383 PDF | ISBN 9781628955934 ePub
Subjects: LCSH: Authors, American—Homes and haunts—Michigan | American literature—Michigan | Michigan—In literature | Bookstores—Michigan | Libraries—Michigan | Michigan—Intellectual life | BISAC: LITERARY CRITICISM / American / Regional | TRAVEL / Special Interest / Literary | LCGFT: Literary criticism
Classification: LCC PS283.M5 D473 2026 | DDC 810.9/32774—dc23/eng/20260420
LC record available at https://lccn.loc.gov/2026010413

Cover design by Amanda Frost
Cover art is "Piping Plover," 1834, by Robert Havell after John James Audubon. National Gallery of Art, Washington, DC. CC0 1.0 Universal.

Visit Michigan State University Press at *www.msupress.org*

To our parents and grandparents
—Jack, Dave, and Patrick

All through my boyhood and youth, I was known and pointed out for the
pattern of an idler;
and yet I was always busy on my own private end, which was to learn to write.
I kept always two books in my pocket, one to read, one to write in.

As I walked, my mind was busy fitting what I saw with appropriate words;
when I sat by the roadside, I would either read,
or a pencil and a penny version-book would be in my hand,
to note down the features of the scene or commemorate some halting stanzas.

Thus I lived with words.

—*Robert Louis Stevenson*

Contents

CENTRAL/SOUTH CENTRAL MICHIGAN

SOUTHWEST MICHIGAN

NORTHERN LOWER MICHIGAN

UPPER PENINSULA

PART TWO. ABSOLUTELY EVERYTHING (ALMOST) TO KNOW ABOUT MICHIGAN AND BOOKS

Introduction

In 2012 and 2016, brothers born and raised in Michigan published two books excavating and extolling the state's forgotten literary heritage. The volumes were entitled *Ink Trails*, taking readers on both real and imaginary journeys throughout the peninsulas that uniquely define our state.

Inspired by Michigan's past and looking to a bright future, each brother sat down in his writing den and celebrated prose and poetry created in and/or about the state in line with the highest literary traditions.

We wrote about how Michigan's forests, dunes, farmland, and water have served as a cradle of creativity for the three dozen (plus one) authors profiled. For those most influenced by their Michigan towns or cities, we showed how something special in their communities, as small as a village green or vast as the urban sky, helped foster their art.

As the third love letter to Michigan stories and the authors who wrote them, this book explores the inspiration, passion, and writing that it takes to create a Michigan story. Through in-depth investigative chapters and shorter "squibs," the three authors engage writers as they tell stories, share their love of reading, and give advice for aspiring writers. The book displays Michigan's rich literary legacy to the nation, while also giving students of all stripes an opportunity to learn firsthand how to be inspired to read and write. It reveals intricacies and diversity of stories and storytellers. The inspiring passion and spirit that these authors and poets express through their art is the ultimate learning experience.

After one *Ink Trails* book presentation, a couple revealed how they had taken the volume with them on road trips, saving the relevant chapter for reading at the site where the profiled author had drawn inspiration. They had used it as a guidebook, enriching their lives and appreciation of our state. Exactly our intent. Another reader related that the books had warmed his heart by revealing something new about places that he and his wife had visited and grown fond of. He had gained heightened affection and felt more of a sense of community. Precisely.

Applying this concept as we did to Michigan appears to have been unprecedented. We were unaware of parallel works across the Atlantic, one published in 2000 by the National Trust and authored by Christina Hardyment (*On the Writer's Trail: 20 Great Literary Journeys*; *Literary Trails: British Writers in Their Landscapes*). A $10 purchase in a Lower Peninsula used bookstore opened the page to Hunter Davies's *A Walk Around the Lakes* (London: Weidenfeld and Nicolson, 1979), in which the lives and works of the "Lake Poets" including Samuel Coleridge and William Wordsworth are a key subject during an exploration of England's Lake District. We of Michigan know, of course, that our almost one hundred thousand square miles are a great lake district—with eleven thousand inland lakes and shoreline on four of the five Great Lakes.

Since '16, we have been lobbied by devotees of the Wolverine State's writing legacy for another book. Fans of the prior volumes have contributed suggestions for new studies. Additional justification for this volume lies in the divisiveness and negativity so rampant nowadays and in popular culture's obsessiveness with myths and counter-myths. The lingering effects of the 2020 pandemic continue to cause a different type of shelter-in-place, one within the soul, where wellsprings of hope seem to be running dry. Books, we submit, are essential nutrition for a literacy-benighted world.[1]

To do justice to the names we've collected along the way, and to avoid overtaxing the reader, a number of the chapters in this issue are more in the nature of sketches. We trust these pieces, as well as the lengthier studies, serve as proper accounts. What about those whose words were not written down by them but are original only in oral form? We've not excluded such words, finding the spoken word just as valuable. We've opened up the scope of writers in this volume to include journalists, public figures, and some notable Michiganders who completed few works but whose voice deserves remembrance.

The pens of several writing greats have been stilled in the interval between the second volume and this, and thus Jim Harrison and Elmore Leonard are included. Herein is the person who introduced bookmaking to Michigan, a female Native American who created in her own culture, and a Black female who was the most famous American woman of her day. There is a mystery or two—some reposing in utter obscurity, others who achieved fame and had surprising Michigan connections, including a "little house" link. All found inspiration here for their craft. The result: this volume covers forty-seven authors, more than doubling the coverage of the first two.

Would the average reader have thought in 2011 that three books, examining more than seventy authors, could be published with serious attention paid to each writer? We certainly didn't. It's a real joy to have shined the light on a phase of Michigan's cultural legacy that is too often overlooked. And, as proud descendants of Upper Peninsula stock, the dramatic expansion in the inventory of U.P. authors contained in this volume has been highly gratifying.

The chapters in *Ink Trails* and *Ink Trails II* were organized by geographic area, then alphabetically. We've arranged this volume into two parts. Part one follows the same organization as the previous volumes. Part two builds upon the premise of the series by adding selected literary features that readers will find of benefit on their own trails of discovery. Included are bookshops that enhance the bibliophile's enjoyment—they've done that for us—and public repositories that are well worth visiting. Included is the great inventory of libraries in Michigan that deserve patronage: research institutions like the Bentley, Burton, and Clarke; district libraries; city and community libraries; and some other reservoirs of underappreciated value. The Key to Authors that follows next features a bracketed number to denote in which of the three volumes each author is treated.

In a real sense, the reader encounters a cultural history of Michigan within the pages of these volumes that is a rich part of our great Midwest heritage. It is significant that a serious scholarly effort to resurrect the proud position of the Midwest within American letters has marked the last several decades. Jon K. Lauck's *The Good Country: A History of the American Midwest, 1800–1900* (Norman: University of Oklahoma Press, 2022), is a groundbreaking study of the remarkable land of cultural strength in which Michigan has a proud part. Other works of similar nature are cited within this volume.

As with the previous volumes, this book contains a Notes section, providing sources and other relevant information. It is more extensive than its predecessors by necessity.

This guidebook has been designed for any season of the year, all types of weather, and no matter the reader's mood. Take it with you on the road—whether by motorcar, bus, lorry, bicycle, or on foot.

On a glorious summer evening, you can be touring with the vehicle windows open and stop at a roadside table, perhaps spread your plaid blanket or vintage quilt upon the grass, open up your thermos, pour out a favorite beverage, and be captivated by a writer who found Michigan an exquisite destination in travels through life.

Or you can use it for a journey of the imagination. On, say, a bitter winter's day, evening, or night, you can sit deep and comfortably in your chair before crackling firelight with a cup of cocoa and enjoy dreaming of a writer's den that inspired creative impulse somewhere within this Great Lakes State.

The book you hold will take you into urban centers and down rural back roads. It is suitable for times of melancholy, mirth, and mystique. It will help you to learn and to experience and to be thrilled because, your tour guides contend, so is the case with Michigan itself. Each day in Michigan, we submit, is a precious gift.

Our hope is that readers both new to and familiar with our continuing journey among Michigan's wordsmiths will be inspired to see much more about the connections between this place and the books it has spawned. If so, we all will experience a greater appreciation for who we Michiganders have been and who we are—and who we might become. We will foster a culture where people feel they are part of a place where books matter.

Si quaeris peninsulam, amoenam, circumspice is the state motto: "If you seek a pleasant peninsula, look about you." It is a place "where writers grow," according to an article in *Michigan Blue* magazine in 2014. Rich in diversity as is Michigan, the individuals who populate the three books in this series remind readers to seek and to look, to discover and to grow. As Michigan approaches its sesquicentennial in 2035 (when it qualified for admission to the Union) or in 2037 (when finally achieved), that commemoration will be founded on many aspects of our heritage—with literature high among them.

Happy reading and traveling!

Part One

Famous and Forgotten Authors

Southeast Michigan

Harriette Louisa Simpson (Arnow)

Weedkiller's Daughter

July 7, 1908–March 22, 1986
Lived in Detroit and Ann Arbor

Harriette Louisa Simpson was born in 1908 in Wayne County—Kentucky, not Michigan. In 1944, she and her Jewish husband moved into the wartime workers' public housing development known as Emerson Homes on the east side of Detroit near Mt. Elliott and Nevada Street when Harold took a reporter's job at the *Detroit Times*. A child was born to her in Detroit in December 1946.[1] Because of her husband's love for country living, not hers (she loved cities), the couple moved with their two children to forty acres near Ann Arbor. It was an hour commute for Harold; Harriette remained in near proximity to a vibrant urban center, the kind of community she loved. Here, in a cement floor room connecting house and extension known as "the breezeway," sitting on a wooden milk box, plucking on a manual typewriter, the wife and mother engaged late into the night and early into morning at what she had to do: write fiction.[2]

That storyline is the classic understanding of the Arnow/Michigan connection. Her fame, such as it was and is, grew out of writing about the Kentucky hills and the Cumberland River culture of her family, which she left for good in fall 1934 for Cincinnati. In 1954, *The Dollmaker* was published by Macmillan of New York, becoming a bestseller and National Book Awards finalist. The lengthy novel told of a Kentucky family and its challenges after a move to a Detroit public housing complex during World War II.[3] Gertie Nevels served as an archetype for hundreds of thousands of Southerners who came North as cogs in the great Arsenal of Democracy, churning out tanks and planes to defeat totalitarianism around the globe.

The novel began with a child's ride on a mule, perhaps meant to symbolize the mascot for the U.S. Army—the principal arm of Allied victory. Gertie's first impression of Detroit is at the great portal of the Michigan Central Station as a tightly packed press of people hurry up a long ramp into the cavernous concourse, temporarily separating the family members. "Willer Run" is where workers "a maken big money." The children are impressed by the "million cars" on the streets. A snowstorm prompts a different sentiment. The scene sets up the rest of the novel, in which Detroit proves to be no promised land. Tragedy takes a child's life; the hardships associated with the harsh industrial setting flesh out a bleak plot.[4]

Harriette Simpson's introduction to Michigan preceded 1944–1945. In the summer of 1934, her perspectives broadened thanks to a waitress job at a small summer resort near Petoskey. She remembered it fondly: "I found myself in a delightful world of blue water, blue skies, white birches, stump fences, swamps, and with leisure to enjoy it all." Enjoying the "atmosphere of the place" meant fishing (and consuming fresh lake trout and white fish), boating (canoeing by moonlight), woodland walking, witnessing the northern lights, and encountering the artistry of Native Americans in their "beautiful handiwork, especially baskets and moccasins."[5] Indeed, it was the human factor that proved essential:

> Best of all were the people I got to know—owners, workers, and guests, many of whom were from Michigan and through them I learned something of the many ways of life in the state.

After the tourist season of 1937 ended, she lived rent-free in one of the resort's cottages. The setting enabled Simpson to do something she had yearned to do:

> There, I could write in peace and quiet. The urge to write had grown ever stronger. . . . So, there in a cottage among the birches by a lake, I worked on what was to be my first book, a novel of life in the Kentucky hills.

Working and staying in Michigan also enabled a visit to extended family in the Detroit area. It proved inspirational as she "became acquainted with the city and the surrounding country." She was especially attracted to Ann

Arbor, saying, "My awe of the University of which I had heard so much was almost matched by delight in the tree-filled town with its stately homes; and all around it the farmers' fields in which cattle grazed almost to the city limits. Better yet were the farms out from the town." The end of gas rationing after V-J Day enabled weekend drives and weeklong trips "getting acquainted" with the Arnows' "new homeland" in Michigan, which is how they found the forty acres on a gravel road north of the town where only a chicken house still stood:

> Yet, much remained: ancient fruit trees and a large grape arbor with flowers and shrubs all over. Many of these, especially lilacs and bush honeysuckle, had escaped to grow along the road shoulders with the wild grapes and raspberries, alders, swamp dogwoods, and other native shrubs and vines. Also flourishing in the never-plowed earth of the road shoulders was a succession of wild flowers beginning with marsh marigolds and ending with purple asters. Sometimes equally beautiful were the field flowers in the fence rows and scattered among the grass and clover of the pastures that adjoined our place.

Over time, while she visited great libraries in Ann Arbor and Detroit and dug up artifacts on the farmland dating back to the 1840s, the wheels of an uncaring civilization minimized the bucolic setting, dried up the natural ponds, banished wildlife, and replaced a preserve with "progress." She bemoaned what was going and gone.[6]

Fifteen years after her greatest success, Arnow published *The Weedkiller's Daughter*. Set in a Detroit suburb, the main character was again a woman who clashed with a father far more comfortable with the use of pesticides and plastics in an era of dawning environmental concern. Gertie Nevels appeared again, but the novel focused not on those who left rural homesteads behind but urban dwellers for whom Eden Hills—their community—ought to better represent original conditions in the Book of Genesis. Napalm bombardments were engulfing Asian greenery; American boys were becoming doused with Agent Orange in unprotective Army clothing. Nature was not the enemy, Arnow stressed. Transplants could survive and thrive under the right conditions. Sales of the novel were mediocre (less than fifteen thousand copies in 1970) compared to the multiple printings required for its predecessor. The 1970 book received few reviews when published, not many positive, but Arnow enjoyed the opportunity in an interview to boast that readers had written to say "it's the best book [she's] ever written."[7]

The graves of the Arnows are found back in Kentucky. Harriette died in Ann Arbor in 1986, a year after Harold. On her desk was an incomplete and still unpublished manuscript of a Civil War novel, *Belle*, set in the Bluegrass State. History—not the textbook-derived version—was her igniting fuel, and Detroit's industrial scene "helped Arnow's focus on social and political issues." Her advocacy of civil liberties found expression in an incomplete short story, "The Un-American Activities of Miss Prink," about a schoolteacher in a factory-worker neighborhood who is caught up in the McCarthy red scare of the 1950s. Students and fellow instructors clamor to hear an endorsement of anti-Communist activities, but Miss Prink, grounded on Patrick Henry and the American tradition of freedom of speech, spoke up against the crackdown.[8]

Michigan settings enabled Arnow to portray lives dealing with conflict. The peaceful beauty of the Great Lakes State balanced the ugliness that the world too often enables.

Selected Works

The Dollmaker (1954)
The Weedkiller's Daughter (1969)
The Collected Short Stories of Harriette Simpson Arnow (2005)

Grace Lee Boggs

Detroit Spring

June 27, 1915–October 5, 2015

Intellectual, author, organizer, and community builder in Detroit

Detroit's place in American history as a fertile breeding ground for ideas about the economy, work, and race relations is often overlooked. But if the life and works of Grace Lee Boggs are protected and preserved, that role will persist in American memory.

Born in Providence, Rhode Island, Grace was one of seven children, the daughter of Chin Lee and Yin Lan Ng, both of whom emigrated from China in 1911. Her father was twenty years older than her mother, who was his second wife. Grace described her father as "an old-fashioned tyrant." Grace said he "never saw my mother as an individual, never understood why she was so unhappy or why learning to read and write English and becoming an American in her own name meant so much to her. He never spoke directly to her unless he was shouting back at her."[1]

Grace's mother concluded that American men treated women with greater respect than Chinese men because a white American doctor helped her give birth to Grace's sister on the steerage floor during the voyage to the United States. "As a result," Grace wrote, "she fell in love with America and began dreaming of the day when her children would be grown so that she could go to school to learn how to read and write enough English to become an American citizen in her own right."

Her mother treated Grace "as a symbol of her oppression," which had resulted in a life spent at home tending to the children. Grace added that "the more unhappy she [Grace's mother] became with her life, the more envious she became of mine."

Her father, who arrived in America with fifty cents in his pocket, became a successful entrepreneur, owning and operating a Chinese restaurant in New York City. But it was also in New York City that Grace became aware of racial discrimination. Her father was able to obtain land to build a house only by putting the name of his Irish contractor on the deed; restrictive covenants barred land sales to non-Caucasians. Using the subway en route to school, Grace and her siblings were the object of stares from other passengers, making the children feel something about them was wrong.

Her father's lucrative business provided a middle-class life, and his support of education for his children freed Grace to pursue an advanced degree. Grace's precocious intelligence did the rest. She completed eighth grade before turning twelve. At sixteen, having received a $100 per year scholarship, she enrolled in Manhattan's Barnard College, one of only three students of color.

In 1935, Grace graduated with a bachelor's degree in philosophy, a choice of knowledge that evolved in part from her discovery at age eighteen that as society's assumptions about reality and meaning faltered, individuals "who get an almost voluptuous pleasure from grappling with ideas" embark on the work of developing a new philosophy of meaning. The social suffering of the Depression reinforced her consideration of values. "All I knew was that I was feeling the need to think for myself," she said. "What other people had discovered, what other people thought was no longer enough for me."[2]

A scholarship enabled Grace to attend Bryn Mawr and obtain a doctorate in philosophy in 1940. There were no teaching jobs available to female Chinese Americans in that era. A department store manager told her that the store did not hire "Orientals." Grace moved to Chicago, living rent-free in a small downstairs apartment that teemed with rats. She found a job paying $10 a week at the Philosophy Library of the University of Chicago.

One of Grace's formative experiences as an advocate for change was the proposed March on Washington organized by A. Philip Randolph. In 1941, as U.S. domestic industries ramped up for war and employment boomed, Randolph protested that employers flush with taxpayer money were not hiring Black people in substantial numbers. He threatened to fill Washington with protestors, a prospect unsettling to President Franklin Roosevelt. To head off the march, FDR issued an executive order banning discrimination in the defense industry.

"I learned that a movement begins when large numbers of people, having reached the point where they feel they can't take the way things are any longer, find hope for improving their daily lives in an action they can take together," Grace wrote in her autobiography.[3] Impressed by the power of the Black community to drive change, Boggs decided that "what I wanted to do with the rest of my life was to become a movement activist in the black community."

Grace's ideological journey took her through the Workers Party, the Socialist Workers Party, and the Trotskyite movement. She teamed with the revolutionary C. L. R. James and others in what the *New York Times* called "tortuous dialectical analyses that described the Soviet Union variously as 'a degenerated workers' state,' a 'state capitalist' system and 'autonomous Marxism.'"[4] She read Marx, Hegel, and other philosophers grasping with questions of work and class.

After moving to Detroit to be part of the change fermenting there, Grace invited James "Jimmy" Boggs, an African American Alabama-born author and auto worker to her house for dinner. He complained about the food she served and the music she was playing and then asked her to marry him at the end of the evening. She agreed—to her surprise. Their marriage in 1953 lasted until his 1993 death.

Jimmy Boggs had ridden the rails and worked odd jobs before migrating to Detroit and working in a Chrysler plant, where he would toil for twenty-eight years. He was active in union organizing and desegregation causes. He and Grace forged an intellectual as well as an emotional partnership, eventually becoming better known in other nations than they were in Detroit.

While an activist for a fundamentally new approach to the economy, Jimmy did not operate out of malice against the ideals of his country of birth. Grace wrote that "Jimmy believed revolutions are made out of love for people and for place. He often talked about loving America enough to change it. 'I love this country,' he used to say, 'not only because my ancestors' blood is in the soil but because of what I believe it can become.'" Grace said proudly that "when he [Jimmy] rose to speak his mind, he would speak with such passion, challenging all within hearing to stretch their humanity . . . he would often bring down the house."[5]

For a time, Jimmy and Grace promoted the Black Power movement, hosted Malcolm X, and attacked organized labor for too often collaborating with management. The Federal Bureau of Investigation was said to have tracked them. Writing was central to their thinking and expression. Grace was the author or co-author of nine books, two of which had contributions from Jimmy. She was also author of a featured column in the Black-owned

Michigan Chronicle until her late nineties. "They have established an international reputation as radical thinkers and writers," the *Detroit Free Press* observed in 1975. "They have traveled through much of Europe and Africa on lecture tours. Their books have been translated into French, Italian, Japanese, Spanish, and Catalan."[6]

One of the issues with which Grace constantly struggled was the destructive power of conventional capitalism. At one point in her life, she advocated for its replacement:

> [T]he material abundance produced by rapid economic development has turned the American people, including workers, into mindless and irresponsible consumers, unable to distinguish between our needs and our wants. . . . Our challenge is to continue the evolution of the human race by grappling with the contradiction between our technological and economic overdevelopment and our human and political underdevelopment.[7]

Her thinking evolved as the decades passed with more emphasis on community change. Initially skeptical of the approach pursued by Dr. Martin Luther King Jr., Grace came to embrace nonviolence as she became a catalyst for reform in Detroit. She called the 1955–1956 Montgomery, Alabama, bus boycott one of the first examples in the United States "of two-sided transformation, both of ourselves and of our institutions. Inspired by the twenty-six—year-old King, a people who had been treated as less than human had struggled for more than a year against their dehumanization, not as angry protesters or as workers in the plant, but as members of the Montgomery community, new men and women representing a more human society in evolution."[8]

Grace had little tolerance for a victim mentality among those who, along with their ancestors, had felt the sting of discrimination. She and Jimmy published a pamphlet, "Crime Among Our People." They wrote,

> It is now widely believed that anyone who has been a victim of oppression and who has been imprisoned for anti-social behavior, should not be judged as responsible for his actions, but only as a victim of oppression. . . . Those of us who are serious about transforming our society must evaluate and criticize anti-social behavior and must stop making excuses for actions that are inexcusable.[9]

The first order of business, she said, was to reform oneself. She moved away from talk of an abrupt toppling of the entire economic system to steady community progress toward solutions. "She realized change had not come from within the government or from putting pressure on the institutions of power."[10] She wrote, "If we want to see change in our lives, we have to change things ourselves."

Still, she deplored what she called World War Four, "the Empire of Money' against Humanity. The Empire of Money seeks to impose the logic and practice of capital on everything, to turn every living being, the Earth, our communities, and all our human relationships into commodities to be bought and sold on the market."[11]

At another point, she said:

> The meaning of revolution must also undergo a dialectical change. Fighting on the side of humanity against the empire of money, we need to go beyond opposition, beyond rebellion, beyond resistance, beyond civic insurrection. We don't want to be like them. We don't want to become the political class, to simply change presidents and switch governments.
>
> We want and need to create the other alternative world that is now both possible and necessary. We want and need to exercise power, not take it.[12]

Grace was an organizer of an all-minority ticket on the 1964 general election ballot. She attracted twenty-six votes statewide for her candidacy for the Michigan State University Board of Trees, running under the banner of the Freedom Now Party. She was undaunted, but it was her only try for elective office and intended to make a point, not secure a victory.

Despite her visibility and reputation, the woman who had once been little Grace Lee had difficulty writing about her achievements. Brought up in a Chinese family, she was socialized into thinking of herself only in relationship to others rather than as an individual. As an adult, she was teased for her "passion for anonymity." Commenting on a first draft of her autobiography, an independent reader observed that she was self-effacing to a fault. Grace rewrote the manuscript.

Her most accessible and powerful written work is the autobiography *Living for Change*. She acknowledges mistakes as well as triumphs and reveals herself as a doctrinaire transformed by experience. Studs Terkel , a renowned

American historian and writer, said the book was "more than a deeply moving memoir, this is a book of revelation."

She supported looking at the whole rather than parts, defining common and overarching challenges to a sustainable and humane society. Nearing ninety, she attended an Environmental Justice Symposium in Washington, D.C., where approximately five hundred advocates developed an agenda to combat degradation of the built environment, not simply wilderness areas. Addressing lead poisoning and disproportionate air and water pollution impacts in minority and low-income neighborhoods were among the proposals of the new movement.[13]

The evolution of Grace and James's thinking resulted in two social incubators. In 1992, the Boggs' co-founded Detroit Summer, a community-based youth empowerment and engagement program, described as "an intergenerational, grassroots, multicultural youth collective based at the Boggs Center in Detroit, Michigan, with the goal to empower young people to improve their communities and stand up for what they believe in."[14]

In 2013, Grace established the James and Grace Lee Boggs School, a community-based charter school with a curriculum focused on Detroit. Its mission is "to nurture the transformational leadership capacities of individuals and organizations committed to creating just, productive, conscious, and ecologically sustainable communities."

Her husband died in 1993. Grace had more than two decades of purposeful action remaining. Her reputation grew nationally and internationally. Legendary journalist Bill Moyers interviewed the ninety-two-year-old Grace in 2007 for his Public Broadcasting System show.[15] "In her twilight, Grace Lee Boggs shines brighter than ever," said a reporter.[16]

She lived long enough to see the beginnings of a rebirth for her adopted city.

> Detroit, which was once the symbol of miracles of industrialization and then became the symbol of the devastation of deindustrialization, is now the symbol of a new kind of society, of people who grow their own food, of people who try and help each other, to how we begin to think, not so much of getting jobs and advancing our own fortunes, but how we depend on each other.[17]

Upon her death in 2015, *Detroit Free Press* reporter Nancy Kaffer described Boggs as an "Activist, civil rights pioneer, public intellectual and prolific writer."[18] Saddened by her passing, President Barack Obama said, "Grace dedicated her life to serving and advocating for the rights of others . . . Grace's passion for helping others, and her work to rejuvenate communities that had fallen on hard times spanned her remarkable 100 years of life, and will continue to inspire generations to come."[19]

Selected Works

George Herbert Mead: Philosopher of the Social Individual (1945)
The Invading Socialist Society (1947)
State Capitalism and World Revolution (1950)
Facing Reality (1958)
Revolution and Evolution in the Twentieth Century (1974)
Women and the Movement to Build a New America (1977)
Conversations in Maine: Exploring Our Nation's Future (1978)
Conditions of Peace: An Inquiry: Security, Democracy, Ecology, Economics, Community (1991)
Living for Change: An Autobiography (1998)
The Next American Revolution: Sustainable Activism for the Twenty-First Century (2011)

Elizabeth Margaret Chandler

Voice of Liberation

December 24, 1807–November 2, 1834
Resident of rural Lenawee County

At the top of the gravestone in the family cemetery in Raisin Township, Lenawee County, is a single term representing the inhabitant's vocation and her talent: "Author." According to the Clements Library in Ann Arbor, a more specific title would be "abolitionist writer." A modern-day teacher recorded that "she used her pen to wage war on slavery."[1] Her duration in this state was all of four years, and her move here cost her life. That short time was marked, however, by her launch of the first anti-slavery society in the Territory of Michigan. A marker in Adrian commemorates that legacy, adding how she produced poems to support the abolition movement.[2] She became a member of the inaugural class of honorees when the Michigan Women's Hall of Fame was founded in 1983—in significant part because of her authorship.

Tragedy beset Elizabeth Margaret Chandler early: her mother died soon after Elizabeth's birth and her father when she was nine. Both belonged to the Religious Society of Friends—colloquially known as Quakers. Raised by family in Philadelphia, she attended school until age thirteen. Then began her authorship of items that would be published in newspapers, always unattributed, attaining regularity at age sixteen.

When eighteen years of age, Elizabeth merited recognition for a poem entitled "The Slave Ship" concerning the defiance of a kidnapped African about to be carried in chains across the ocean into a life of servitude.[3] Her Quaker sisterhood, and general sentiment in Philadelphia, contributed to her attention to fighting this evil. Slavery was still lawful in the State of New York until 1827; Delaware, her home state, did not outlaw it until after the Civil

War. Slavery persisted in Pennsylvania, where she grew up, because the 1780 "Gradual Abolition Act" had only freed persons born after that enactment and in certain circumstances. In 1830, the U.S. population approached thirteen million, and more than two million were enslaved. Free Blacks totaled just over three hundred thousand; half lived in the North. She encountered a number of them in the city of brotherly love.

Her poem was republished in *Genius of Universal Emancipation*, an abolitionist newspaper published in Baltimore. Its editor, Benjamin Lundy, brought her aboard in 1829 to edit "The Ladies' Repository" section. She continued in that role, insisting on anonymity, still making contributions to other anti-slavery publications even after moving with her brother Thomas and other family to Michigan in 1830. Lundy claimed she was "one of the most accomplished and powerful female writers of her time." Moreover, "she was the first American female author" to center her writing on the justice and merits of abolishing slavery on the continent.[4]

The Chandler family settled in Logan (later Raisin) Township near a Friends meeting house built by a leading family, the Comstocks.[5] Her brother's farm "was pleasantly situated on the margin of the river Raisin," so pleasant that Elizabeth christened it "Hazlebank" for the sweetness of the locale. It promoted, rather than detracted from, her inspiration to write: "From this, her quiet and secluded retreat, emanated some of the choicest productions of her pen, that have been submitted to the eye of the public. She had contracted a fondness for rural life, and delighted in nature's varied scenery."[6]

Her activities included helping found the Logan Female Anti-Slavery Society in October 1832, for she felt "surely a more important cause has never called upon the energies of the nation."[7] Her effort was aided by Laura and Charles Haviland, who had moved nearby in 1829. Laura Haviland would write of how her family, "with others, united with Elizabeth Margaret Chandler, who organized in our neighborhood the first anti-slavery society in our State." She would also quote her friend and fellow worker in support of the duty of women on the side of righteousness:

> Shall we behold unheeding
> Life's holiest feelings crushed?
> When woman's heart is bleeding,
> Shall woman's voice be hushed?[8]

In the spring of 1834, Elizabeth came down with "a remittent fever"—the term typically employed for malaria or cholera. Although impossible to prove, it is likely that she contracted cholera during an epidemic in which Detroit is estimated to have lost one-seventh of its population. Cholera often proved fatal in an era that had yet to understand the causes of infectious disease.[9] Her decline was gradual but progressive, yet "during the whole period of her protracted affliction she manifested an uninterrupted tranquility of mind, a firm reliance on the truths of Divine revelation, and a perfect resignation to the will of her Heavenly Master."[10] She died in November at age twenty-six.

The last stanza of the last article she sent in to the *Genius* focused on the evil against which she had devoted most of her writing:

Prayer! for those who, day by day,
Weep their bitter lives away;
Prayer, for those who bind the chain
Rudely on their throbbing vein,
That repentance deep may win
Pardon for the fearful sin!"

One of her works serves as a fitting conclusion to a rich life cut short:

The Sylvan Grave.
Lay me not, when I die, in the place of the dead,
With the dwellings of men round my resting place spread,
But amidst the still forest, unseen and alone,
Where the waters go by with a murmuring tone;
Where the wild bird above me may wave its dark wing,
And the flowers I have loved from my ashes may spring;
Where affection's own blossom may lift its blue eye,
With an eloquent glance from the place where I lie.
Let the rose and the woodbine be there, to enwreath
A bright chaplet of bloom for the pale brow of death;
And the clover's red blossom be seen, that the hum
Of the honey-bee's wing, may for requiem come:
And when those I have loved, 'midst the changes of earth,

The clouds of its sorrow, its sunshine of mirth,
Shall visit the spot where my cold relics lie,
And gaze on its flowers with a tear-moisten'd eye—
Let them think that my spirit still sometimes is there,
My breath the light zephyr that twines in their hair,
And these flowers, in their fragrance, a memory be,
To tell them thus sweet was their friendship to me.[11]

The cemetery is on private land, in a field south of East Valley Road and east of Breckel Highway.

In October 1853, renowned anti-slavery activist William Lloyd Garrison disembarked at the depot in Adrian on a tour of Midwest engagements. Thomas Chandler greeted and took Garrison to his home to enjoy "the cordiality of Western hospitality." After several lectures and before departing for further appearances in Detroit, the publisher of *The Liberator* "spent an hour alone at the grave of Elizabeth . . . and pencilled a sonnet on the post of the railing erected around the deceased, expressive of my estimate of her virtues, and the feelings of my heart." In a letter to his wife, Garrison waxed poignantly about the site where Chandler's aunt also was interred:

> They are buried on a rising elevation in a large wheat field, which is seen conspicuously at a considerable distance—half a dozen young and thrifty oak trees standing in a row on one side of the enclosure. To me it was hallowed ground, and, while standing there, I renewed my pledge of fidelity to the cause of the enslaved while life continues.[12]

A dozen more years would pass before that cause reached its fulfillment.

When rain falls on the free soil of Michigan covering her grave, it helps renew the sources of the meandering *La Rivière aux Raisins* that gathers nearby, a stanza by the "Author" capturing the contentment inherent in knowing that all things work together for good to those who love:

The verdant sod around my feet,
The treasure of its flowers may spread,
And close embowering branches meet,
In fresh'ning coolness, o'er my head.[13]

Selected Works

Ladies' Repository columns in *Genius of Universal Emancipation* published as Benjamin Lundy ed., *Original Essays, Documents and Facts Relative to the Subject of African Slavery*, Vols. I–III (1830–1833)

The Poetical Works of Elizabeth Margaret Chandler with a Memoir of Her Life and Character (1836)

Godfrey Dell Eaton

Brutally Blunt Iconoclast

October 11, 1894–June 16, 1930
Born in Plymouth; lived in Jackson, Redford, and downtown sections of Detroit; University of Michigan–Ann Arbor graduate

> Died. Geoffrey Dell Eaton, 36, founder-editor of the young critical magazine *Plain Talk*, onetime literary editor of the *New York Morning Telegraph*; of heart disease; in Manhattan.

Time magazine reported this sad news in a survey of the day's memorable events involving births, marriages, and engagements. It did not mention Eaton's authorship of a controversial book, praised in 1941 as "a milestone in the development of American realism." A major New York house had published it in 1925, crediting "G. D. Eaton" as author. The obit mentioned nothing of his background before New York City. It also got his first name wrong, which was Godfrey; he merely went by Geoffrey.

The milestone book, *Backfurrow*, disappeared almost immediately after publication, thanks to its publisher. Such an incongruous outcome can only come from perfidy, one might believe. Actually, George Haven Putnam, publisher and owner of G. P. Putnam's Sons of New York, returned from abroad to find a manuscript on his desk that criticized rural manners and morals with vigor. Negotiations produced a few edits, but the author refused to back down from the essence of his views. Putnam lived up to the letter of their contract; he printed the book with the minimum of publicity. Then, he blocked further marketing and essentially killed sales. The author soon turned to an outlet in which he had more control over the final outcome of his work.

Plain Talk became the platform. In the first issue released in October 1927, editor Eaton described the new periodical's purpose:

> What! Another Magazine?
>
> Even so. And, what is worse, a magazine with a mission, dedicated within the limits of human fallibilities and prejudices, to Tolerance, and naturally to locking horns with Intolerance. To this end it will be inconsistent, foolish, incongruous, unreasonable, good-humored, bad humored and even hodge-podge, but never dull. It will be even more an aim with us to be interesting than to be tolerant—and our muttered prayer is that liveliness won't conflict with tolerance. We have never liked double funerals.
>
> We shall sincerely try to make you laugh over one article, grow thoughtful over another and denounce us with a thousand damns at the third. The editor issues a standing invitation for you to come up and shoot him, and says that if you mistake one of the publishers for the editor, so much the better—one less boss.

With humor and irony, Eaton went on to explain his enlistment "in the fight to preserve individualism in this country." Here was a lover of words who sought to defend freedom of expression and to eschew writing anything "flannel-mouthed or insipid."[1]

How came this barely thirty-year-old to be in such a position? In 1900, he and father William, a druggist; mother Mary (Staneback); and younger brothers Harold W. (age four) and Rudolph W. (age two) lived on Sixth Street in Jackson. William died in 1912 and was buried in Detroit's Grand Lawn Cemetery. The draft card G.D. filled out in June 1917 gave his address at 44 Sibley, working as office manager for the Fred M. Foster (Truck) Company of Detroit.[2] He described himself as tall, slender, dark blue–eyed with light brown hair. His service records show he was inducted into the U.S. Army on March 5, 1918, in Detroit, trained at Camp Greenleaf on the Chickamauga Civil War battlefield, and was discharged in May 1919 because of illness. He carried the rank of Private First Class and appears to have been a hospital attendant at Camp Merritt, New Jersey, without going overseas. A flu epidemic took many ill in late 1918, perhaps contributing to his own illness.

After the war, Eaton entered the University of Michigan. He was on the staff of *The Michigan Chimes*, a "magazine of campus opinion." The next semester he reported for the university's summer school newspaper, *The Wolverine*, and became its literary editor in the following school year while "arousing the campus" by making his own "contributions to well-known magazines." The following year found him again the summer literary editor.[3]

As a member of the class of 1923, he graduated in June, a Phi Beta Kappa honoree in the Literary College. In December, it was announced that he had accepted a position at Scribner's, the world-famous New York publisher, "editing and advertising language text-books."

This history failed to reveal the underlying tenor of his collegiate career. An alumni publication noted his undergraduate status as "Campus *enfant terrible* for some time."[4] The university banned Eaton from campus publications more than once. The first occasion arose from an article in the *Daily* on the Great War in which he charged most professors of history with being "senile, simple and misguided asses." *Backfurrow* earned him yet another embargo after the head of student publications remembered the three-year-old ban and re-imposed it. Eaton reacted by launching *The Tempest*, "a fiery little magazine, which appeared twice a month until he graduated and attacked the university administration outrightly." The administration regarded him as a radical and "an enemy of society." Most students had a different take, because of the "certain saving grace of humor in his articles." The greater part of the faculty also enjoyed Eaton's work because of its high scholarship.[5]

His alumni weekly reviewed Eaton's first novel with praise:

> *Backfurrow* is distinctly a farm novel, devoted to the celebration of all that is monotonous and drear in present-day life on a small farm. This is its aim, and it is successful. It is written without gloss and without glamor; it belongs to the documentary type of literature that is determined to see honestly and to expose fearlessly the less-often-explored corners of contemporary life.
>
> *Backfurrow* is an earnest piece of work; it is solid, "all of a piece." Its matter and its manner are so much a part of each other that they must have grown together. The book is crude, strong, unlovely; it is a flower of the soil of the American small farm.

Other critics gave the farm novel varying grades. H. L. Mencken concluded: "There is not much finesse in the story, but it is moving. Few first novels show so much seriousness or so much skill."[6] Others regarded it as a worthy successor to the American naturalism movement expressed in Edgar Lee Masters's *Spoon River Anthology* and Sherwood Anderson's *Winesburg, Ohio*. Eaton's work debunked the unblinking view of farm life as virtuous due to its "hymn of hate" and pessimism.[7] Another critic called it "mediocre" and "grim."[8] The book "described the frustration of the small farmers in mid-Michigan" overcome only via illicit living.[9] A less pejorative review called it "proletariat," even though Eaton was no communist. It was not "propaganda," said another critic, but fiction "strongly built, highly unified in its essential nature as narrative. It is a good novel, remarkable for the number and variety of its characters and for the vividness of its total impression."[10]

The setting for a "fight for existence" was far from bucolic, introduced with the first sentence:

> In a cluster of hills of mid-Michigan lay a fifty acre farm, with the original old worm rail fences marking it off from the neighboring and larger farms, which stood on more level ground, the slopes bordering the small farm being left to wood lots. These gave it an added touch of isolation which was hardly relieved by the double row of trees flanking the narrow and seldom traveled road that marked the western limits of the farm.

An old house with rickety porches, cracked and broken windows, loose shingles, and rotten odors rounded out the location. The poorly dressed protagonist was atypical for mainstream novels: "the boy had not been born of wedlock." It ended as it began, in melancholy, the boy now a man, gazing blankly as he remembered people from his past, being called in from the porch to dinner and finally, silently relenting.

In January 1927, Eaton penned "Not Generally Known" for *McNaught's Monthly*, an article launching his monthly contribution to the independent review publication. The item surveyed developments in the literary world. The issue also reported that a piece Eaton had written "on the abolition movement is awaiting publication," a follow-up to December when his writing had been misinterpreted as a defense of slavery. A letter to the editor from Battle Creek (and another from New York City) took Eaton to task for his viewpoint. Eaton had recently excoriated higher education in the *Telegraph*, accusing Harvard, Princeton, and other colleges with using entrance requirements to exclude persons of Jewish, Italian, and African ancestry. He did not mince criticism of a slanted academic atmosphere: "As state after state, especially in the South, falls before the poltroonish attacks of dunghill dumbbells, the educational situation will become so obviously bad that every civilized man will go abroad for his training."[11] In April, *American Mercury* published his story on Harriet Beecher Stowe exposing her rise and collapse as a literary star.

Eaton likely wrote his own biography for a page in *Plain Talk*, justifying his hiring:

> He was born in Plymouth, Michigan, in 1894, and went to the Detroit public schools, but after two years in high school there his father's death threw him into journalism, and he worked on Detroit newspapers until the United States entered the Great War. He served with a great deal of heroism for a year and a half on the New Jersey front, after which horrors of war he returned to Detroit in a pacifistic state of mind.
>
> He entered the University of Michigan in the fall of 1919—and the war really started! His articles in the *Michigan Daily*, the campus newspaper, threw the students and faculty into an uproar, and in 1922, following an article in the *Smart Set* magazine—then under the editorship of H. L. Mencken and George Jean Nathan—on the University of Michigan, he was badly beaten one night by two men, one of them a member of the Varsity football team.

It also mentioned working for the Associated Press upon his arrival in New York. A less tongue-in-cheek recital appeared as an epitaph in the same graduate publication that had followed his short career:

> Death came after an illness of a few weeks, and was caused by paralysis and heart failure.
>
> Mr. Eaton was a native of Plymouth, Michigan, and entered the University in 1919, after having served during the World War. He came to college with his health impaired by service, and his mind embittered. Almost at once he achieved notoriety for himself by writing violent letters appearing in the *Daily* under the initials G.D.E. A fearless opponent of complacency, G. D. Eaton drew down upon his head the wrath of many prominent faculty members. By the student body he was either admired for his courage, or despised as a radical, but no one remained neutral. In 1923 he was elected to Phi Beta Kappa, an honor which he refused with a gesture of disdain. He had voiced his opinion of honor societies more than once, and he did not alter this opinion. In 1923 he was graduated with honors. These he could not refuse. Shortly after he left college his novel, *Back Furrow*, appeared, an autobiographical work, tainted with the bitterness which never left him. For a time he was on the staff of the Associated Press in New York City, and

contributed to magazines, notably the *American Mercury*, but for the last three years has devoted all of his time to the development of *Plain Talk*.[12]

Eaton was yet another victim of the War to End All Wars. He had been sent to university by the U.S. government "because of disabilities incurred during the war." He stood first academically among the 240 veterans so supported, and he graduated in the top 5 percent of his class of 1,800.[13]

G. D. Eaton was buried in section 16 of Detroit's Grand Lawn Cemetery. His gravestone is an accurate record—except for its last line:

Novelist, Journalist, Book Critic, Linguist
Founder Of "Plain Talk" Magazine
Born In Plymouth, Mich. Oct. 11, 1894
Died In New York, N.Y. June 6, 1930
U.S. Veteran Of Foreign Wars

His mother, to whom he had dedicated *Backfurrow*, outlived him and, most likely, included the last line. Her son might not have crossed the Atlantic, but she apparently felt his premature death came about because he did, indeed, answer—and was changed by—the call of his country to serve.

Selected Works

Backfurrow (1925)

J. Oscar Frenette

The Great Voice of the Good Historian

May 21, 1926–December 8, 1997
Lived in Bloomfield Hills, worked in Detroit

An audiobook is one that is not eyeballed; it is heard as a voice recording of a book. The text is read by the author, a celebrity, a trained talent, or—in the age of AI—a "bot" with the capability to mimic the synergy of human voice. The book is accessed not by the holding and physical turning of pages but by mechanical functioning: the technology of a phonograph record, cassette tape, compact disc, the internet, or electronic means of some sort. In 1986, the Audio Publishers Association formed to advance the growth of the new medium. Audible, Spotify, and other formats have been increasing in usage. In 2021, a quarter of the American population listened to at least one audiobook. It is not just a function of a busy society, for many patrons simply enjoy a good listen.

Some sources claim Dickens's *A Christmas Carol* was the first audiobook—that is, the first book read aloud over radio. Perhaps the most infamous is the radio play broadcast on October 30, 1938, by the Mercury Theater, Orson Welles directing, of H. G. Wells's *The War of the Worlds*. Perhaps the record for the longest audiobook reading tenure belonged to Dick Estell (1926–2016), "the Radio Reader" of WKAR-FM in East Lansing, whose voicing of book texts for a half-century gave pleasure to many thousands of public broadcasting listeners. WJR-AM of Detroit, broadcasting from the Golden Tower of the Fisher Building in midtown Detroit as "The Great Voice of The Great Lakes," celebrated its centennial in 2022. Edgar A. Guest was one of its early talents, and the station maintains a tradition of airing much local content. With a signal reaching Cape Cod and Puget Sound,[1] it has long carried stories of the Great Lakes to a wide audience.

In June 1967, a native of Sudbury, Ontario, joined the station after stints at WSOO-AM in Sault Ste. Marie and WPON-AM in Pontiac. With a uniquely authoritative voice, Oscar Frenette served in various capacities on both sides of the microphone, including public affairs director. According to his nomination to the Michigan Journalism Hall of Fame, though, "the 'gem' of Mr. Frenette's on-air work has been 'Sketches of Life and Things in the Great Lakes Area,' for which he has earned the reputation as Michigan's poet of the airwaves." The program had achieved status as "an important historical and educational feature."[2] It, and the sonorous voice that read its scripts, was so familiar to the radio audience that another recipient of such honors, Dick Purtan, featured a lampoon of "Sketches" on his own FM radio show for a number of years.[3]

Those all-caps scripts fill a banker's box at the Bentley Historical Library, proof that Frenette wrote hundreds and carefully researched and edited each before airing. More than one file is labeled "possible," for many stories remained when he left WJR in 1994. Three years later, he died at age seventy-one. Recipient of many accolades, Frenette had been invited to the Board of the Historical Society of Michigan in 1982, and he contributed several articles to its *Chronicle* publication. One entitled "The Fascination of History" began: "History is full of mystery and drama and adventure." Long after his school days, Frenette had become intrigued with history, and the nation's bicentennial commemoration helped spur that interest. Many WJR Sketches intentionally "had a historical flavor," requiring a significant investment of time and energy: "A daily feature on radio is similar to doing a daily column in a newspaper. It requires a great deal of research and at first I wasn't sure how long I could keep it up. But the interest grew with the learning." The combination of voice, study, and writing contributed to each program becoming a "theater of the mind," according to a colleague. In one, Frenette "literally walked the listener through the beauty of Cranbrook gardens with the chief gardener. You could see the flowers and you could see the rolling hills."[4]

His subjects were wide-ranging. A number spoke of attributes of the Great Lakes such as its lighthouses and several on its tree species; one extolling a "two-nation vacation"; another on unusual place names; a meditation on the Northwoods of Michigan; one referencing the St. Clair Flats; and several on various aspects of the Detroit area such as Elmwood Cemetery, the log cabin in Palmer Park, and the unimpressive two-story white frame house occupied by Ulysses S. Grant in the 1840s. Frenette called attention to the upper state in several stories, one about the ghost town of Victoria in the Ontonagon

River area and the famous "Copper Boulder." He celebrated that it was home to two of Michigan's human-made wonders—the Mackinac Bridge and Soo Locks—and six of its eight "natural wonders": Mackinac Island, Pictured Rocks, Tahquamenon Falls, Keweenaw Peninsula and Brockway Mountain Drive, Porcupine Mountains and Lake of the Clouds, and Isle Royale. One of Frenette's tales celebrated Annie "Big Annie" Clemenc, a twenty-five-year-old woman who helped rally the Calumet community behind the copper miners of the Keweenaw during their 1913 strike. Annie's tale became the centerpiece of *Women of the Copper Country* by Mary Doria Russell, which was chosen by Michigan Humanities for the 2021–2022 Great Michigan Read. The program aims to connect Michigan residents by deepening readers' understanding of Michigan and its society and humanity.

Frenette bragged about the state's roadside parks (a State historical marker near Iron River marks "quite likely America's first such facility"). He wrote "Detroit During the War of Independence" and the "Johnston Encampment at the Soo in '92" for the *Chronicle*. He shared the discovery that he lived in an area that was "a constantly changing panorama," reaching from prehistory through "the clash of cultures between the Europeans and the native Americans" to the "dynamic" forces changing "the landscape for good and bad."[5]

A modest home on Tullamore Drive in Bloomfield Hills spoke of the humility with which he approached his work and community service. Among other causes, he volunteered for the Board of the Detroit Historical Society in 1982 to restore Fair Lane, the Henry and Clara Ford home in Dearborn. The American Bar Association and the National Conference of Christians and Jews paid him tribute for advancing understanding and eradicating prejudice in human relations.

The young Frenette would have been shocked to find that history no longer "was a bore" to the elder version. Everything—town, building, place—"has a story." For two decades, he wrote and read those stories over the airwaves, enlivening the appreciation of listeners for the heritage of lands and lakes that is, for those with ears to hear, simply fascinating.

Robert Hayden

The Freedom to Respond to Life in His Own Way

August 4, 1913–February 25, 1980
Received bachelor's degree from Wayne University (today Wayne State University) and master's degree from the University of Michigan, was professor of English literature at the University of Michigan

The story of Robert Hayden is that of a gifted man who fell in love with poetry while still a teen and knew he wanted to be a poet. He said years later that he didn't choose to be a poet any more than he chose to be born. Growing up as a Black man from a broken home among modest economic circumstances in the early decades of the twentieth century, he faced numerous obstacles throughout his life, yet he never complained. He worked diligently at his art in obscurity and finally received his due as a major American poet after years of toil.

Hayden learned essential lessons about human nature as a youth in Detroit and was educated in its public schools and at universities in Detroit and Ann Arbor. He came home to Michigan to cap his professional career at the University of Michigan. He felt freer here than in the South, where he taught for two decades, and his heart was always in Michigan. Today, he is buried here, his journey completed.

Robert Hayden was born Asa Bundy Sheffey on August 4, 1913, in Detroit. His birth parents, Asa and Ruth Sheffey, divorced, and at age two his mother placed him with neighbors, William and Sue Hayden, when she departed Detroit to search for work in Buffalo, New York. The Haydens acted as foster parents, renamed him Robert Earl Hayden, and brought him up as their own son.

Hayden grew up in the Paradise Valley section of the east side of Detroit, near St. Antoine Street. Though the area was mostly inhabited by African Americans, there were also Germans, Italians, and Jewish people in his diverse neighborhood. His foster family was, to use his own word, poor. He helped his foster father deliver coal from a horse-drawn wagon and later remembered standing in line for sacks of flour. The memory was humiliating. Of the neighborhood, his feelings were mixed. He recalled learning at a young age about the good and bad sides of humanity:

> [G]hetto life as I knew it was full of contrasts. Violence and ugliness and cruelty. We kids were exposed to the grim realities . . . in spite of all our elders could do to protect us. But there was beauty, there was gentleness too. There was a vividness of life, an intensity of being. . . . And there were people who retained . . . a sheltering spiritual beauty and dignity—my mother and my foster father among them—despite sordid and disheartening circumstances. I love the memory of those people.[1]

His experiences while growing up in Detroit were the basis for numerous poems including "The Rabbi," "Homage to the Empress of the Blues" (based on a performance by famed singer Bessie Smith at a local theater), "Witch Doctor" (about a corrupt local preacher), and "Mourning Poem for the Queen of Sunday" (the story of a woman who sings in a church choir who dies from bullet wounds). He paints a vivid picture of the neighborhood in his poem "'Summertime and the Living . . . '":

> No roses there in summer—
> oh, never roses except when people died—
> and no vacations for his elders,
> so harshened after each unrelenting day
> that they were shouting-angry.
> But summer was, they said, the poor folks' time
> of year. And he remembers
> how they would sit on broken steps amid
>
> The fevered tossings of the dusk, the dark,
> wafting hearsay with funeral-parlor fans
> or making evening solemn by
> their quietness. Feels their Mosaic eyes
> upon him, though the florist roses
> that only sorrow could afford
> long since have bidden them Godspeed.

A source of tension in the neighborhood was "the menace of white authority—policemen, welfare workers, landlords. We were at their mercy, and they didn't see us as human beings."[2] In his poem "Elegies for Paradise Valley," he writes:

> I saw the hatred for our kind
> glistening like tears
> in the policemen's eyes.

On occasion, his birth mother would return to Detroit to visit young Robert, or he would visit her in Buffalo. He described her as beautiful and said she encouraged his bookishness, though she was not well educated. He had no relationship with his natural father, whom he met only once on a visit to Gary, Indiana.[3] Of his foster father, he wrote in "Those Winter Sundays":

> I'd wake and hear the cold splintering, breaking.
> When the rooms were warm, he'd call,
> and slowly I would rise and dress,
> fearing the chronic angers of that house,
>
> Speaking indifferently to him,
> who had driven out the cold
> and polished my good shoes as well.
> What did I know, what did I know
> of love's austere and lonely offices?

Life in his household was not easy. His foster mother, trapped in an unhappy marriage, inflicted her anger on Robert by whipping him. Of his home life, he later said, "worse than the poverty were the conflicts, the quarreling, the tensions that kept us most of the time on the edge of some shrill domestic calamity. . . . We had a terrible love-hate relationship with one another, and dreadful things happened I can never forget. They turned me in upon myself."[4]

He describes corporal punishment in his poem "The Whipping":

> She strikes and strikes the shrilly circling
> boy till the stick breaks
> in her hand. His tears are rainy weather
> to woundlike memories:

My head gripped in bony vise
of knees, the writhing struggle
to wrench free, the blows, the fear
worse than blows that hateful

Words could bring, the face that I
no longer knew or loved. . . .
Well, it is over now, it is over,
and the boy sobs in his room,

And the woman leans muttering against
a tree, exhausted, purged—
avenged in part for lifelong hidings
she has had to bear.

Born with poor eyesight, Robert wore thick eyeglasses, and was unable to play games outside with other children in the neighborhood. He sought solace from a young age in books borrowed from the library, reading fanatically. He began writing stories and plays by age twelve. In his teens, he started reading poetry, then composing his own poems, and became obsessed, preferring it to fiction and drama. In an unfinished autobiography, he wrote that he turned to poetry after being called "sissy," "four-eyes," and racial slurs.[5]

After graduating from Northern High School in 1930, he obtained a scholarship to the College of the City of Detroit (later Wayne University, today Wayne State University) and studied there beginning in 1932. He majored in Spanish (he described himself as "intensely interested in Latin America, in everything Spanish"),[6] wrote and directed plays, and continued writing his poetry. After he had completed all but one course toward his degree, Hayden began working for the Federal Writers Project, part of the Works Project Administration, interviewing former slaves in Michigan.[7]

One of Hayden's favorite poets was African American: the renowned Langston Hughes. A key event in Hayden's life occurred when a friend arranged for Hayden and Hughes to meet for lunch while Hughes was in Detroit. Hayden showed his poetry to Hughes, who told him his poetry displayed talent but lacked individuality. Nonetheless, Hayden was encouraged and continued writing.

Meanwhile, Hayden wrote music and drama criticism for the *Michigan Chronicle*, a weekly newspaper concentrating on African American news. In the summer of 1938, he began attending classes for a master's degree in English literature at the University of Michigan in Ann Arbor, before returning to work in the autumn. He would continue studying there during succeeding summers.[8]

Two significant events occurred in Hayden's life in 1940. First, a volume of his poems titled *Heart-Shape in the Dust* was published in pamphlet form. Though the poems were good, they displayed socialist political leanings in their depiction of the life of the working class, and Hayden would later renounce them. Second, he married Erma Morris. Erma was a pianist and piano instructor, and the two shared an interest in the arts.

The following year, in the autumn of 1941, Hayden began school full time in Ann Arbor. He studied under the famous English poet W. H. Auden, who was teaching at the university during the 1941–1942 school year. Auden advised Hayden to abandon writing poems with political themes and to incorporate more symbolism into his poems to demand more from his readers. His poems became more profound as a result of Auden's tutelage. In 1971, Hayden described Auden as "undoubtedly the greatest poet writing in English today."[9]

While at Michigan, Hayden won two Hopwood Awards for poetry, named after a university alumnus, Avery Hopwood, who became a successful Broadway playwright and who endowed the awards at the school. The awards gave him much-needed confidence. Hayden knew two other students who would become prominent writers: the playwright Arthur Miller and Kenneth Millar, who would go on to write detective fiction under the pseudonym Ross Macdonald.

In 1942, Erma gave birth to their daughter, Maia. The Haydens lived variously at 326 Beakes, 722 Haven, and 204 S. State in Ann Arbor. In 1944, Hayden was awarded a bachelor of arts in Spanish from the now-renamed Wayne University and a master's degree from the University of Michigan. The latter gave him a fellowship, and he made his living teaching from 1944 to 1946.

In 1946, Hayden was offered a position teaching creative writing and English literature at Fisk University, a predominantly African American institution, in Nashville, Tennessee. Reluctantly, he accepted. Years later, he remarked that "although I had experienced segregation in Michigan, I was appalled by the southern brand, which I thought worse because it drew the lines between black and white so much more sharply, made everyone conscious of race in an unhealthy, a nasty way. It was obscene, dehumanizing."[10] His poem "Tour 5" recounts a journey by car on Southern roads, during which the narrator—Hayden himself—feels the searing, unspoken hatred of a White service station attendant for Hayden and his dark skin.

> We stop a moment in a town
> watched over by Confederate sentinels,
> buy gas and ask directions of a rawboned man
> whose eyes revile us as the enemy.
>
> Shrill gorgon silence breathes behind
> his taut civility
> and in the ever-tautening air,
> dark for us despite its Indian summer glow.

By this time, Hayden had evolved his own theory of poetry. "I see things as symbolic, and I think of my poems as a way of coming to grips with reality," he said in a 1976 interview with journalist Jo Thomas. "All the great prophets of the world have spoken in poetic terms. The only way to explain great truths is to express them in metaphorical terms."[11] He saw poetry as more than the expression of an emotion: "the rhythm, the images, the connotations of words, the tone, are all essential parts of the meaning. . . . [W]hat a poem says is really not more important than *how* it makes its statement."[12] Further, "a poem should have silences. For me the silences of a poem are as meaningful as its sounds. All my best poems have silences in them. There are things in them that are not expressed, that are all the more strongly suggested because they are not stated."[13] He revised and rewrote his poems extensively, sometimes taking years to polish them to perfection.

In the 1940s, Erma and Robert, who was brought up in the Baptist church, became members of the Baha'i faith. According to Hayden, Baha'i members believe in the "oneness of mankind and the oneness of all religions." He said that the Baha'i faith "asks you to change yourself. You don't see things in political, but in spiritual and human terms." He observed that "the real revolution has to be an inner, spiritual revolution." He said that Baha'is believe that after a period of great turmoil, "would come a new society, a new social order characterized by justice for all, a new vision of mankind." He said that his religion occupied a central place in his life and influenced his poetry.[14]

In 1948, Hayden co-wrote a book of thirteen poems with Myron O'Higgins titled *The Lion and the Archer*. A *New York Times* reviewer took notice, praising both poets. The next collection of his poems was not published until 1955 and a longer volume was published in 1962. In the meantime, Hayden continued teaching at Fisk, where he was promoted to associate professor, and writing poetry, but both were full-time occupations, and the burden was enormous. During this period, he sometimes grew despondent. In letters to Langston Hughes, who was now a friend, he described himself as "doomed to be a pamphlet poet, a periphery poet," and "discouraged."[15]

Another disappointment followed. In 1966, Fisk University hosted a Black Writers Conference. Hayden came under criticism from some participants for not devoting his poetry to civil rights and for not being militant in his poems about the search for equality for his people. Hayden defended himself by arguing that he was a poet for all of humanity, not just Blacks, and that artists must be free to choose their own subject matter. "As a poet, I want the freedom to respond to my life in my own way," he insisted. He defined himself "as a poet first. I don't want to make a political issue out of the fact that I'm black. I'm not a separatist or a nationalist. I believe in bringing people together."[16] Years later, the memory of the criticism would send him into a private rage.

Ironically, some of his most famous poems deal with the Black American experience. "Middle Passage" explores the rebellion of Cinquez on the Amistad, "The Ballad of Nat Turner" is the first-person narration by the leader of a slave revolt, "Runagate Runagate" depicts a slave escaping to freedom in the North ("And before I'll be a slave / I'll be buried in my grave"), "Frederick Douglass" exalts its subject, and "El-Hajj Malik El-Shabazz" is a poem about Malcolm X.

Also in 1966, Hayden was awarded the Grand Prize in Poetry at the First World Festival of Negro Arts in Dakar, Senegal. And for the first time, a volume of his poems, *Selected Poems*, was published by a major American publishing house. His poetry began to attract the attention it deserved.

In 1969, he returned home and became professor of English literature at the University of Michigan. New collections of his poems were published in 1970, 1972, 1975, and 1978. He served as the consultant in poetry to the Library of Congress, what is now termed the Poet Laureate of the United States, and was the first Black to be so honored, from 1976 to 1978. Other honors included the Russell Loines Award for poetry from the National Institute of Arts and

Letters in 1970, election as a fellow into the Academy of American Poets in 1975, induction into the American Academy of Arts and Letters in 1979, and several honorary doctorates. He was celebrated alongside other American poets at a White House reception hosted by President Carter and his wife Rosalynn in January 1980.

Late in life, for all that he had endured, Hayden was not bitter about his own struggles or that of his people. He remarked, "I have a great belief in America as a kind of microcosm. All the races and all the cultures seem to meet in this country. . . . One can see the great diversity and the things that bind us and make us one."[17]

On February 24, 1980, the University of Michigan honored its star poet by hosting a conference on Robert Hayden, featuring readings of his poetry, discussions of their meaning, and music and a play based on his poems. Hayden, who was suffering from cancer, was unable to attend, but when a number of attendees stopped by his house later, he left his sickbed and greeted them. He died the next evening. Hayden is buried in Fairview Cemetery in Ann Arbor. His house at 1201 Gardner was granted historic status by the City of Ann Arbor in 2023.

Upon his death, his University of Michigan colleague, professor of English literature Laurence Goldstein, wrote that "Hayden ranked among the greatest of contemporary poets of any color."[18] Robert Pinsky, who served as U.S. Poet Laureate from 1997 to 2000, observed in 2024 that Hayden's poetry was "masterful, profound work" and showed "greatness of spirit."[19] Robert Hayden, who had set out in life feeling unwanted by family and society, who had made it his life's mission to become a poet of distinction, had finally gained the acceptance of his peers.

Selected Works

Heart-Shape in the Dust (1940)
The Lion and the Archer (1948)
Figure of Time: Poems (1955)
A Ballad of Remembrance (1962)
Selected Poems (1966)
Words in the Mourning Time (1970)

The Night-Blooming Cereus (1972)
Angle of Ascent: New and Selected Poems (1975)
American Journal (1978, 1982)
Collected Prose (1984)
Collected Poems (1985)

Caroline Mathilda Stansbury (Kirkland)

Can You Go Home Again?

January 11, 1801–April 6, 1864

Moved to Detroit, settled Pinckney in the 1830s, wrote about early Michigan

After westward migrators initially bypassed its southern tier as too swampy to settle, Michigan became a "boom" destination once the falsehood was exploded in the 1830s. All kinds of interested parties were drawn here: speculators, sons who would not inherit their father's farm, families seeking a new start to an unsuccessful life. Among them came a married couple who, on the surface, seemed unlikely to leave the Northeast for the uncertainty of the wild Midwest (then known as "the Northwest" or, simply, West).

Caroline Mathilda Stansbury was born in 1801 in New York City to a prominent family, eldest of eleven children, with a mother of literary ability. She had attended a fine school for young women and excelled scholastically, knew French, German, Italian, and Latin, and "was one of the very best educated women in America."[1] William Kirkland had been born in 1800. He graduated from Hamilton College in 1818, taught there as a tutor, and opened a school in Geneva in the Finger Lakes region of New York in 1828. Their marriage on January 10, 1828, presaged academic pursuits. Two children were born in New York, two in Michigan.

In 1835, William Kirkland accepted the job of principal for the new Detroit Female Seminary, and the family of six moved to the growing city on the strait. Enlarged with the birth of a daughter there on August 19, 1835, the Kirkland contingent soon began acquiring land in Livingston County and, by end of 1836, owned eight hundred acres. William's father owned another five hundred, and Caroline's brother became business manager for the properties. The Kirklands moved to the wilderness in 1837 and founded

Pinckney, named for William's brother, platted on August 9.[2] Another male child, also a William, was born there on March 8, 1838.

It was a rough go. In 1843, the family returned to New York, dreams of profit having exploded, and within three years William died. Caroline provided for her bereaved family by teaching, writing, and editing. In July 1847, she began publishing the *Union Magazine of Literature and Art*,[3] in which, among other pieces, she serialized chapters of a work entitled "Western Sketches." She penned introductions to the works of others.[4] She reviewed books in the *North American Review*. She also wrote her own, which grew upon the foundation of three works published about the Michigan experience.

The first was *A New Home—Who'll Follow?*, published in 1839, with a second edition in 1840 and third in 1841.[5] Caroline used a pseudonym, Mrs. Mary Clavers, hoping to remain anonymous in case any neighbor was offended, especially by heavy reliance on dialogue that fell short of the finest parlors of New England. She nonetheless incurred hostility, providing a reason for moving back East. The success enabled *A Forest Life* (1842) and *Western Clearings* (1845) to issue as sequels.[6]

These three volumes did not whitewash the difficulties of the backwoods life. Cutting through the "timbered land" of Michigan over muddy tracks, only to experience a just-born community without many advances of civilization, proved unromantic. Yet Kirkland could not help but be taken by the natural beauty encountered in the wild, "clothed" in burr-oaks and "haunted by the red deer":

> When I made my first visit to these remote and lonely regions, the scattered woods through which we rode for many miles were gay in their first gosling-green suit of half-opened leaves, and the forest odours which exhaled with the dews of morning and evening, were beyond measure delicious to one "long in populous cities pent." . . . I picked upwards of twenty varieties of wild-flowers—some of them of rare and delicate beauty;—and sure I am, that if I had succeeded in inspiring my companion with one spark of my own floral enthusiasm, one hundred miles of travel would have occupied a week's time.
>
> The wild flowers of Michigan deserve a poet of their own.[7]

Why did these works merit favor? The opinion of one of America's most famed writers, Edgar Allan Poe, answered:

> Unquestionably, she is one of our best writers, has a province of her own, and in that province has few equals. Her most noticeable trait is a certain freshness of style, seemingly drawn, as her subjects in general, from the west.
>
> The cause lay not so much in picturesque description, in racy humor, or in animated individual portraiture, as in truth and novelty. The west at the time was a field comparatively untrodden by the sketcher or the novelist. In certain works, to be sure, we had obtained brief glimpses of character strange to us sojourners in the civilized east, but to Mrs. Kirkland alone we were indebted for our acquaintance with the home and home-life of the backwoodsman.[8]

Her home became a leading literary salon where Poe and other American writers gathered. She traveled abroad and met Charles Dickens and Robert and Elizabeth Barrett Browning. A 1953 reissue of her first book assessed her career. *A New Home* had made her "a literary figure of international proportion," constituting "a classic expression of a new and indigenous American literature." She had not engaged in dialects or fashionable conventions; instead, she delivered "a consistently serious realistic treatment of a way of life" soon to vanish.[9] She also wrote—of course—from a woman's standpoint, revealing the hardship of life in a rural community without romance or reductionism. A common theme in all was a desired rise in the level of the civil and political situation of women.

The Depression Era Writer's Project survey of Michigan included a chapter on literature, oriented from a chronological viewpoint. Listed were the well-known: James Fenimore Cooper, Henry Rowe Schoolcraft, Henry Wadsworth Longfellow—plus Caroline Kirkland.[10] The circle of her friends included Louisa May Alcott.[11] Her descriptions of the life of early settlers have formed the basis for historical/sociographic studies.[12] She is still regarded among some academics as "a major contributor to American literature" for revealing the life experienced in the rural Michigan of the 1830s as statehood was achieved. To quote one pithy reviewer, she "may well be one of the most underrated and underestimated literary observors of human character we have yet to ignore."[13]

Her second book—appearing in two volumes—began by responding to criticism:

> My neighbor, Mrs. Rower, says, indeed, that there are books enough in the world, and one too many; but it will never do to consult the neighbors, since

> what is said of a prophet is doubly true of an author. Indeed, it is of very little use to consult any body. What is written from impulse is generally the most readable, and this fact is an encouragement to those who are conscious of no particular qualification beyond a desire to write. People write because they cannot help it. The heart longs for sympathy, and when it cannot be found close at hand, will seek it the world over.
>
> We never tell our thoughts but with the hope of an echo in the thoughts of others. We set forth in the most attractive guise the treasures of our fancy, because we hope to warm into life imaginations like our own. If the desire for sympathy could lie dormant for a time, there would be no more new books, and we should find leisure to read those already written.[14]

Sympathy was a trait that Kirkland exhibited notably through anti-slavery advocacy. When the Civil War ensued over that cause, she supported Union soldier relief efforts. Her death in 1864 prevented witnessing the culmination of the costly effort to end human bondage within the United States. It would be well over a century before her fade into obscurity would be reversed and her writing regarded as among the front ranks of American writers. That reevaluation has revealed at least two pen names she used: Mrs. Mary Clavers and Aminadab Peering. The Bentley in Ann Arbor holds a photographic collection, and hundreds of her personal letters have been published. For someone now seen as a precursor to the style that Mark Twain made famous, her fame and association with Michigan are no longer unrecognized.

Selected Works

A New Home—Who'll Follow? (1839)
A Forest Life (1842)
Western Clearings (1845)

Elmore John Leonard Jr.

The Dickens of Detroit

October 11, 1925–August 20, 2013

Graduate of University of Detroit Jesuit High School and University of Detroit, employed by Campbell-Ewald Advertising Agency, long-time Detroit-area resident

The ineluctable motive of advertising is to sell. Clients hire ad agencies to boost sales and profits. When "Dutch" Leonard presented himself in 1949 at Campbell-Ewald's office in the General Motors Building on West Grand Boulevard in Detroit, he quickly absorbed that *Mad Men*–like culture. Copywriters squeezed into "cubicles no bigger than they had to be to hold a man and his typewriter."[1] From their feverish imaginations arose immortal jingles like "See the USA in Your Chevrolet." Leonard contributed to the firm's production—and within a few years became a sales tool himself in a *New Yorker* ad (issue of October 6, 1956). The agency's "rising young writer" was a "connoisseur of words" who emphasized character and an economy of phrasing in his three published novels, inspired by the style of Ernest Hemingway.

Were they good enough to have sold well? At twenty-five cents a pop, these entries in Dell's pulp fiction line were affordable. Reviews suggested, however, that they were the work of a talented but inexperienced author. Their genre, classic Western fiction, followed the precedents of Owen Wister and Zane Grey. Like these best-selling writers, born in Pennsylvania and Ohio respectively, Leonard came to the arena without actual experience. He based his early work on insights he gained about the West through subscribing to *Arizona Highways* magazine. Not until 1995 did he make the *New York Times* bestseller list.

The Leonard family came to reside in Michigan in 1934 after stints all over the United States ended when General Motors called Elmore Senior, a dealer location scout, to the Motor City. One, in New Orleans, welcomed Elmore's birth. The family chose Highland Park as home, with its three square miles of tree-lined avenues and boulevards, bearing street signs such as Avalon, Monterey, and Tuxedo, with over fifty thousand residents. Industrialist Henry Ford had made it the site for the first motor vehicle moving assembly line factory along Woodward Avenue, and an iconic postcard image showed streets overflowing with Ford Motor's workers beneath the massive Albert Kahn–designed complex. Chrysler's main operations and offices stood on Oakland Avenue. An S.S. Kresge "five and dime" held down the opposite corner from the looming Sears Roebuck's department store on Sears Street. A lumber company at 15853 Hamilton, Tom's Quality Market at 12811 Woodward, and McLellan's printing shop at 12–14 East Buena Vista were part of the coterie of small businesses that serviced shoppers. Over time, Highland Park grew famous world-wide as the birthplace of a living wage and cradle of mass production.

The Leonards lived on the west side of Woodward at 70 Highland in a newly built tile-roofed Spanish-Revival building holding forty other apartments. The schools ranked high, as did the municipal services provided out of the elegant City Hall. The Beaux Arts–style McGregor Public Library had opened its bronze doors a year after Elmore Junior's birth. Senior's salary of $5,000 a year enabled the son to attend a prestigious parochial high school on Seven Mile Road in Detroit since the family, including mother Flora, were staunch Catholics.[2] Elmore Junior and his elder sister Margaret no doubt enjoyed motion picture titles displayed on the theater marquis at 13843 Woodward Avenue and at the RKO Uptown movie house on the street's west side at Six Mile, just a short streetcar ride north. Margaret was more interested, however, in the printed word and "developed an affinity for reading and often read to her younger brother."[3]

Classmates at University of Detroit High bestowed his lifelong nickname "Dutch," borrowed from a Detroit Tigers pitcher. When he received his diploma in 1943, Leonard could take pride in his Jesuit training—rigorous, challenging, and thought-provoking. A war was on, and his attempt to volunteer for the U.S. Marines failed because of poor eyesight; instead, he was drafted into the U.S. Navy. In 1946, Leonard returned from service in the Pacific in the "Seabees" construction battalion via the magnificent Michigan Central Station. Entitled to attend college on the G.I. Bill, he chose the private Jesuit college known as the University of Detroit. Located near Livernois and West McNichols/Six Mile Road, almost next door to Highland Park, the main campus featured a clock tower erected in the 1920s to honor students and alumni who served in the First World War. A number of the buildings on the campus evoked a Western theme, with the signature orange tiled roofs and white-washed walls of Spanish Mission heritage.

The first post-war yearbook in 1947 provided evidence of the student body's mindset: a page of names of students who had not returned from service; a two-page spread entitled "Surrender" with photographs from the September 1945 ceremony on the deck of the U.S.S. Missouri in Tokyo Harbor; a prayer for peace; a credo opposing totalitarianism and racism; images of young people who had replaced uniforms with civilian dress, exchanging military transportation for "The DSR"—Detroit Streets and Railway transit. When the Academy Awards were announced that year, the hands-down winner was *The Best Years of Our Lives*, a realistic portrayal of war veterans and their adjustment to civilian life.

Dutch adjusted well. He gained membership in the Alpha Chi National College Honor Society (or "AX"), an American collegiate fraternity that recognized achievement in general scholarship. He met and married fellow student Beverly C. Cline. Her photo on page sixty-five in *The Tower* portrayed a diminutive woman with a victory roll hairstyle that accentuated dark locks. The romance did not require a lengthy courtship, for the couple were married in 1949 upon his graduation. It was not a completely happy year: Elmore Senior died of a cerebral hemorrhage at age fifty-five after moving to New Mexico and was buried there. Flora passed away in 1990, Margaret in 2007; both are buried in a cemetery in Little Rock, Arkansas.

The post at Campbell-Ewald was made possible by the peacetime boom in the American consumer market, the domestic auto industry, and in the nation's birthrate. Over seven million vehicles were domestically produced during 1951. In 1954, president and former general of the Army Dwight D. Eisenhower proposed an interstate highway system, funded by 1956 legislation, that paved the way for North American manufacturing to increase beyond ten million vehicles. The firm's largest client, General Motors, became the leader of the Big Three domestic auto industry and provided the engine for Campbell-Ewald to rival New York ad agencies in importance. The City of Detroit had achieved its population apogee, the Ford Highland Park plant no longer produced automobiles, and the influx of wartime workers presented social and economic challenges that no government leader seemed amenable to addressing.

When Leonard began extracurricular writing, his stories did not center on or even mention the landscape that was changing under his feet. Instead, they featured the Old West of ranchers, gunslingers, U.S. cavalry, and Indigenous peoples. His first published piece, "Trail of the Apaches," appeared in the December 1951 issue of *Argosy* magazine with the subhead, "In this land, a man's life took on a different meaning. Each day it was a prize he won for his vigilance." The first publication to put his name on the cover—as "E. J. Leonard, Jr."—was *10 Story Western Magazine* in October 1952, obtained for a quarter, in which "Red Hell Hits Canyon Diablo!" grabbed at the prospective buyer's attention. Dutch later explained why he wrote in this genre from inside the city limits of Detroit:

> I wanted to make money right away and I chose Westerns because of the market. You could aim for *Saturday Evening Post*, *Colliers*, *Esquire*, *Argosy*, *Adventure*, and a number of pulp magazines, like *Dime Western*, that were still in business. I liked Western movies and they were big in the Fifties.[4]

How did he write with any authenticity from Midwest environs? Detail derived from the subscription and the resources of the Detroit Public Library Main Branch down Woodward.

Not until 1959 did a story appear under his byline in a setting other than the West. In "The Bull Ring at Blisston," Leonard located the story in Detroit (and elsewhere) and portrayed a grittiness that resembled Ross Macdonald.[5] His style and storytelling interested an agent, who sought and added him to her stable while insisting he not quit his day job. Leonard hit real success in 1961 with *Hombre*, a Western novel with a multi-racial protagonist, made into a 1967 movie with Paul Newman.[6] Florida became a favorite setting, and Mississippi is the setting for *Tishomingo Blues*. A number of his stories became motion pictures, adding significant revenues to the enterprise.

By 1974, when the Sunday edition of the *Detroit Free Press* included a "Lively Arts" section and locally penned book reviews, Leonard was ensconced in an upper-office suite on Pierce Street in Birmingham, not far from the Lathrup Village house with basement that also served as writing studio. His day job was creative writing "most every weekday from 9 to 5:30," reaping a lucrative six-figure income stream by "methodically cranking out novels and movie scripts" at the rate of "five clean pages a day." That production rate yielded a book or screenplay two or three times per year. "Iron discipline" had brought him wealth, a measure of fame, and the ability to hire a researcher. Succeeding years powered his progression up the ranks until achieving the National Book Foundation's lifetime achievement award in 2012. By then, he lived and worked from a fine Bloomfield Hills residence. His standing bemused him; after all, he had written for "entertaining primarily, and about selling what I write for as much money as I can get."[7]

The contribution to Leonard's fame from celluloid adaptations—thirty or so—proved instrumental in winning acclaim for his writing. In some cases, he authored the screenplay, endeavoring to make the movie align with the book and avoid the Hollywood penchant for telling a far different story from that in the text.[8] A whole generation became aware of Leonard thanks to *Get Shorty* (1990) by MGM in 1995 and *Jackie Brown*, the 1997 film based on *Rum Punch* (1992). Both rely on south Florida as an integral factor in their *noir* atmosphere. In between came the *New York Times* bestseller *Maximum Bob*.[9] In 1969, Leonard bought a small motel in Pompano Beach for Flora to enjoy and to rent out. In a 1985 *Rolling Stone* interview, he explained how in visiting her, he came to see that Miami and its environs could foster a new universe of stories based on their quirkiness. It inspired him to switch from Westerns and dive into a new lucrative genre. In the twenty-first century, the neo-Western television crime series *Justified* brought a Miami lawman to the Midwest in episodes airing in 2023 based on *City Primeval: High Noon in Detroit*, written nearly a quarter-century earlier.

Why did Leonard never relocate? "I like Detroit and its suburbs," he maintained, along with the proximity of family and friends. As he turned more to crime fiction, he had found out "there's an awful lot to write about around here." The progressive deterioration of Detroit, Highland Park, and Flint gave him ready-made material. The Highland Park apartment house became abandoned and derelict. His first Detroit-centered book, *52 Pickup*, appeared in 1974, followed by *City Primeval*, *The Big Bounce*, and *Killshot*, among others. *Up in Honey's Room* (2007) featured settings of his childhood hometown, along with mentions of J. L. Hudson's, Palmer Park, and other familiar locales.

The "Dickens of Detroit"—bestowed because of the multitude of colorful characters he fashioned and the seediness of their settings—died in 2013 after six decades of publishing.[10] His grave in Greenwood Cemetery, Birmingham, steps away from Woodward Avenue, is marked by a U.S. Government–issued military stone, detailing his U.S. Navy service during World War II. Nearby is a vertical granite stone bearing inscriptions of his name, life span, and the appellation awarded to him in 1994, which he enjoyed. Joined together also by thematic strains involving suffering and death, the first Dickens, middle name John, son of a British Navy clerk, is interred within the hallowed halls of Westminster Abbey in London, England. His legacy continues, as does Leonard's, not only on the printed page but in cinematic portrayals, for which both were well suited.

Selected Works

The Big Bounce (1969)
Fifty-Two Pickup (1974)
Swag (1976)
Unknown Man No. 89 (1977)
City Primeval: High Noon in Detroit (1980)
Freaky Deaky (1988)
Killshot (1989)
Out of Sight (1996)
Up in Honey's Room (2007)

Joan Agnes Theresa Sadie Brodel "Leslie" (Caldwell)

G.I. Joan

January 26, 1925–October 12, 2015
Born in Detroit, raised in Highland Park

The eighteen-year-olds in the class of 1943 at St. Benedict's of Highland Park,[1] a thriving city of fifty thousand, graduated into an uncertain and dangerous world engulfed in total war. That summer, a periodic "Michigan Army Casualties" newspaper header listed nineteen new names of killed, wounded, and missing Detroit-area servicemen. One sailor's home at 1130 Collingwood Street was stricken when news came of his making the ultimate sacrifice.[2] More than ten thousand Michiganders would die in uniform during the global conflict, and untold thousands came back forever altered to a state far different from the home they had left behind. After the long Depression, the region had emerged as an industrial powerhouse—the Arsenal of Democracy—for its round-the-clock production of armaments and materiel critical to the U.S war effort.[3] American technology employed by a diverse work force undergirded its military; the Arsenal's army of workers included persons of color and battalions of women each hailed as "Rosie the Riveter."

Joan Brodel did not attend her classmates' graduation; she had another role to perform. Known as Joan Leslie, she had just finished as "[Fred] Astaire's New Dance Partner" in *The Sky's the Limit* by RKO Pictures with Astaire playing a military pilot. The year prior, she had co-starred as wife to Jimmy Cagney's George M. Cohan in *Yankee Doodle Dandy*, unabashedly a morale-boosting war film.[4] Her performance as Gary Cooper's love interest in the highest-grossing movie of 1941, *Sergeant York*, supported his Academy Award win and the nation's involvement in the Second World War.

In the summer of 1941, as storm clouds of war gathered, Leslie had alighted from the cars at the Michigan Central Depot for a visit with old friends and a personal appearance at the Vogue Theater's showing of *The Wagons Roll at Night*, a Metro-Goldwyn-Mayer motion picture.[5] It was her eighteenth movie, and she had yet to turn seventeen. She made the cover of *Life* magazine's issue of October 26, 1942.

Soon, Leslie would play herself in the central figure of America's sweetheart in Warner Brothers' 1944 *Hollywood Canteen*, a morale-boosting cameo-studded film inspiring confidence in U.S. victory. A wounded soldier on leave wants only to meet her—not Eleanor Parker, Alexis Smith, nor Barbara Stanwyck. Leslie had become filmdom's ideal "girl next door."

The war won, turning twenty-one, Leslie challenged the studio system and broke her stifling contract. Newfound creative freedom enabled her to appear in independent films that broadened her oeuvre. Her last celluloid appearance came in a 1991 television movie, leaving a quarter-century of retirement in which to complete her memoirs. An unfinished autobiography contained fascinating revelations of a storied career, including her early years in Michigan.

In the only published retrospective of her work, however, it was not acting that she highlighted. "I'm so proud I was a part of it," Leslie wrote in 2012, about the Canteen at 1451 North Cahuenga in Los Angeles. From 1942 to November 1945, entertainers and employees of the motion picture industry donated time and effort to provide American servicemembers with food and lasting memories of talking and dancing with women they idolized on screen. Every Tuesday after work, Leslie's father drove her to the club from a Hollywood studio where she served sandwiches, cake, and coffee; sat with men in uniform to talk about their families back home; signed autographs; and danced. Her most vivid recollections were not of fellow stars and their devotion of free time, but of the faces of the soldiers. When they talked about their hometowns and families, she could hearken back to pre-war Detroit.

Rather than seeking credit, Leslie venerated the patrons' service to countrymen in the worldwide fight for freedom: she asked, after "what they did for us, how could we not do our best for them?" At the Canteen, "they" was a term not limited to Caucasian soldiers and performers, and its policy of integration "was an achievement the black press emphasized" during the war.[6] Musical numbers in *Hollywood Canteen* included the Black performers of the Golden Gate Quartet.

Leslie had come a very long way from a modest home on Midland Street in Highland Park, attendance at St. Benedict's and Our Lady of Lourdes churches, living in the Woodstock Apartments on Peterboro Street, and vaudeville performances on Detroit-area stages. An ad for one booking invited those ready "for the next thrill" after the Ohio State–University of Michigan football game to visit the Marine Room on Jefferson Avenue to see the singing, dancing, and comedic troupe.[7] In part, her musical talents would be honed when the Brodel sisters performed in New York at the Cotton and Harlem clubs alongside performers such as Bill "Bojangles" Robinson. Playing an eighteen-year-old in the 1940 Warner short *Alice in Movieland*, her small-town character engaged as equals with a Pullman porter played by Clarence Muse, marked by his single-handed bolstering of Alice's confidence without stereotypical dialect.[8]

Her work contributed to four Best Picture nominees while being coached not to "sound so Midwestern."[9] But that trait was a big part of her appeal. Even when Leslie turned her career to more complex parts, as in the 1947 noir *Repeat Performance*, she connected with audiences. She married for life in 1950, had twin daughters,[10] and devoted her remaining years to family, charity, and an unblemished, scandal-free legacy.

When Leslie died at age ninety in 2015, tributes poured in: "Girl-next-door movie star of the 1940s"; "Versatile actor from Hollywood's golden age"; "A Hollywood Girl Next Door"; and "Hollywood golden age ingénue."[11] Turner Classic Movies honored her memory during a night of films in January 2016, with film historian Robert Osborne praising her as "one of the nicest people I ever had the pleasure of knowing in Hollywood."

When the once-lost and restored *Repeat Performance* emerged at a film festival in 2007, its star made a personal appearance and compared the story line (the protagonist gets to live out an alternative reality) to the 1946 classic *It's a Wonderful Life*.[12] It featured Mexican muralist Diego Rivera's art for set decorations, honoring the creator of the immortal *Detroit Industry* at the Detroit Institute of Arts. Perhaps a published autobiography would have restored Leslie's position as one of the great lights—and true role models—from the Golden Age of American Cinema.[13]

Philip Levine

Blue-Collar Bard

January 10, 1928—February 14, 2015

Born in Detroit, author of poems about gritty Detroit childhood and youth factory jobs

Poetry arises from and in seemingly inhospitable places. Some poets write of trees and lakes, while others tell stories of urban life. Still others delve more deeply into the experience of the latter through work. Philip Levine was one of these. Much of his work concerned the impact of factory labor on the human spirit. The subject would contribute significantly to his selection late in life as the Poet Laureate of the United States.

As Philip described it, his parents were Russian Jews who emigrated to the United States not for religious reasons but to survive.[1] Although the family was not observant, Levine in his youth felt the sting of prejudice, later pointing to Henry Ford and Father Charles Coughlin, a Detroit-area Catholic priest who gained a national following with a radio program on which he promoted anti-Semitic views.

Philip Levine was one of three sons. Patriarch Harry Levine, owner of an auto parts business, died when Philip and his identical twin brother, Eddie, were age five. The family struggled through the Great Depression. "I was born in the wrong year and in the wrong place," he wrote in the poem "One for the Rose." A critic called its namesake book one of "penetrating honesty, the kind of honesty that makes you wince with recognition and remembrance."[2]

The family needed income, so Philip Levine joined the workforce at age fourteen, laboring at, among other places, a soap factory, a bottling plant, Chevrolet Gear and Axle, and Detroit Transmission. Levine told the *Los Angeles Times* fifty years later that "he enjoyed physical work at first. He believed working with his hands would leave his mind free for poetry."

Reality proved otherwise, at least for a while, Levine said, but in the end the experience shaped his sensibilities. "I felt myself wearing down. I wasn't going to have the strength or will to keep writing. Now I see that it made me as a poet." Levine's poem *Growth* describes his life at the soap factory:

The oil drums
of fat would arrive each morning,
too huge for me to tussle with,
reeking of the dark, cavernous
kitchens of the Greek and Rumanian
restaurants, of cheap hamburger joints,
White Towers and worse. They would
sulk in the battered yard behind
the plant until my boss, Leo,
the squat Ukrainian dollied them in
to become, somehow, through the magic
of chemistry, pure soap

Levine started down the path to a poet's life when, at Central High School, a teacher lent him a book of verse by Wilfred Owen. He began writing poems, relying on the words and the cadence of the Old Testament. But it was at Wayne University (now Wayne State University) that Levine began composing serious poetry. Among the influences he later mentioned were T. S. Eliot and Dylan Thomas.[3]

In his National Book Award–winning 1991 collection, *What Work Is*, Levine wrote:

We stand in the rain in a long line
Waiting at Ford Highland Park. For work.
You know what work is—if you're
old enough to read this you know what
work is, although you may not do it.
Forget you. This is about waiting,
shifting from one foot to another.

In the 1985 poem *Sweet Will*, Levine described a night of factory life:

The man who stood beside me
34 years ago this night fell
on to the concrete, oily floor
of Detroit Transmission, and we
stepped carefully over him until
he wakened and went back to his press.

It was Friday night, and the others
told me that every Friday he drank
more than he could hold and fell
and he wasn't any dumber for it
so just let him get up at his
own sweet will or he'll hit you.

The first member of his family to receive a college degree, Levine earned two, a bachelor's and a master's in English. In 1957 he also earned a master's in poetry from the Iowa Writer's Workshop.

Levine met poet John Berryman at the workshop, and the latter became a seminal influence as his teacher. Berryman's collected poems would later win the Pulitzer Prize and the National Book Award. Levine called Berryman "entrancing and magnetic and inspiring" as well as demanding of his students. He was the best teacher Levine ever had, he said. "Berryman, of all the people I ever studied with, was the one who gave me insight into how to become a better poet, and I saw the ferocity with which he pursued poetry. I thought: 'I'm going to have to be that ferocious if I'm going to make it.'"

Iowa was where he met his second wife, Frances Artley. They remained married for the rest of Levine's life. She earned a steady paycheck the couple needed by teaching speech and drama at Florida State University in 1954–1955. Levine was crafting poems and beginning to place some in literary periodicals. A one-year fellowship at Stanford paved the way for a teaching job at the University of California at Fresno (Fresno State) in 1958, where he remained for thirty-five years. He also taught at Tufts University, Columbia University, and New York University.

Although he left Michigan after graduating from Wayne and never lived in the state again, Levine did not leave the subject matter of a blue-collar life behind. To Studs Terkel, he explained his choice of industrial work for verse:

> It was at an early age, when I was working in factories and also trying to write. I said to myself, "no one is writing the poetry of this world here; it doesn't exist!" And it didn't. You couldn't find it. I took a vow that I was going to do it, and goddamn it, it didn't matter how long it was going to do it.[4]

Asked whether he had ever considered writing poems about life in academia, Levine replied, "Who the hell wants to read about the life of a professor? Do you? I don't."

On the Edge, Levine's first book, was published in 1963. It won praise for his poems' "cutting edge." Critic Webster Schott said in Levine's work "sex, love, physical pain, abandoned buildings hurt, and his diction is his own."[5]

The proud local *Fresno Bee* proclaimed in a headline, "Fresnan's First Book is a Sellout" and it was—in the city where he taught.[6] Levine did not dwell on his success, telling the reporter he had already finished another volume of poems that would be published soon. For much of his career, Levine's books sold modestly, but 1991's *What Work Is* sold more than forty thousand copies.

In 1968, Levine returned to Detroit and recorded his impressions in a poem:

> A winter Tuesday, the city pouring fire,
> Ford Rouge sulfurs the sun, Cadillac, Lincoln,
> Chevy gray. The fat stacks
> Of breweries hold their tongues. Rags,
> paper, hands, the stems of birches
> dirtied with words

By 1983, Levine had authored eleven books of poetry and acquired a national reputation. In a feature article published that year, his students saw more than a poet, several told the *Fresno Bee*. "He gave me encouragement to be myself," said Sherley Williams, who had gone on to become a published poet herself. "And that is one of the things I have always found most precious about him—that he is able to recognize talent and help that talent discipline itself without imposing his own style on you, or making you feel that you have to write like him to be good."[7]

Levine's blue-collar years left a lasting distaste for the industrial system. He told interviewer Bill Moyers that what made him most angry was "American capitalism. Its heartlessness. And American racism. The conditions that are imposed upon the poor by the rich . . . you never get over it."[8]

Joyce Carol Oates commented of Levine in the *American Poetry Review*: "He is one of those poets whose work is so emotionally intense, and yet so controlled, so concentrated, that the accumulative effect of reading a number of his related poems can be shattering." Oates dubbed Levine "a visionary of our dense, troubled mysterious time."[9]

In 1994, the *Los Angeles Times* found the sixty-six-year-old Levine marveling over his good fortune to make a middle-class living instead of sweating for a paycheck. But poetry wasn't child's play. Levine handwrote his works with a fountain pen, sometimes waiting for words that didn't arrive. Where did his best work come from? "In academics they teach us to trust the brain and not to trust the imagination," he said. "I say trust the imagination. It is furtive. Submit to it."

In 2011, at age eighty-three, Levine was named U.S. Poet Laureate. Librarian of Congress James Billington, who made the selection, called Levine "the laureate, if you like, of the industrial heartland. It's a very, very American voice. I don't know that in other countries you get poetry of that quality about the ordinary workingman." The *New York Times* echoed the description with the headline, "Voice of the Workingman to be Poet Laureate." The *Detroit News* described him as the Walt Whitman of industrial Detroit.

Expressing his gratitude for the honor, the humble Levine said his best writing had happened long before. "I find more energy in my earlier work," he said. "More dash, more anger. Anger was a major engine in my poetry then. It's been replaced by irony, I guess, and by love."[10]

Becoming poet laureate so late in life brought surprises to Levine and others who thought they had known him. "People like my doctor or the guy who sells me wine or the people in my gym come up to me and say, 'Oh, Phil, this is marvelous.' Some of them didn't even know I was a poet," he told the *New York Times*.[11]

Becoming poet laureate also increased his fan base. "Now there are mobs of people when I read poems. I read at a high school in Pennsylvania, and there were 600 people." He contrasted that with a 1969 reading from his second book at the University of San Francisco, when no one showed up.

Levine collaborated with jazz saxophonist and composer Benjamin Boone on a project blending poetry and music. The resulting CD, *The Poetry of Jazz* was released posthumously in 2018. It contains fourteen Levine poems and performances by Levine and Boone and notable jazz musicians.

Levine tackled subjects besides factory life, including his life in Spain and the Spanish anarchists of the 1930s. The family lived in Spain in both 1965–1966 and 1968–1969. In his youth, Levine had identified with Spanish revolutionaries. A commentator said, "He felt an affinity between the Catalan city and Detroit, both places where common ideals could be crushed."

Levine's work merited a whole volume of analytical accolades titled *On the Poetry of Philip Levine: Stranger to Nothing*. Published in 1990, it contained more than eighty essays of appreciation by critics and other poets. He won two National Book Awards and a Pulitzer Prize, among other honors.

A journalist summed up Levine's impact on poetry:

> His work was not to every critic's taste. Because of its strong narrative thrust, frequent autobiographical bent and tendency to shun conventional poetic devices, some reviewers dismissed it as merely prose with line breaks. Others found monotony in his revisiting the same themes again and again. But many admired his deceptively simple style, which could belie the carefully worked out cadences beneath its colloquial surface. They also praised Mr. Levine's unabashed use of poetry as a vehicle for radical social criticism, noting his frank explorations of the nature of masculinity and his cleareyed depictions of working-class lives and the immigrant Jewish experience.[12]

Levine died of pancreatic cancer in Fresno in February 2015. His poetry endures, a chronicle of the reality of blue-collar life in his time. In the posthumously published *The Last Shift*, Levine wrote his own epitaph, including one poem that a critic said was a "tremendous performance." The Michigan-born poet escaped the monotony of assembly line life to make art of the struggle of generations for upward mobility and society's respect.

Selected Works

Not This Pig (1968)
Pili's Wall (1971)
Red Dust (1971)
They Feed They Lion (1972)

1933 (1974)
The Names of the Lost (1976)
Ashes: Poems New and Old (1979)
7 Years From Somewhere (1979)
One for the Rose (1981)
Selected Poems (1984)
Sweet Will (1985)
A Walk with Tom Jefferson (1988)
New Selected Poems (1991)
What Work Is (1991)
The Simple Truth (1994)
Unselected Poems (1997)
The Mercy (1999)
The Bread of Time: Toward an Autobiography (2001)
Breath (2004)
Stranger to Nothing: Selected Poems (2006)
News of the World (2009)
The Last Shift (2016, published posthumously, edited by Edward Hirsch)

Edmund G. Love

Whimsy and Woe

February 12, 1912–August 30, 1990
Born in Flushing, lived in Flint in later childhood, returned to Flint in retirement

Edmund Love lived a life spanning small-town Michigan and subways; the local breakfast stop and the staggering assortment of restaurants in New York City; tongue-in-cheek humor and heartbreaking tragedy. Contrasts characterized Love's years.

Love lived early on in the little town of Flushing, population nine hundred, about eleven miles west-northwest of Flint.[1] As he remembered it more than fifty years later, life in Flushing during those years was everything a boy could want—plenty of playmates, parents who shooed their children out to play, colorful local characters, natural places to explore, and best of all, trains.

In the first decades of the twentieth century, railroad was king as a means of traveling more than a few miles. That was changing with mass production of the automobile. Young Edmund would see that transition take place, but not before he became smitten with the powerful locomotives, getting to know engineers and the distinctive cry of each engine. "When I look back at my early life, I find myself inclined to relate everything to the railroad," he said.

With his family, Love moved from Flushing to Flint when he was twelve. The city was no sleepy burg. Enticed by the rapid expansion of General Motors in the 1920s, thousands flocked to Flint. The experience of moving from country to city left a deep impression on Love that he would explain decades later in published memoirs.

After graduating from the University of Michigan with a master's degree in fine arts, Love taught at Flint Northern High School from 1937 to 1941, then served in World War II before pursuing his writing career in New York City. The *New Yorker* published his nonfiction. Scraping along financially early in his Gotham years, he came upon the material of which his best-selling book, *Subways are for Sleeping*, was made. Originally an article in a 1956 issue of *Harper's* magazine, the story became a book the following year.

In ten chapters, Love told of ten men and women, most homeless, living on the ragged edge of society in New York City, some by choice. In the parlance of the day, Love called them "bums," but no disapproval was intended. The author admired some of them for the craft they used to survive, some to thrive. Several readers questioned whether all the "bums" and all their adventures were nonfiction.

The book's title derived from one of the stories. Henry Shelby, a graduate of the University of Michigan and a former public school teacher in Lansing, has run out of money to pay for lodging. Without a home, he sometime sleeps at a shelter but prefers the subway. Boarding a train between midnight and one o'clock, he sleeps while riding to the end of the line and back. Occasionally he takes odd jobs to earn spending money, but when he has enough, he returns to the streets. Henry doesn't mind the complications of the homeless life. Things seem "so easy and natural." He and the author meet occasionally to discuss philosophy, world problems, and their lives.

"I don't know how long I'll live this life," he tells Love. "I don't have much trouble. I've never gotten drunk and lain in a doorway . . . I haven't had to beg. I'm just not going to look at the future."

Another character is Martha Grant, "the girl who wore no clothes." The description is nearly literal. Keeping to herself except for a comely arm reaching out of her apartment for a yogurt cup on the windowsill, Martha manages to win the lust of both Love and his friend George Brothers. When Love visits her, she is clad in only two bath towels. She manages to remain in her apartment despite not paying her rent, and when three men appear at her door to evict her, she stands *au naturel* and, flabbergasted, they flee. Soon the bills are paid; Martha manages to seduce the author, George, a dentist, and even a police detective into supplying money—and in return she gives nothing but sweet talk.

Kennebunc (a pseudonym chosen from the loose proximity of his birthplace to Kennebunkport, Maine) is an ironworker too bruised to continue in his line of work after twenty-eight years. He moves to New York, sleeping in doorways at night and washing the windows of both residential and commercial buildings at five cents per frame. Every Monday morning, he walks to construction sites looking for a fight, exchanging insults with the workers. "Sooner or later he would manage to be more insulting than insulted. A few blows would be struck and Kennebunc would return to Third Avenue, a satisfied look on his face." Kennebunc dies from malnutrition and exposure on a fire escape behind a theater where he has been living.

New York Times critic Oliver Prescott said the book was "humorous, pathetic and [an] extremely interesting excursion into ways of life as strange to most gainfully employed citizens as those of Papuan head-hunters."[2] In the *Hartford Courant*, A. L. Malabre called it "a vivid picture of one aspect of living in New York."[3]

Love elaborated on his view regarding "bums" at a women's club in Binghamton, New York in 1959. No more than 20 percent of the city's homeless, he said, were alcoholics. Many of the rest were clever but were in "open rebellion against everything. They are on strike against something—probably themselves."[4]

Peculiarly for a book revealing so much of the underbelly of New York City, in 1961, *Subways* became a cheery Broadway musical, adapted by Betty Comden and Adolph Green, famous for *Singin' in the Rain*. The *Daily News* liked it but not too well, calling the production "just noisy, energetic and good-natured." The musical attracted a flurry of publicity when its producer, David Merrick, banned two *Boston Globe* critics from the play's opening in Boston, calling one of them incompetent. That critic, Kevin Kelly, although forced to take in the musical in Philadelphia, praised it as "lively and lighthearted."[5]

The research for *Subways* had a fortuitous result in Love's personal life. He met the woman who would become his wife in the New York Public Library, where she was head of reference and he asked her for material on homeless persons.

Love was distinguished for more than writing. In the 1950s, on a whim, he set out to eat at all of New York City's approximately 5,600 restaurants. By the time he reported on his quest in a 1964 *Saturday Evening Post* article, he had dined at 1,750 (in alphabetical order according to the city's Yellow Pages) at an estimated cost of $18,000. Why did he do it? "I got interested in restaurants because I was hungry." He forecasted the completion of his culinary odyssey in 1980. It is unlikely he ever finished the job.[6]

Michigan appeared in both Love's fiction and nonfiction. In the amusing trifle *A Small Bequest*, he remembers a 1934 road trip to the Upper Peninsula to inspect a piece of land no one had known his grandfather owned until his will was read. After a series of misadventures with travel companion George French, in a 1916 Buick touring car whose aged tires frequently give out—and after a half-day wait at Mackinaw City for a car ferry to cross the Straits—they arrive at a rustic resort known simply as Charlie Fuller's camp on Manistique Lake.

The comedy has to do with porcupines, timber wolves, a beautiful and inaccessible young woman, cheapskate resort owner Charlie Fuller, and the land, which turns out to be swampy acreage impossible to build a cabin on. Love sells it to a rival of Fuller for $500.

One Love work is a Civil War yarn based on fact, *A Shipment of Tarts*, called to Love's attention by friend and Michigan-born Civil War historian Bruce Catton. In 1862, Gen. William Tecumseh Sherman orders Captain Thomas K. Poole to round up the sixty-eight prostitutes doing business with his soldiers in Memphis, put them on a boat, and ship them north to Cairo, Illinois, never to return. Trouble is, the people of Cairo and other towns to the north have advanced word of the cargo and want nothing to do with the tarts. In desperation, Poole has the boat renamed and the passengers disguised. And that is not the end of the adventure.

"Love has done an excellent job with a story that could easily have become an example of 'True Confessions,'" critic Florence Winkler said in the Lexington *Herald-Leader*. The *Nashville Tennessean* complimented Love's "great ingenuity."[7]

Undoubtedly the work of Love's most deeply rooted in Michigan is *The Situation in Flushing*, a fond and perhaps occasionally fictional memoir of his youth in the 1910s and 1920s. Published in 1965, the book vividly describes an assortment of characters, some of them oddballs, and memorable local events, including a fire at his school and a train wreck.[8]

A prominent character in the book is the railroad that passes through sleepy Flushing. Young Edmund is fascinated by trains from the age of four. At the age of six, he can imitate the whistles of different engines and draw pictures of them. He aspires to be an engineer when he grows up.

On the book's first page, Love centers his youth at a turning point in U.S. history:

> I was born into a world that ceased to exist almost as soon as I came into it. In the first twelve years of my life rural America was swept away as completely as though it was a picture on a blackboard that had been suddenly erased. The

> technological revolution that had been creeping into the large cities flooded through the country. It came so suddenly and the changes were so thorough that most people didn't realize that the old way of life had gone.

On a summer Sunday evening in 1923, the eleven-year-old Love noticed a procession of cars through Flushing. Peering from the automobile windows were faces he did not recognize. They belonged to people from Flint, Saginaw, Montrose, and other towns and cities out for a Sunday drive. This was new to Love. "I didn't know it, but I was looking at a whole generation of Americans who for the first time had been freed from the environment in which they had always lived." The pace of life in Flushing would never again be measured by the howl of an oncoming locomotive.

The Situation in Flushing won Flushing national notoriety. The *New York Times* raved that the book was "enchantment pure and solid . . . This is an exceptionally good book." In addition to its colorful characters, the *Times* said, Love had written a social history of sorts. "His subject is one aspect of a considerable moment in our nation's life: the decade when [we] moved from rural to urban, from simple to complicated, from a relatively self-sufficient society to an industrialized one." *Detroit Free Press* columnist Judd Arnett raved that the memoir was "a rare and sensitive piece of writing, full of humor and yet centered on a theme which needs repeating in a nation hell-bent on liquidating its past. The 'moral' of Mr. Love's book is that all change is not necessarily good."[9] The *Saturday Evening Post* published a thirteen-page spread on the book, including a reminiscence by Love.

But the local reception wasn't uniformly positive. Several locals who had lived in Flushing during Love's youth accused him of taking liberty with the facts. A Mrs. John G. Rulison wrote to the author to complain that he'd distorted the character of Percy Benjamin as a shiftless alcoholic, causing hurt to his descendants. Love responded that no offense was intended and that it was difficult to distinguish local myth from fact. More than fifty years after the publication, a news service reported *The Situation in Flushing* was still touching off a tizzy.

There is some reason to believe that Love was a fabulist. He describes Flushing's Ira Sayre as a powerful thirty-year veteran of the Michigan Legislature. The state's legislative record has Sayre as a one-term state senator, elected in 1898. Love mentions his father briefly played major league baseball, but there is no record of him doing so.

A particularly interesting—and apparently accurate—portrait is of Joe Gage, a prizefighter turned barber and the only Black man in town. He wins local acceptance and outcompetes the town's two other barbers. Although genial, he stands up for himself when one of his rivals tell his customers not to patronize a Black man's business, using a racial slur. Joe drops by the competitor's shop and threatens to break him in two if he ever uses the insult again. The competitor doesn't.

Love continued his memoirs with a second volume, *Hanging On: or How to Get Through a Depression and Enjoy Life*. The sometimes-ribald memoir walks the reader through the 1930s. Love's family goes from the comfortable middle class to a cliff-hanging near-poverty. The family sheds "the help," and Love's stepmother goes from "a charming gracious person who was given to playing bridge and going to teas and other social functions" to a gray-haired worrier scrubbing the kitchen floor on her hands and knees.

Despite it all, through doggedness and occasional luck, Love scrapes together enough money to get a teaching certificate at the University of Michigan, write a novel that catches the eye of famed editor Maxwell Perkins (the midwife of works by F. Scott Fitzgerald and Thomas Wolfe), and suffer a string of romantic failures. He manages to find humor in even the grimmest of events.

Tragedy darkened Love's later years. His daughter was murdered in 1967 while on holiday in London. Twenty-year-old Shannon was stabbed to death by a mentally ill acquaintance. Three months later, Love led a New York *Daily News* reporter through his deceased daughter's room, untouched since her death. "His face was ashen," the reporter observed.[10] "There are still some bad moments," Love said.

Remarkably, Love bore no ill will against his daughter's killer. "This isn't the kind of thing that fills a man with a need for revenge," Love said. "Think of it: it's terrible for a 19-year-old boy to go through the rest of his life with something like this." He added, "Don't fit me for a halo, or anything."

Returning to Flint later in life, Love continued to publish. He also took time in 1980 to write the sports page of the *Detroit Free Press* when the Detroit Tigers announced they would retire the uniform number of Hall of Fame outfielder Al Kaline. "As an old-timer who can still recite Tigers lineups from way back in the 1920s . . . I think it is high time we honor Charlie Gehringer and retire his number 2."[11] The sports editor agreed.

Love died of a heart attack in 1990. Obituaries from the *Free Press* to the *New York Times* remembered him primarily as the author of a book that became a Broadway musical and of a memoir about childhood in Flushing. The latter places him firmly among the ranks of writers who have not just reported on but immortalized a time and place in the state's and nation's history.

Selected Works

Subways Are for Sleeping Signet (1958)
War is a Private Affair (1959)
Arsenic and Red Tape Signet (1960)
The Beautiful and Anxious Maidens (1962)
An end to bugling (1963)
The Situation in Flushing (1965)
A Shipment of Tarts (1967)
Set-up (1980)
Hanging on Or, How to Get Through a Depression and Enjoy Life (1987)
A Small Bequest (1987)

Ross Macdonald

The Transference of Guilt

December 13, 1915–July 11, 1983
Received master's degree and PhD from the University of Michigan

Some fiction writers write to divert the reader, to entertain. Others write to explore deeper, more pressing social or psychological issues. The best do both. In the genre of detective fiction, one of the very best writers who did both has a Michigan connection. His pen name was Ross Macdonald, and he was widely acclaimed in his day as the best in the genre since famed authors Dashiell Hammett and Raymond Chandler.

Ross Macdonald detective novels are set in sunny, post–World War II Southern California. They are a seductive world of beautiful weather, economic prosperity, and smiling, tanned faces—the epitome of the American Dream. Yet lurking behind this utopia is a subterranean world where underhanded financial dealings, economic struggles, family betrayal, and murder occur—the true world behind the facade.

Macdonald was active from the 1940s through the 1970s. His novels were praised for elevating the detective story to the status of literature. As a youth, he led a rebellious, delinquent life. As an adult, he was fascinated by the darker side of human nature and portrayed it in his work.

"Ross Macdonald" was actually a pseudonym of Kenneth Millar. Millar was the author of twenty-four novels published between 1944 and 1976. Eighteen of these novels feature a narrator named Lew Archer, a divorced former police officer working as a private detective out of a cheap office on the Sunset Strip. Archer's specialty is finding missing persons. Clients hire him to locate absent daughters, girlfriends, or business partners. In his quest to track the person of interest, he stumbles upon a deeper mystery and is compelled to explore a dark realm of deception involving criminality and family strife.

His journey introduces the reader to a world of corruption and psychological estrangement under the unblinking eye of the Western sun.

Ken Millar was born on December 13, 1915, in Los Gatos, California, to Canadian parents. His father was a former newspaper editor, his mother, a former nurse. When he was only four years old, his parents separated, and he relocated with his mother to live in his grandmother's household in Kitchener, Ontario, Canada, and later in numerous rooming houses. Because his mother was in poor health and impoverished, he was often forced to reside with relatives across Canada. Late in life, he admitted feeling responsible as a child for his parents' estrangement.[1] He said the absence of his father during his childhood was the "central, original fact" of his life.[2]

A troubled young Ken bullied his classmates. He was initiated into childhood homosexual experiences at age eight.[3] At age twelve, he drank himself to inebriation for the first time and later referred to himself as a "semi-juvenile delinquent."[4] Yet the street-smart Ken also became an avid reader. A Kitchener pool hall where Millar spent much of his time featured illegal slot machines in the back, whose presence was tacitly condoned by city law enforcement. In fact, illegal dice games, bookmakers, and slot machines were not uncommon throughout the city. When Ken read Dashiell Hammett's detective fiction for the first time, he experienced a revelation. Here, he thought, was displayed the real world of the city, the furtive and corrupt world the politicians and police in a city like Kitchener tolerated yet pretended did not exist.[5] Perhaps there was a division between surface respectability and deviant behavior that he recognized within himself as well. Years later, this division would feature prominently in his fiction.

Somehow, Ken matured and turned his life in a different direction. A student with great promise, he graduated from high school in Kitchener, then from the University of Western Ontario in 1938 after studying English literature and history. He next married the gifted, strong-willed Margaret Sturm, whom he had known in high school. After further study at the Ontario College of Education, Ken returned to his high school to teach for two years. Seeking to expand his intellectual horizons, he spent two summers enrolled in courses at the University of Michigan in Ann Arbor, 180 miles from Kitchener. Eventually, he started full-time study in the master's degree program in English literature in the autumn of 1941 in Ann Arbor with wife and two-year-old daughter at his side. His goal, at first, was to acquire the skills needed to become a lifelong teacher of English literature.

Neither Ken nor his wife was enamored of Ann Arbor; in fact, Margaret reportedly "hated" it.[6] Ken taught undergraduate students to help pay for his expenses, and the Millars lived modestly at 1020 Hill Street. Nonetheless, Ken's experience there was central to his later success as a writer. Not only was he exposed to a highly rigorous curriculum in his chosen field, but he had the great fortune to study under the famed English American poet W. H. Auden, who was teaching at the university that semester. Auden, coincidentally, was a fan of detective fiction. Auden offered to accompany Ken to New York City, where Auden would introduce him to important figures in magazine publishing. Though Ken declined, he saw Auden as a brilliant, inspirational figure who recognized his potential and who, because he took detective fiction seriously, "legitimized" Ken's eventual choice to write in that genre.[7]

Ken and Margaret had a marriage that was sometimes turbulent. They screamed and hit one another, and Millar sometimes even "shook or slapped" their young daughter Linda.[8] Like Ken, Margaret was blessed with talent. While they still lived in Kitchener, Ken encouraged Margaret, an avid reader of detective fiction and stay-at-home mother, to write her own mystery novel. He made suggestions and edited her work; a major New York publisher accepted the novel for publication, and the reviews from the critics were positive. Ken wrote his own his first novel—*The Dark Tunnel*—while still a graduate student at Michigan, an ominous tale about Nazi spies lurking among the faculty at a midwestern university modeled after the University of Michigan. The discerning reader can perceive strong campus resemblances to Angell Hall, the Power Plant, the Ruthven Exhibit Museum, Palmer Field, and the underground steam tunnels crisscrossing central campus, where the narrator frantically eludes pursuing Nazis. The novel was published in 1944 to favorable reviews.

After earning his master's degree, Ken joined the U.S. Navy in 1944 and was posted on a ship in the Pacific Ocean as a signals officer. Margaret moved to California and continued writing, eventually signing a contract with Warner Brothers to adapt one of her novels for the screen, though the movie was never produced.

After the war, the Millars lived in Santa Barbara, California, then relocated to Ann Arbor in 1948, where Ken began researching and writing his PhD dissertation while once more teaching undergraduate students. By this time, four of his novels had been published. Though he had resolved to become a professional writer, he wanted the financial security an advanced degree would offer were it necessary for him to continue teaching. He resided at 4810 Jackson Road, then 204 Burwood Place. The Millars returned to Santa Barbara following the school year. Ken's mother talked often of California when he was a child, and he had always pictured it as a promised land.[9] Ken and Margaret settled in, and the two started writing fiction full time. During a brief final stay in Ann Arbor in 1951 completing and defending his dissertation on the English writer Samuel Taylor Coleridge, Ken was awarded his PhD. Millar lived the rest of his life in his beloved California, though upon his return that year, he appears to have suffered a nervous collapse.[10] A few years later, he started seeing a psychiatrist, addressing anger issues stemming from his childhood.[11]

In the late 1940s, Ken began writing a series of detective novels featuring a narrator named Lew Archer. Because his wife had by now published a number of mystery novels under her married name, Margaret Millar, Ken decided to write his Archer novels under a pseudonym. Borrowing his father's first and middle names, he chose the name John Macdonald to grace the cover.[12] The first Archer novel, *The Moving Target*, was published in 1949 and received plaudits from the critics. Later in the *Archer* series, he expanded the name to John Ross Macdonald, before finally settling on Ross Macdonald. The latter was the name that would become famous in detective fiction.

The Lew Archer novels are elaborately plotted. Typically, while following leads tracking a missing person, Archer encounters a multi-layered enigma of which the missing person plays only a part. As he plunges headlong into the case, he becomes committed to uncovering the final truth and endangers his own life. On occasion, Archer acts unethically, searching people's possessions without permission or not telling the police all he knows about a case. As the mystery unfolds and the case grows more complex, he begins forming tentative conclusions and divulges those conclusions to other characters in the story. At some point, Archer stops confiding in others. When he unveils the solution to the deeper mysteries at the end, the effect is electrifying, for there is always a final surprise the reader will not have foreseen.

By design, the *Archer* novels brought something new to detective fiction. Ken wrote for the common man, not fellow scholars of literature, yet introduced elements of what he called "high culture" into his works.[13] He wanted to avoid superficiality; terming solutions to the mystery in the whodunit detective novel "too easy," he slammed mystery authors Ellery Queen and Erle Stanley Gardner, whom he said felt "freed from the responsibility of developing character" and who displayed tragedy "without facing reality."[14] And he made greater use of imagery, of simile and metaphor, than had other detective fiction writers, "to relate the overt action to the inner lives of the characters."[15]

Perhaps inspired by his own unhappy childhood experiences, Ken chose to incorporate into his work what he labeled the "gothic": "the dark side of human life and human experience . . . which emphasizes the strange, mysterious, and the unexpected." One of his literary heroes was Edgar Allan Poe, the inventor of the modern detective story, whom Ken said "perceived the psychological essence of the American experience in ways that nobody else has." Another was F. Scott Fitzgerald, whose narrator in *The Great Gatsby*, Nick Carraway, inspired Ken to create the Lew Archer character, a mysterious first-person narrator about whom the reader learns little, who records the actions of the other characters as an observer.[16]

What made the Lew Archer novels popular at a time of social disorder in the 1960s was their depiction of family upheaval, of a kind of familial post-traumatic stress disorder. In interviews, Millar said the Archer novels displayed the "transference of guilt from one generation to another," a kind of familial original sin. Often, his characters are shown to be self-destructive as they grapple with the consequences of the actions of an earlier generation. In a psychological sense, they are almost doomed. Some of his characters have been emotionally abused and are vulnerable to further abuse. "People are prepared by people who mistreat them to become the victims of other people," Ken told an interviewer.[17] The novels are set in Southern California, of which he observed, "Life here does have a fairy-tale aspect. It seems unreal until you penetrate to the interior. Unless you really understand how people live here, it looks like a dream, a kind of delightful, movie-like fantasy."[18] After growing up in Canada, Ken wrote his *Archer* novels with an outsider's eye for the California of his time.

Though the *Archer* novels sold respectably and were published in translation in multiple foreign languages, it was only when prestigious mainstream publications highlighted them that the books became bestsellers. In 1969, screenwriter William Goldman wrote a front-page essay on the Ross Macdonald novel *The Goodbye Look* in the *New York Times Book Review*, headlined "The finest detective novels ever written by an American." Ray Bradbury wrote a laudatory review featured prominently in the *Los Angeles Times* one week later. In 1971, Ross Macdonald was displayed on the cover of *Newsweek* magazine. What entranced the critics was not only the novels' psychological complexity—their unmasking of people's conflicted motivations—but also their literary quality. Ken Millar was producing detective fiction on a par with the most distinguished novels. Suddenly, the *Lew Archer* series became a sensation.

Even Hollywood took notice of Lew Archer. Paul Newman starred in two movies based on the *Archer* novels, Peter Graves played Archer in a television movie, and Brian Keith portrayed Archer in a short-lived television series.

Tragically, Ken and Margaret Millar experienced their own family upheaval. At age sixteen, while driving one night under the influence of alcohol, their daughter Linda struck two pedestrians, killing one, a thirteen-year-old boy. She was found guilty of two felony counts, but the court gave her a sentence of probation. At age nineteen, she ran away from college and disappeared. A desperate Ken Millar mounted a publicity campaign, granting interviews with newspapers and television throughout California about his daughter's disappearance. After ten days, she was discovered in Reno and reunited with her parents. She later married and gave birth to a son but died at age thirty-one. A few years later, Ken was to experience the tragedy of Alzheimer's disease, showing early signs of decline in the mid-1970s. It was to take his life in 1983, at age sixty-seven. His beloved grandson, his only descendant, died of a drug overdose a few years later. While Millar's early family misfortunes and personal secrets formed the inspiration for his fiction, in the end fate mocked him, for the course of his later years resembled the sad destinies of the characters in his novels.

Ross Macdonald's 1964 classic *The Chill* was reprinted in paperback in 2022. Its publisher, Vintage Crime/Black Lizard, included a short apology at the beginning, warning that the book reflects its time and place, and that contemporary readers may be offended by occasional characterization and language. This may be true of the *Archer* novels, but by raising the detective story to the level of art, their survival long into the future is assured.

Selected Works

The Moving Target (1949)
The Drowning Pool (1950)
The Way Some People Die (1951)

The Ivory Grin (1952) (also known as *Marked for Murder*)
Find a Victim (1954)
The Name is Archer (1955) (short stories)
The Barbarous Coast (1956)
The Doomsters (1958)
The Galton Case (1959)
The Wycherly Woman (1961)
The Zebra-Striped Hearse (1962)
The Chill (1964)
The Far Side of the Dollar (1965)
Black Money (1966)
The Instant Enemy (1968)
The Goodbye Look (1969)
The Underground Man (1971)
Sleeping Beauty (1973)
The Blue Hammer (1976)
Lew Archer, Private Investigator (1977) (short stories)

Catherine Jane "Kittie" Cuthbertson McCoy

Real McCoys

November 18, 1854–February 21, 1917
Born near Orchard Lake, lived and wrote in Oakland County

Across from a yellow-hued farmhouse in Commerce Township is a free-standing silo, a silent reminder of the farms that used to dominate rural Michigan even in the state's southeastern corner. In 1999, the "Kittie C. McCoy Home" located at 1455 Benstein Road was added to the National Register of Historic Places. Once part of an eighty-acre farm, the 1850s–1860s structure is "a simply detailed two-story gabled-ell farmhouse with a one-story, gabled rear ell . . . on a fieldstone foundation." The "clapboarded building displays plain comer boards and projecting eaves with raking cornices without returns atop a broad architrave/frieze band extending entirely around the house below the eaves." Nearly all windows "are narrow one-over-ones framed in architrave trim." The nomination form, however, advocated listing because of association "with the lives of persons significant in our past," specifically during the period 1879–1910.[1]

Its worthiness, then, was portrayed as deriving from a human factor, not as construction project. The State Historic Preservation Office, supporting the nomination, contended that it met national register criteria as the home of the "poetess of Orchard Lake," Kittie McCoy, who "is important for the recognition given her during her lifetime in the Orchard Lake–Pontiac area for the poetry she produced in the years from the 1870s and 80s until her death in 1917." Many of her poems were published in local newspapers and in a book compilation bearing the bucolic title, *Buds and Blossoms*.[2] Only three hundred were privately printed.[3] One of her compositions was cited in the inaugural issue of *Michigan History* magazine in July 1917:

And let us be sure that our children will know
The story of one hundred years ago—The story of hardship, of toil and of
tears.[4]

Catherine Jane Cuthbertson married Thomas McCoy, a son of two Irish immigrants, on November 18, 1879, in Oakland County. They had five children as well as grandchildren. One was killed in action in Europe during World War II.

There was another writer of Michigan named McCoy, though she is usually known by her maiden name. Iona Fuller, born in Marcellus on January 25, 1906, won the 1939 Hopwood Award for her Mackinac Island novel *The Loon Feather*. During World War II, the book became an Armed Services Edition (ASE) distributed free by Army and Navy Library Services to members of the American military. At a conference honoring these publications in 1983, the Librarian of Congress cited the "ASEs" as an inspiring example of how imagination and determination can entice new audiences into the community of readers. Fuller's second marriage to Raymond A. McCoy enabled her use of that surname before her death on April 12, 1993.[5]

The marker over the poet's grave in the Walled Lake Cemetery (Sec. 3, Row 12), near the "McCoy" family stone, reads "Mother Kittie C." After her husband died, she moved to Milford and served as president of the Monday Literary Club. A more fitting epitaph might have cited her poetic ability and love of writing, once thought to merit preservation in the state's central bibliotheca.

Selected Works

Buds and Blossoms (1896)

Milo Milton Quaife

Prolific Chronicler

October 6, 1880–September 1, 1959
Lived in Highland Park, worked in and wrote on Detroit and Michigan history subjects

Four years before his tragic death on a two-lane road between St. Ignace and Sault Ste. Marie,[1] Dr. M. M. Quaife had been honored by the Algonquin Club of Detroit and Windsor with a published bibliography of his works. It filled forty-one pages.[2] On April 1, 1924, Quaife had become the first editor of the prestigious Burton Historical Collection at the Detroit Public Library. He remained in that post until becoming its secretary, finishing his tenure at retirement in 1947. Among his written contributions were multiple items in the "Leaflet" published bimonthly by the library, relying on the collection, commencing with three in 1924. He also lectured at Wayne State University and the University of Detroit. One of Detroit's dailies called him "the greatest authority on the history of Michigan and the Northwest."[3]

Instead of that latter term, the paper should have inserted "old," thus identifying the Old Northwest Territory—the Midwest states of Ohio, Indiana, Illinois, Michigan, and Wisconsin—rather than the upper corner of the continental United States. Quaife was, indeed, an authority on the Northwest Territory. Born in Iowa, schooled in Chicago, and superintendent of the State Historical Society of Wisconsin, he had both academic and professional qualifications to assume the Burton job. A subsequent tenure of over one-third of a century in the Detroit area entitled him to preeminence among scholars of Michigan's heritage. A columnist correctly termed him "student and historian,"[4] for no author of history can be anything other than a constant learner. One of his key findings was being the first to document Chicago's founding by a male of African descent. His groundbreaking work did not stop there.

Because of his reputation, Quaife was chosen to become an editor of forty-three of the first fifty-seven volumes in the *Lakeside Classics* series published by Illinois-based R. R. Donnelley. He began his involvement with Volume 14, *Life of Black Hawk*, a republication of the Native American leader's autobiography. The editor was a man of his time, as evidenced by such assertions as "the Indian was a savage." He did, however, seek a balance in matters as witnessed by his judgment that "the white race was commonly guilty of cruel injustice to the red."[5] In 1937, Lakeside editions began to include Michigan subjects: *The Bark Covered House* by William Nowlin, originally self-published in 1876; *War on the Detroit* (1940); *My Life on the Plains* by George A. Custer (1952);[6] *The Siege of Detroit in 1763* (1958). This, the longest continuously running series of Americana from 1903 to 2019, was a Christmas gift from the company; thus, public copies in university libraries and the Library of Congress were specially obtained. With their limited distribution, the Lakeside Classics are collectors' gems.[7]

In 1944, the Bobbs-Merrill Company launched a comprehensive history of the Great Lakes. The first treated Lake Huron, written by Canadian scholar Fred Landon and edited by Quaife, followed similarly with *Lake Superior* (Grace Lee Nute, PhD in American history from Harvard University).[8] *Lake Michigan* was wholly Quaife's production. The book jacket trumpeted that all ten volumes—success justified adding another five other lakes—were "under the general editorship" of Quaife, as if to provide an imprimatur. He identified himself at the end of the preface, revealing the book's purpose as to "condense something of the grandeur" of the lake, as "M. M. Quaife, Detroit Public Library." He termed the Tunnel of Trees "the most beautiful driveway in Michigan."[9] In this era predating pre-invasive species introduction, one finds the discussion of ecological subjects focused on the effects of excessive hunting and logging on moose and elk populations.

Quaife's indefatigable writing also included some sixty articles contributed to the *Dictionary of American History*, his original work entitled *The Flag of the United States*, the first half of *Michigan: From Primitive Wilderness to Industrial Commonwealth*, *This is Detroit, 1701–1951: Two Hundred and Fifty Years in Pictures*, and *River of Destiny: The St. Marys*. His study of King Strang, the separatist leader of Beaver Island, was groundbreaking.[10] He was a historian whose energies surveyed a vast swathe of Michigan's heritage, including some obscure chapters that he sought to make more available.

In 2018, the Chippewa County Historical Society reprinted *River of Destiny* to commemorate the 350th anniversary of the founding of the Soo. Quaife contributed the first half on the history of the Saint Marys River; Joseph and Estelle Bayliss wrote the rest, and the local library bears their name for a generous bequest. It was en route to visit the Baylisses that Quaife and his spouse, who survived, were involved in the fatal vehicular accident on the Mackinac Trail.[11] The couple then lived at 56 Louise Avenue in Highland Park, a spacious double-gabled two story, emblematic of the best of the city. It still survives today. Quaife's grave is in White Chapel Cemetery, Troy, and whether his works endure is questionable. Scholarship has since evolved, opening new and renewed emphasis on the diversity he touched but did not fully explore. His prolific coverage of the Great Lakes, the Midwest, and Michigan showed his appreciation for "the Good Country" of Middle America, where democracy made its greatest advance, where a rich cultural heritage developed, and where this heartland deserved a central place in our country's history and in attention by historians of succeeding generations.[12]

Selected Works

The Kingdom of Saint James: A Narrative of the Mormons (1930)
Lake Michigan (1944)
Michigan: From Primitive Wilderness to Industrial Commonwealth (1948)
This Is Detroit, 1701–1951: Two Hundred and Fifty Years in Pictures (1951)
River of Destiny: The St. Marys (1955)
Forty-Six Years: The Published Writings of Milo M. Quaife, 1910–1955 (1956)

Gabriel Richard

Michigan's Gutenberg

October 15, 1767–September 13, 1832

Lived in Detroit for thirty-four years as a leading public servant

Housed at the Sacred Heart Major Seminary on Chicago Boulevard in Detroit is a major collection of important written materials. The seminary proclaims its part of the Gabriel Richard Library as a "definitive highlight of the collection," since the entirety was parceled out early in the twentieth century among the Archdiocese of Detroit, the Detroit Public Library, and the University of Michigan. Among the seminary's holdings are Richard's handwritten journals and autographed books.

While such materials are of interest to the rare book collector, the collection is also noteworthy to every Michigander for its original owner's contributions to the state's literary heritage. Richard brought the first printing press to Michigan, which published the first newspaper and some of the first books on these shores. He was among the founders of the institution that today boasts almost forty locations and an inventory of over sixteen million items, making it the second largest research library by number of volumes in the United States.

Gabriel Richard, born in France just after its disastrous North American war with England, was ordained a priest of the Society of Saint-Sulpice, an intellectual order focused on education, in 1790. Two years later, he emigrated to the United States to escape the excesses of the French Revolution. He lived in Maryland and on the frontier before making his way to Detroit in 1798. He was far from physically imposing, but his work encompassed many spiritual and cultural pursuits that grew his popularity. As a civic leader, he helped Detroit rebuild from the fire of 1805 and is credited with its resurgent mottos.[1] He represented the Territory of Michigan in the U.S. House of Representatives during 1823–1825; he carried with him a letter of introduction as a "belles lettres scholar."[2] His community work during a cholera epidemic brought about his death at the age of sixty-four. His remains are interred within the Basilica of Ste. Anne de Detroit where annually an exhibition displays his letters, books, and artifacts. Numerous parochial schools in Michigan bear his name.

Richard (pronounced reesh-ARD) played a major role in the American policy of westernizing the Native population. His legacy, as with many of his contemporaries, cannot be understood properly without consideration of the cultural conflicts to which he contributed.

He also was a benefactor of the literary and educational needs of the people. In 1808, he traveled to Baltimore, purchased a small hand-operated printing press, and brought it back overland to Spring Wells (the area east of the Rouge River) to the house of fellow Frenchman Jacques Lasselle.[3] The prominent Lasselle family had built relationships with the Indigenous people through fur trading and acting as official interpreters in treaty negotiations.[4] The first newspaper appeared on August 31, 1809, but it was not the first item printed via such technology. According to Detroit's early historian, Silas Farmer, "one or more books were printed before the paper was issued." That first issue contained an advertisement whereby the publisher proposed to print several works, such as "Nine Days' Devotion of the Sacred Heart of Jesus; a Manual of Agriculture; cards of small pictures for the study of history, geography, etc.; and a Cyclopedia of Anecdotes for children.'"[5]

It is not obvious that the priest acted as publisher, so perhaps the honor of being the first in Michigan Territory to issue a book should be bestowed on another. Some evidence exists of a printing press as early as 1777, but it only issued proclamations, not a folio-based publication.[6] Some credit might be awarded to John McCall, whose name appears on a pamphlet out of Detroit in 1797.[7] It was James M. Miller who employed the Richard-procured press and supply of type to issue a twelve-page booklet on August 1, 1809, entitled *The Child's Spelling Book; or Michigan Instructor: Being a Compilation from the Most Approved Authors*. It was, says an expert in American printing history, "not the earliest printing in Michigan—but the most significant." And he credited Richard with authorship.[8]

Without books, there can be no bookshops. The book trade commenced in a concerted fashion in 1817 when the proprietors of a newspaper "sought to encourage literary taste and increase their profits by selling books as well as papers."[9] Detroit has been home to some great bookstores down through the decades.[10]

Richard helped found "The Catholepistemiad of Michigania" in 1818 for the purpose of establishing a university level of learning in the territory. His co-founders were John Montieth and Judge Augustus Woodward, who secured a territorial law on August 26, 1817, authorizing creation of the institution in Detroit. Montieth and Richard held the first professorships. In 1837, the school relocated to Ann Arbor where it has become the largest in the state.

A statue of Richard stands on another center of public education, Wayne State University in Detroit. Commissioned by lumber baron and historian Bela Hubbard in 1884, statues of Richard and three other Frenchmen instrumental in the opening up of the Great Lakes region—Cadillac, Marquette, and de la Salle—can be viewed on a pedestrian walkway near the university's Faculty and Administration Building and Towers Residential Suites at 695 West Kirby. They had stood outside the original Detroit City Hall; it was demolished in 1961.

The Basilica of Sainte Anne de Détroit stands tall in its eighth iteration, dedicated in 1886. Its twin towers rise just north of the taller supports for the Ambassador Bridge as it carries an international route over the Detroit River. Trucks queue up beyond a screening wall that separates the church structure on now-closed Howard Street at St. Anne from wheel-carried commerce. Mexicantown is nearby, split by a wide channel of concrete. The award-winning Detroit Riverwalk is within pacing distance, providing a pathway east toward Belle Isle and a park named for the cleric beyond. Less than a mile away is the Michigan Central depot structure, its incredibly painstaking restoration reflecting the hope that renewal is always possible.

One can wonder how Richard would react to changes in the publishing world, with audio and electronic forms sometimes supplanting traditional printing. After all, he introduced technology here that was designed to spread the reach of knowledge. Given the cleric's devotion to words, perhaps his response would be *avec enthousiasme*. But he still would bring the press.

William Penn Adair Rogers

Our Nation Turns Its Lonely Eyes

November 4, 1879–August 15, 1935

Appeared on Michigan stages, honored with school naming in Redford, etc.

A century ago, the cover of *Time* magazine featured an Oklahoman of Native American heritage whose name had become synonymous with good humor and pointed witticisms. Will Rogers performed in circuses, rodeos, vaudeville, motion pictures, and practically anywhere he was invited, including Detroit.

> As the headline feature at the Capitol for the week starting today will be presented the famous stage and screen star, Will Rogers, in person. Mr. Rogers has just terminated a long engagement with the Ziegfeld Frolics. For his Detroit appearance the celebrated gum-chewing, lariat-throwing, quaint philosopher of the stage has arranged a special act which brings him forth with his leathern chaps, his cowboy hat and his ever trusty lariat, and with a new line of patter of the sort which has made him famous, and which deals with current topics of the day in a dry and highly amusing manner. For Mr. Rogers and his special act will be afforded the proper atmosphere in the way of scenic backgrounds, thus making the offering at once one of the most enjoyable seen in Detroit in many a day.[1]

According to the Smithsonian, Rogers "brightened the dark days of the Great Depression with words of compassion and common sense."[2] He also helped people cope with a social experiment that went very wrong. From 1920 until repeal in 1933, Prohibition ruled America, drove much harmless enjoyment underground, and gave powerful impetus to organized crime. In Detroit, the Purple Gang gained notoriety. So, too, did Etta Mae Miller.

The forty-eight-year-old mother of ten was convicted in December 1928 of her fourth offense of selling liquor (two pints this time) in violation of the Michigan Prohibition statute. As a habitual offender, she received a mandatory sentence of confinement at the Detroit House of Correction in western Wayne County for her natural life.[3] Many objected, not the least of which was Rogers, who addressed a communication to the 4,665,000 inhabitants of the state in whose name the criminal complaint had been initiated:

Will Rogers's Suggestion to the State of Michigan

> To the Editor of The *New York Times*:
>
> For her fourth offence in selling liquor the great State of Michigan may send the mother of ten children to the penitentiary for life. I guess that will just about blot out the liquor business in the State. I suppose she was the last one selling. Any woman that tries to raise ten orphan kids in that cold State not only ought to be allowed to sell booze, but the State should furnish it to her to sell, and guarantee that it was pure. That would make her the greatest life saver in Michigan.
>
> It certainly ought to be a lesson to people with ten children to never move to Michigan.[4]

Rogers's humor helped him deal personally with the traumatic experience of his ancestors. He was Native American, born in Oklahoma where the Trail of Tears terminated. Michigan's tribes avoided that fate when they struck a deal with the federal government in the 1800s that enabled their remaining in the Great Lakes State on portions of home grounds. The Treaties of 1836 and 1855, in which the Anishinabek maintained certain ancestral rights, made unnecessary the U.S. Army installation at Fort Scott in Indian Territory along the Kansas/Missouri border that had been designed to keep them on the reservation. That story—the escape from forced removal, thanks to saying no—has begun to emerge again thanks, in part, to signage recently installed along M-185 ringing Mackinac Island and at the newly recommissioned Biddle House featuring the life account of Agatha Biddle, Odawa leader.

Had Rogers been born in Michigan, his career might have been as hunter or fisherman. Instead, he catapulted into status as the leading "wag" of his day, a humorist who could poke fun at nearly anyone without offense but never based on fake news. Despite the "Suggestion," Henry Ford became a close friend, and the two were photographed at Greenfield Village in the year before Rogers died. At his death, newspapers lamented the loss of one who contributed so much to "world amity."[5] He had capably stepped into the role of quintessential American humorist founded by Benjamin Franklin (whose career in ink, as printer, became the profession that gained him notice and fame) and enhanced by Mark Twain, mixing wry humor, folksiness, and barbed observation.

Such a legacy led the educational authorities in south Redford Township to christen a school after the Native American celebrity.[6] Opened in 1955, the T-shaped, subway tile–clad, one-story structure served the growing Baby Boom generation whose parents found affordable housing in the area near Fenton Avenue between Schoolcraft and Glendale. From 1957 until 1961, one of the authors of this work attended that institution, successfully negotiating kindergarten (Mrs. Truesdale) through the third grade (Mrs. Davis). It offered to the inquisitive a solid library in which books of many descriptions could be perused. One, however, bedeviled the budding reader: he borrowed a red-covered volume on several occasions, feeling bound to read every page or else regard himself as a loser. His valiant effort continually foundered after page one hundred when the contents detailed a worm-infested meal served to the hero of the piece while rotting away in a prison.[7]

In 2022, after having been repurposed and then mothballed, the mid-century modern structure, which to youthful eyes resembled a Kenner's Girder and Panel building set, fell to the wrecking ball. Others, including Stillwater's in Rogers's home state, have shared that ignominy. His legacy deserves better. In September 2023, a columnist wrote about "Where There's a Will, There's the Truth," quoting a number of Rogers's quips about politics.[8] Not everyone has forgotten.

According to the Memorial Museum that keeps lit the flame, Rogers "put approximately two million words in print—six books, more than 3,600 newspaper columns, and scores of magazine articles" in only sixteen years of activity. Some were written in Michigan while on tour, such as this 1929 exemplar of humor about Congress:

Will Rogers Tells About Congress Relief To Congress

> Detroit Mich., May 24. Did you know that the only bill that has already passed the House and Senate and been signed by the President is the bill appropriating the salary of the members of this extra session? The farmers can grow whiskers, the orphans can grow up, the tariff can tear out the vitals of the consumers' purse, but the boys there want theirs in advance whether they deliver any relief to anybody else or not.[9]

These opinion pieces could exhibit vitriol; Rogers was also known to use language insensitive to other ethnicities and not apologize. Perhaps, had he lived to senior citizen status, rough edges might have been smoothed.

Yet Rogers was a generous man, and perhaps that trait best justifies the naming of an elementary school twenty years after his passing. A Michigan-related vignette illustrates the point. Entertainer friend Eddie Cantor (son of two Jews) advised Rogers to invest in a certain stock. "I don't know anything about the stock market," the sage responded. "I'll buy a block of it for you," Cantor volunteered, and, sure enough, the share price increased $20 in a short time before a slight drop. Cantor answered a telephone call: from Detroit, Rogers insisted that the holdings held in his name be sold "at once." Angry over his friend's short-term myopia and greediness at profiting without any skin in the game, Cantor nonetheless complied and mailed a check for over $6,000 to Rogers. Soon, in "return mail from Detroit was a letter from Rogers. In it was the check, endorsed by Rogers and made payable to Cantor's 'fresh-air' camp for poor boys."[10]

Robert Anthony Snow

Gently Falling

June 1, 1955–July 12, 2008

Wrote for the *Detroit News*

One of the obituaries for Tony Snow began: "a conservative writer and commentator who cheerfully sparred with reporters died Saturday." The combination of what some would decry as inherently inconsistent ("conservative," "cheerful") drew attention, but the summary did not adequately encapsulate the life lost. A tribute by Nolan Finley, a colleague at the *Detroit News*, was more apt:

> [W]hen it came to the things you fix with your heart, he was a master craftsman. The recounting of Tony Snow's professional life will note that he was one of the most significant journalists of his generation, that he brought class and civility to a political world that has too little of both, and that his ideas helped shape the concept of compassionate conservatism.[1]

Heart; class; civility; compassion. These emotional terms gave the reader a deeper understanding of character, not content to summarize with faint praise (sparring: argument without landing heavy blows). The curious would want to comprehend how, in a post-Mencken era, Tony Snow would be classed among the most significant in journalism during his short life.

Although the Snow family roots go back generations in Kentucky where Tony was born, he grew up outside of Cincinnati, Ohio. His father Jim was a teacher and administrator at Princeton High School in Sharonville, a suburb of the river city, during Tony's youth. Before his graduation in 1973, he had become editor of the school newspaper. In 1979, he was hired as an editorial writer for the newspaper in Greensboro, North Carolina. Three years later, he came to Detroit as deputy editorial page editor for the *Detroit News*, a time when, as the seventh largest in the nation, it led its chief competitor, the *Detroit Free Press*, in circulation, advertising, and profitability. Since the World War I era, the paper has followed principles of journalism laid down in a succinct guidebook:

> Formation of a newspaper's ideals comes through a process of years. The best traditions of the past, blending with hopes of the future, should be the writer's guide for the day. . . . [T]he principles under which the staff should work, in striving toward those journalistic ideals to which this paper feels itself dedicated [and] summary of the best practices of the profession follows:
>
> The *Detroit News* should be:
>
> Vigorous, but not vicious.
>
> Interesting, but not sensational.
>
> Fearless, but fair.
>
> Accurate as far as human effort can obtain accuracy.
>
> Striving ever to gain and impart information.
>
> As bright as possible, but never sacrificing solid information for brilliancy.
>
> Looking for the uplifting rather than the depraved things of life.
>
> We should work to have the word RELIABLE stamped on every page of the paper.
>
> The place to commence this is with the staff members: First, getting men and women of character to do the writing and editing; and then training them in our way of thinking and handling news and other reading matter.[2]

Snow found a home for his values at the venerated Detroit institution, which celebrated its sesquicentennial in 2023. He moved to the conservative *Washington Times* in 1987, served in the White House for President George H. W. Bush, then returned to the *News* in 1993 to write a nationally syndicated column on public affairs. It appeared in more than two hundred outlets. Another effort appeared in a Hillsdale College publication entitled "American Journalism and the Constitution," extolling the ambit and benefits of the First Amendment.[3]

A column from 1995 spoke to how the issue in K-12 schools was "not that too many kids get punished, but that too few receive the education they deserve." Snow spoke from experience, hailing "from a family of teachers," and subbing in a Cincinnati high school. A bright but bored student acted out;

instead of addressing the root cause, "pedagogues . . . did the easy thing": they just passed him through the system. Instead of the discipline and challenge that would have helped him achieve his potential, Tony (ironic, the same first name as Snow) ended up shot to death. In about five hundred words, the conservative writer advocated for tough schools—not where "toughs" reign supreme, but where high expectations prove to kids that they are worthy of high academic investment.[4]

Working for a Detroit publication had another benefit. He met Jill Ellen Walker, a fellow employee, and they married in 1987. In February 2005, Snow received a diagnosis of cancer of the colon, reminiscent of the disease that had taken his mother's life prematurely. Treatment brought remission until a recurrence in April 2007. Soon after, he delivered the commencement address at Catholic University, enjoining the graduates: "I want you to remember that it's not about you. It's a hard lesson—a lot of people go through life and never learn it. It's to submit willingly, heart and soul, to things that matter." On December 6, 2007, Snow delivered a speech entitled "Overcoming Adversity: Beating the Odds and Passing the Tests" at College of the Ozarks in Missouri. His contest with disease ended seven months later. The funeral was held at the Basilica of the National Shrine of the Immaculate Conception in Washington, D.C., emblematic of his fervent faith.

Nolan Finley also wrote that Snow "was drawn by the history and his place in it, by what he saw as the deep privilege of serving his country." Pulitzer Prize–winning political columnist George F. Will, a former Michigander, wrote a fond epitaph: "There is nothing more perishable than the reputation of Washington media types. But not in the case of Tony, who still is widely and fondly remembered, perhaps because he is emblematic of a better time."

The passage of years since Snow's death just after the Fourth of July already evokes a certain nostalgia for a time before "fake news." It, and the journalist who was associated with one of Michigan's major publications, are fondly remembered by those who counted on a reliable, solid, and unsensational voice to be a key source for understanding what went on outside their front door. It was a rosier time when debate did not require destruction of an opponent's person and newspapers were not hiding behind paywalls.

David Augustus Straker

To Raise and Reconcile

July 11, 1840–February 14, 1908

Moved to Detroit at age forty-eight; wrote, died, and was buried there

The preface ended with a specific date—August 1, 1888—and location—"Detroit, Mich." The title—*The New South Investigated*—suggested an exposé of that region's fragmented post–Civil War society after the end of legalized slavery. The preface, however, conveyed a hopeful view of the Reconstruction Era. How could a Detroiter take up the subject from a home in the Midwest so far away? One reason: the author of this two-hundred-page set of policy recommendations and wisdom was a distinguished lawyer who had been elected several times to the legislature of a southern state. A dozen years of his life had been invested in the sunny South. He also brought to the subject a special qualification, for he was of African lineage.

David Augustus Straker was born free on Barbados, the easternmost island in the Caribbean. Receiving an excellent education, he became a schoolmaster at the age of seventeen. He was inspired to come to the United States soon after the Civil War and participate "in the uplifting of his race" in the reconstructed South as a teacher of freedmen in Kentucky. He flirted with the ministry but opted for the bar, graduating from Howard University Law School in 1872.[1] That same year, he married Annie Carey of Detroit, a descendant of a grandfather born in Guadeloupe. An uncle, John D. Richards, "was well-known in Detroit circles and served as a delegate to the 1864 National Convention of Colored Men" held in October 1864.[2] Frederick Douglass served as convention president, and the gathering approved a Declaration of Wrongs and Rights and an address to the people of the United States, hoping that the future "may bring to us all the blessings of equal liberty" instead of "the woes of slavery and continued social degradation."[3] The list of attendees "would leave any student of African American culture star struck."[4] Annie's obituary would mention her local presidency of the Colored Educational Improvement Society.[5]

Improvement of the condition of Americans of African descent and of race relations in general was the watchword for lawyer Straker. He worked in the U.S. Treasury Department in Washington; as customs inspector in Charleston, South Carolina; in the practice of law in Orangeburg; and as victorious candidate for the State Legislature in 1878 and 1880. In 1882, he became dean of the Allen University School of Law in Columbia, an institution founded in 1870 by the African Methodist Episcopal Church. He served there until 1884 when he resumed practicing law, serving as president of the 1883 National Convention of Colored Men at Louisville.[6] The couple moved to Detroit in 1887 where his legal work blossomed with a multi-racial clientele.[7] The Strakers lived at 230 Bagg Street (today, Temple).[8]

The New South Investigated was published within a year of the move. It exuded hope, for great changes had been occurring in the region, Straker wrote, wrought initially by the "destruction of slavery," and since the youth of today and tomorrow were poised for their enjoyment. New industry, new architecture, and the prospect of a "better understanding between the people" were blossoming. If the region's citizens would embrace the reality of the constitutional impetus for a more racially equal society, "there are enough inherent possibilities in the South to make it a great section of our country." That region had much to be proud of in the early history of the Republic, but as "the theatre of human slavery," it had betrayed the nation's founding principles upon which "*all* of its citizens" were to "enjoy the fullest opportunity for intellectual, industrial and moral advancement." Greater educational opportunities must be afforded to those who were denied this avenue to advancement in the "Old South." The performance of people of color in the great universities of the North—"Harvard, Yale, Princeton and Ann Arbor"—proved their capacity. Social and political conditions still needed major improvement. Prejudice existed in both the North and South, but Straker believed that "time will heal all of this." He looked forward to when the races would all gather at "the feast of reconciliation and good feeling," a day when "all race feeling will disappear." He believed that era was "near" for "Our country."[9]

The same year of the move to Detroit, on August 15, 1887, William W. Ferguson and a friend entered the European Hotel Restaurant run by Edmund G. Gies at 10–14 Monroe Street.[10] The establishment had one room with two sides: in the restaurant portion were tables with white tablecloths and fine glassware, with an electric fan to cool patrons, while the "saloon side" contained uncovered tables and beer glasses. The two men of color sat in the finer portion, but a server informed them, "I can't wait on you here." Why not? The waiter replied, "We cannot serve you kind of people here. It is against the rules of the house to serve colored people in the restaurant. If you want anything to eat, you will have to go on the other side of the house." Ferguson appealed to Gies, who upheld the discriminatory policy and, when the matter went to court, freely admitted to the practice "for no other reason than that Ferguson was a colored man."

Straker represented Ferguson and initially lost his case in the Wayne County Circuit Court. The judge instructed the jury that the plaintiff was entitled, under the law and, specifically, the 1885 Michigan Civil Rights Statute, to full and equal accommodations with all other citizens. He also advised that the defendant should win "as long as the accommodations offered are substantially the same"—which amounted to an endorsement of "Jim Crow" practices under which segregation by racial classification was permissible. The case went to the Michigan Supreme Court, which adopted Straker's argument:

> The fault of this instruction is that it permits a discrimination on account of color alone, which cannot be made under the law with any justice. As far as it relates to the right of a restaurant keeper to make rules and regulations based upon other considerations, the charge is of no concern in this case, and we shall not express any opinion as to its correctness. But in Michigan there must be and is an absolute, unconditional equality of white and colored men before the law. The white man can have no rights or privileges under the law that are denied to the black man. Socially people may do as they please within the law, and whites may associate together, as may blacks, and exclude whom they please from their dwellings and private grounds; but there can be no separation in public places between people on account of their color alone which the law will sanction.[11]

Six years later, the U.S. Supreme Court ruled to the contrary in the infamous *Plessey v. Ferguson* "separate but equal" holding—a doctrine that ranked with the *Dred Scott* decision among that tribunal's execrable precedents. Not until *Brown v. Board of Education* in 1954, a lifetime after *Ferguson*, did the law of the land keep pace with Michigan's jurisprudence.

Straker's achievement and expertise received acclaim from many quarters, and he was elected in 1893 to Circuit Court Commissioner of Wayne County despite his "uncompromising Republican" allegiance, defeating white candidates in an overwhelmingly Democratic Party jurisdiction. In 1895, he was elected president of the National Federation of Colored Men of the United States of America, founded to bring an end to lynchings in the South.[12] He launched and wrote for the *Detroit Advocate*, a short-lived weekly newspaper.[13]

Much could still have been anticipated in life and letters from "the foremost Negro lawyer on [the] continent,"[14] but he was cut off before reaching seventy. Like other prominent Detroiters, Straker was buried in Elmwood Cemetery, where the Straker tombstone marks the final resting place of the couple in Section S, Lot 10.

On New Year's Eve of 2000, Detroit Mayor Dennis W. Archer opened a copper box that had been secreted a century earlier by his predecessor, William C. Maybury. The time capsule contained letters from fifty-six Detroit citizens containing impressions of their contemporary circumstances and predictions for the future. Maybury's was addressed "To His Honor, The Mayor of Detroit in 2001 and to the generation whose privilege—and I hope pleasure—it will be to read the letters in this box contained." They had been compiled "at my request by men and women prominent in the activities of Detroit at the close of the nineteenth Century" and for this principal benefit: "From testimony so transmitted you will be the better able to discern what advancement you have made from the modest beginnings of which we are witnesses."

D. Augustus Straker was among the women and men of prominence whose writings were enclosed. His topic: "The past, present, and future of the colored race in Detroit." In a beautifully elegant hand, he wrote:

> The 19th century found the colored people of Detroit a race of slaves altho slavery is not known ever to have < had > a foot hold here. The incoming of the 20th century finds every man, and woman, & child of the colored race, enjoying complete freedom under the law. The 19th century found the colored race in Detroit, ignorant, uneducated, poor, and unenlightened, save with few exceptions. The 20th century dawns upon us with every school door in the City of Detroit, wide open, welcoming within its walls, every colored, as well as white child, of our common citizenship, and from whose precincts have come, educated, and well equipped colored men & women, who have

filled high positions of honor and trust—The 19th century found laws upon the Statute books of our State, which deprived the colored man and woman of enjoyment of every civil, and social < privilege > participated in by our white fellow citizens—The 20th century finds the colored citizens of Detroit in the enjoyment, and right to go, and enter every public place established for public accommodation—The 19th century found the colored race poor and in many instances homeless, because of the low wages and restricted opportunity to labor, and receive adequate wages—The 20th century finds a large per cent of the colored race in Detroit, the owner of their residences. In the past, enough was not earned for any part to be saved. On the incoming of the 20th century a large number of our colored citizens are depositors in our Savings Banks, and some carry a fair commercial account in the transactions of their business—The moral status of the colored race in Detroit with the advantages afforded, compare most favorably with that of any other race of people similarly situated. No laws discriminate between the races on account of Color—These achievements have been brought about by the pioneer energy of such veterans among the colored race as William Lambert. Ben De Baptiste: John Richards, Geo. Parker and others. And now as to the future of the colored race in Detroit.

If we should augur from the past, and present, we have the brightest expectation for the future. Two elements must enter into the future progress of the race. One by the white race and the other by the colored themselves. This element is *equal opportunity*. This and this only remains to test the true development of the race. In the past this was wholly denied the colored race, in the present it is but partially employed—we look to the future for its completion. We ourselves must be ready for the wider opportunity to come. May one hundred years hence find us in the full enjoyment of those rights and privileges which prejudice now deny us. A prejudice does now exist on the fringe of the 20th century—I predict that the sunlight of a more perfect understanding of the Fatherhood of God & the brotherhood of man will drive out the demon < prejudice > and when the 21st century arrives he will find no resting place in the beautiful City of the straits.[15]

That century has arrived, yet the need remains for an association of barristers founded in 1990 that pursues a mission "to increase minority representation in the legal profession, support and encourage legal practice opportunities for minorities, and facilitate equal justice for all citizens."[16] A

Michigan Historical Marker once commemorated Straker where his house was torn down in 1926 for the Fort Wayne Hotel. Although installed a decade after the June 1967 days of unrest, the marker became victim to scrappers who also ruined the interior of the historic hotel. Recently, however, a plan to renovate the structure into residential space was announced as part of the "District Detroit" development.[17] Detroit's comeback remains a work in progress; so do America's race relations. Straker's hopefulness still speaks: "God speed the hour," he wrote, when all citizens of "our country" will exhibit "aught of malice or uncharitableness."[18]

Selected Works

The New South Investigated (1888)
A Trip to the Windward Islands; or Then and Now (1896)

Raoul Gustaf Wallenberg

Truly "Rudy"

August 4, 1912–disappeared January 17, 1945
Attended University of Michigan in Ann Arbor

If only he had lived. If only he hadn't been swallowed up by the surviving totalitarian regime near the moment of triumph over an equally barbaric dictatorship. If only he had personally enjoyed the plaudits justifiably awarded for his efforts during World War II to save targets of Nazi torture and murder. If only he could have penned his memoirs, recounting for posterity how he mustered the courage to stand up to unbridled power.

The story of Raoul Wallenberg has become well known thanks to book and video treatment of his extraordinary deeds while working in Budapest in cooperation with the U.S. War Refugee Board. Employed as secretary within the Swedish legation, Wallenberg actively sought to protect Jewish people from persecution under the Hungarian Nazi regime. Estimates vary of the number saved, but it is agreed that thousands benefited. After Soviet forces gained control in Hungary in early 1945, Wallenberg vanished. His death under Soviet authority is not disputed, only the date.

What is lesser known about this Schindler-like hero is his fondness for university days in Ann Arbor. "Rudy," as he was known to fellow students, first attended the architecture program at the University of Michigan in 1931. He lived in a 1910 Dutch Colonial at 308 East Madison Street, would walk to the Michigan Union for breakfast, and took classes in Lorch Hall, a historic structure on Monroe at Tappan, also known as the old Architecture and Design building. The current naming honors Professor Emil Lorch, of German heritage, who designed the building as part of elevating the school of architecture into prominence. Lorch was Rudy's mentor. Upon graduation in 1935, Wallenberg received the American Institute of Architects silver medal as U of M's most outstanding student.

On November 25, 1936, Wallenberg wrote to Lorch from Nice, France, asking guidance for obtaining a position in the field. Lorch suggested he first gain experience in Europe and then return to America for an architectural career. It never happened; the Second World War intervened to shape the young man's next steps. His letter on the twenty-fifth however, stands as a tribute to the experiences the future humanitarian enjoyed while living and studying in Michigan, with overtones of the work he would shoulder as a diplomat:

> My thoughts very often go back to you and your school. Now that my work in South Africa and Palestine is at an end I have had more time to remember the wonderful three years and a half which I spent in Ann Arbor. Many times I have thought that since I am likely always to have one foot abroad I should at least see to it that "abroad" would mean America. . . . I feel it a pity to turn my back on architecture after all the good times it has given me. I believe the building industry has an enormous development ahead for the next few years in America and I would like to do my share in the great things that are to come. Please tell me if you think that conditions *now* are such that I would have a chance of finding a paid job as draftsman in New York or Detroit. . . . I have so much of a longing to come to America again that I would be coming over on much less than a definite offer for a job.[1]

These words remain a poignant tribute to mentor, school, and graduate, all collaborating on a legacy of creativity during a horrific era well known for the intentional and wanton destruction of cultural resources.

Although the university demolished the East Madison home in 2024, it established a Wallenberg Institute, has a Wallenberg memorial, and awards a Wallenberg medal. In the nation's capital, 100 Raoul Wallenberg Place SW is the address on a portion of Fifteenth Street SW where the United States Holocaust Memorial Museum is located. A Holocaust museum in Farmington Hills, a Holocaust Memorial in the Frederik Meijer Gardens and Sculpture Park near Grand Rapids, and a dozen State historical markers speak to Jewish heritage in the Great Lakes State, including one on Atwater Street in Detroit memorializing "Jewish Soldiers in the Civil War." It was erected in 2007 not far from the Lorch-designed Belle Isle Bridge; the program in its latest phase was launched in 1955 in legislation signed by Governor Gerhard Mennen Williams, born in 1911, of German heritage, then forty-four years of age.

Alumnus Wallenberg would have turned forty-three that year. If only he had lived.

Laura Ingalls Wilder

Little House in the Tallest Store

February 7, 1867–February 10, 1957
Made a revelatory appearance in Detroit

From 1932 to 1943, Wisconsin-born Laura Elizabeth Ingalls authored and published a celebrated series of eight children's titles commonly known as the *Little House* editions. The books presented a rather idealized version of rural Midwest life and achieved widespread commercial success, selling tens of thousands of copies. On September 11, 1974, a television adaption of the books premiered and quickly became highly popular. The program earned nominations for best series and remained on the air until 1984. In January 2025, streaming service Netflix announced a reboot of the program, seeking to capitalize on its continuing appeal. According to Nielsen, viewers in 2024 spent 13.25 billion minutes watching the old series. Videos bolstered the reputation of Wilder's books: worldwide book sales now approach seventy-five million copies.

Before her death in 1957, Ingalls made her first and only appearance at a writer's event—in Detroit—explaining antipathy to additional public engagements because she had something to say about her work, "and once she said it, that was enough."[1] Her target audience at the fourth annual "Week of Authors" presented by the J. L. Hudson department store was children: the final segment on Saturday afternoon, October 16, 1937, featured four juvenile book writers, Wilder as the final speaker because of her most recent volume.[2] She reminisced about her "wonderful" pioneer childhood and the unfolding plan to use such memories for an unprecedented lengthy series of historical novels. The values exhibited by her parents of courage, self-reliance, and integrity, seen through the eyes of an impressionable girl, filled these books and would inspire future young readers.

Wilder's remarks were revealing for adults and critics as well. Her approach in *On the Banks of Plum Creek*, as with the whole series, had been consistently applied:

> Every story in this novel, all the circumstances, each incident are true.
>
> All I have told is true but it is not the whole truth. There were some stories I wanted to tell but would not be responsible for putting in a book for children, even though I knew them as a child.[3]

Some readers and reviewers believed the books were autobiographical. Wilder insisted they were true, and she spoke elsewhere of her extensive efforts to get facts straight. Harper and Brothers subtitled *Plum Creek* as *The True Story of an American Pioneer Family*. Wilder and her publisher also denied that daughter Rose Wilder Lane had provided key assistance. Documents found after her death in 1968 proved Rose, a professional editor, had been a key contributor through powerful suggestions, critiques, and edits to each volume. Laura enjoyed, in Rose, a silent partner.

The collaboration between mother and daughter constitutes a rich backstory of shared feminine creativity, rather than detracting from the *Little House* oeuvre. What Laura published held truth and had a large basis in historical events, but her books were not literal, completely factual truth. As editor Maxwell Perkins said, "a reader is meant to enter into a novel as if it were reality, and so to feel it."[4]

Hudson's downtown store sprawled over the city block at Woodward and Gratiot. At over two million square feet, the building took second to Macy's Manhattan store. Its claim to fame, however, came in height: at twenty-five floors, it was the tallest department store in the world in 1937—and a dozen years later.

In May 1949, the Detroit Public Library did something it had never done by naming a new branch facility after a living person.[5] At eighty-two years of age, Wilder did not feel comfortable attending the ceremony at 6815 East Seven Mile Road. She had to be content with handwriting a thank-you note:

> Dear Friends,
>
> Although I am not present, I join with you in being glad that you now have a Branch Library in your comunity [*sic*].
>
> I am proud and grateful that it has been named for me and that my "Little House Books" will be among the ones you may read.

> Unless you have lived, as I did, where books were scarce and so prized greatly, you can not realize how wonderful it really is to have a whole library so convenient for your use.
>
> With congratulations and all good wishes.

A letter on June 2 to the library director repeated the sentiment: "The Branch being named for me is such a wonderful thing that at times it has seemed incredible." The east side resource moved to permanent quarters at 7140 East Seven Mile in a formal dedication on February 6, 1967. The program bragged how Detroit's branch was "the first in the world to be named in honor of this great American."[6]

Wilder's luster lost some glow with the revelation of her daughter's involvement and a closer look at her language. She employed terms of disrespect for Native and African-Americans that were natural to some speakers of the era. An American Library Association award once named for Wilder, honoring authors and illustrators whose books have made a lasting contribution to the genre, has become the Children's Literature Legacy Award. In place of myth has arisen a more complicated understanding about Wilder's works and how memory served as foundation, not as limit; yet, even though "brilliantly edited" to shape memory into fiction, "the truth about our history is in them."[7]

Children's books can be acquired at more than five hundred Hudson Booksellers across North America, principally in airports. History lovers make the connection, since none exists corporately to the mezzanine-level J. L. Hudson book department that provided excellent customer service, including free home delivery, before the flagship store closed in 1983 and was demolished in 1998. A "Hudson's Detroit" tower now rises nearly seven hundred feet on the block, the billion-dollar development to hold retail, office, residential, and hotel functions. The Wilder branch has reopened on Seven Mile Road after needed refurbishment.

Laura Ingalls Wilder traveled more than seven hundred miles from Mansfield, Missouri, to speak to young people from in and around Detroit. She made a Great American road trip in a late-model Chrysler airflow automobile rather than travel by train. She came in order to relate words of importance about an era of American life no longer to be found.

The *Little House* stories continue to speak at the first quarter pole of the twenty-first century.

Central/South Central Michigan

Lawton Thomas Hemans

Pure Michigander

November 4, 1864–November 17, 1916

Mason-area resident, wrote two seminal books on Michigan history

In spring 2023, the Capitol of Michigan shuddered as if from a Midwest earthquake. No geologic event had occurred; instead, biology was at play in the form of the Cannabis sativa plant, its regulation, and profitable sales thereof. A former Speaker of the House of Representatives offered a guilty plea in federal court to accepting a bribe in return for easing a marijuana licensing requirement. It was then but the latest in a long history of corrupt behavior to beset Michigan government since the first state election, rendered by an artist to permanently expose unseemly conduct.[1]

Never a hint of scandal approached the fifty-two-year life and career of the Democratic candidate for governor of Michigan in 1908 and 1910. Lawton Thomas Hemans was a son of an English-born blacksmith and farmer, whose 1915 death notice called him an honorable man. Upon her death in 1918, Frances Lovinia (Sherwood) Hemans was simply described as a well-known resident of Ingham County, underscoring her fine character. Their son had, wrote his wife, "a great soul, great in the little things as well as in the larger affairs of public life." From humble beginnings, he became a public school teacher, graduate of the University of Michigan law school, elected commissioner of the Ingham Circuit Court, appointed member of the Michigan Railroad Commission, member of the House of Representatives, mayor of Mason, and delegate to the 1907 constitutional convention. His reputation gained him the gubernatorial nomination, twice.

He was also a writer. He became a member of the literary club of Mason at age twenty-seven, and he was serving as its president at the time of his death. Hemans was not the first to pen a history of the Great Lakes State. That honor belongs to James H. Lanman in 1845, soon followed by Electa Maria Sheldon, whose book *The Early History of Michigan, from the First Settlement to 1815* appeared in 1856.[2] Hemans's rendition, however, went through several printings beginning in 1906 and totaling at least nine editions, the last appearing in 1920, as did an edition of *Life and Times of Stevens Thomson Mason the Boy Governor of Michigan*.[3] The biography was a posthumous issue; the author had died of stomach cancer in the Kellogg sanitarium at Battle Creek. He was buried in Maple Grove Cemetery in Mason.

Wife Minnie Pauline Hemans had written a preface for the Mason book. She outlived their legacy, dying in 1956 after their son, Charles Fitch Hemans, had disgraced it. Although a U.S. Army officer in World War I, member of the University of Michigan board of regents, and attorney, Charles was implicated in two major Lansing bribery scandals. The "Baron of the Bathroom"—earned because it was in lavatorial space he conducted his payoffs—does not appear to have authored any publication. Perhaps a penitent exposé would have restored some standing. The parents' Federal-style house remains neatly standing in Mason at 624 South Lansing Street at the corner of West Cherry, a county historical marker affixed to its white-hued siding.

Subsequent heritage surveys of the state have been written, some detailed, none better than a thematic masterpiece by Bruce Catton in *Michigan: A Bicentennial History*.[4] The state's greatest historian painted a picture of a conflicted Michigan, one that embraces and wastes its natural resources, that enshrines high ideals in its Constitution while discriminating against peoples whose crime is being different from their persecutors, that is both optimistic and all grit thanks to its turbulent past.

The Hemans name, virtually forgotten now, endured much in the mid-twentieth century. Perhaps it is worth remembering for the two attempts to record much of Michigan's storied past as well as the other service of this "great soul." Many state officials attended his 1916 funeral, and a eulogist framed the classic contradiction coursing through Michigan political history, of grace versus graft: "Happy the state which can stand beside the open grave of a great man, without a cloud upon its pride at having had such a son."[5]

Selected Works

History of Michigan (1906)

Life and Times of Stevens Thomson Mason: The Boy Governor of Michigan (1920)

John Theodore Herrmann

Genius Is Not Enough

November 9, 1900–April 9, 1959

Born and grew up in Lansing, attended University of Michigan, buried in Mount Hope Cemetery

They were born less than a year apart, spent formative years in Michigan, and met in Paris after World War I. They died two years apart. Both the Hemingway and Herrmann families had cottages on Walloon Lake. John T. Herrmann's younger brothers, twins Robert and Richard, were friends with Ernest Hemingway's younger sister Sunny. Ernest loved Herrmann's clothing store, a tailor shop in downtown Lansing—among the state's largest and finest—and the hand-me-down suits gifted by his friend. As authors, they shared the "editor of genius," Maxwell Perkins of Scribner's Sons fame. Both claimed charter member status in the "Lost Generation" group of expatriates who met in Paris cafés to drink European wines while crafting their literary efforts. Herrmann and wife Josephine Herbst, a respected (and perhaps better) author herself, visited their famous friend at Key West and Caribbean points. Hemingway was six feet tall; Herrmann was three inches taller.

The comparison ends there. Hemingway's first novel, *The Sun Also Rises*, achieved critical and financial success. Herrmann's first, *What Happens*, published initially in France, was banned from importation into the United States. The U.S. Copyright Office denied Herrmann's application for registration. Books deemed obscene were not eligible for copyrighting.

Why this reaction? In 2016, *What Happens* was deemed a Michigan Notable Book by the Library of Michigan. Citing its ban and first American publication the year before, the press release summarized its plot: "tells the coming-of-age story of Winfield Payne, a young man from a wealthy Michigan family. Winfield's struggles to make his way in the world are complicated by his awakening sexuality and fickle affections. He wants to be a hero but modern life isn't made for heroes."

A contemporary opined that Herrmann "had fled laodicean America" because it "deprived him of the force to have powerful experiences." Still, he "did not know how to use his life or his talent." He "surreptitiously worshiped the agrarian states" of the Midwest, pining away for "the red barns of the old bucolic America."[1] His short writing career is evidence of the internal conflict he could not resolve.

The yearn to write began maturing in high school when he served as journalist and newspaper correspondent. Despite the banning of his first book, Herrmann gained some positive press with the next offering. In December 1928, the *Detroit Free Press* told its readers that a new "full length novel" entitled *Engagement* had been published that was "in every way a modern novel." Perhaps an encomium from world-famous "Papa" might help, but Hemingway was reluctant to write blurbs for fellow authors, claiming he had no facility for it. Still, he composed an endorsement for his friend's *Summer Is Ended*, published in fall 1932: "John Herrmann writes of the tragedy of the human heart as truly as any writer who ever lived." Setting the book in the Lansing/East Lansing area limited its appeal.

Despite praise, none of his books did particularly well. In 2018, a second novel not published during Herrmann's life came into print. *Foreign Born* told the tale of Ernst Weiman, a German immigrant who became a successful businessman in Fairbanks, Michigan (a fictionalized Lansing), until the outbreak of the First World War. Everything of German origin became suspect, and Weiman's heritage proved inconvenient in a society rampant with jingoism. The topic did not appeal to publishers and was shelved.

One of Herrmann's works did appear within U.S. borders just months before Germany elevated a monster as its top civilian leader. Entitled "The Big Short Trip," the short story was published in Volume XCII of *Scribner's Magazine* for August 1932. He had two shorties published the prior year, "The Man Who Had Two Stars" about a Pullman conductor who encountered the Queen of England and "The Gale of August Twentieth." The latter involved a sailboat setting out from Pentwater for a two-week excursion across Lake Michigan, up to Mackinac Island, into the Les Cheneaux archipelago, then back home along the eastern coastline. The severity of an unexpected gale alters the life plans of Roger Martin of "Benton, Mich.," a stand-in for the author's birth city, causing him to vow "if he ever made shore it was his last time on the water." His business problems, delaying a marriage proposal, all became "simple out there in the storm," the bravado of thinking "he was young yet and had plenty of time" before making commitments all vanished before the fury of a Great Lakes tempest. The Herrmanns owned a vessel, and the story evidenced real sailing experience.

The couple's leftist views carried them into association with the Communist Party. They separated in 1934 and divorced in 1940. Herrmann married again, and it was widow Ruth who revealed his death in Mexico, where he had lived for ten years, on April 9, 1959, after serving in the U.S. Coast Guard during World War II and becoming a salesman afterward. He had given up writing soon after his first marriage ended.

The family home stands at 520 North Capitol Avenue, refurbished to the tune of several hundred thousand dollars on the Lansing Community College campus. The English Tudor design, with Norman and French influences, bespeaks refinement and style, fitting for a tailor who had gained status notwithstanding immigrating from Europe, with the impression of conveying lasting value. The State historical marker says nothing about the author who grew up within its walls.

One writer with Michigan roots continues to be regarded as a giant of literature, while the other is virtually forgotten despite his membership in the famous "Lost Generation" writers' stable. Genius is not enough, a critic notoriously wrote in pointed evisceration of a writer (Thomas Wolfe) who had come to fame in 1929. For Herrmann, the saying is even truer, for fame never paid him a visit even after he had long left Lansing.

Selected Works

What Happens (1926)
Engagement (1928, possibly 1925)
Pennsylvania Idyll (with Josephine Herbst, 1929)
Summer Is Ended (1932)
The Salesman (1939)
Foreign Born (2018)

Anna M. Johnson

Hope Daring

July 11, 1860–1945
Lived and wrote in Hastings, Barry County

The gravestone is simple but rather odd to the modern eye. The practice of including a pseudonym or nom de plume—alter ego or nickname—has become far less frequent on grave markers. A modern guide to inscriptions on veterans' headstones and markers announces that the federal government will furnish and inscribe them and does allow "accent marks such as the tilde, ampersand, parenthesis, colon and hyphen" when appropriate.[1]

Apparently, such punctuation was appropriate on the marker for a woman named Anna Johnson in Riverside Cemetery in Hastings. The burial ground is in three sections at 1003 West State Road near the banks of the Thornapple River; this marker is in the north section. It is one of thousands in the cemetery, but a parenthesis does set it off. Aside from birth and death years is found: "(Hope Daring)." No obvious clue to its significance is provided.

One must refer to the 1938 edition of *Who's Who in America* to uncover the reason: "Johnson, Anna ('Hope Daring'), author." The parenthetical inclusion was meant, then, to give Johnson's pen name and identify her as a writer. After giving her birthplace (Bradford County, Pennsylvania), birthdate, and parents' names, *Who's Who* also reported her education at Albion College, vocation as a teacher in "dist. sch. several years," her unmarried status, and her memberships in the Michigan Woman's Press Association, Michigan Authors Association, and Michigan Academy of Science, Arts and Letters. At her residence in Hastings, she was a "Contrb. to Juvenile and religious publications." Following came a list of fourteen works, all between 1901 and 1928, a rich output over such a period.[2]

A few other details appear in another reference dedicated to women.[3] Her Hastings home address was 428 Church Street; in 2026, the house remained standing, a refurbished Victorian, with the original garage providing a clue to how it must have appeared during Johnson's residence. The publication recorded her attendance in the Barry County district schools and Hastings High School before college. Her church: Methodist. Her "recreations: reading, travel." She held membership in the local Women's Club and contributed to "many Sunday-school and church papers."

Johnson's publisher for some works was the American Tract Society.[4] The organization dates back to its founding in May 1825 in New York City for the purpose of publishing and disseminating Christian literature. The Michigan Woman's Press Association had a secular origin in 1890 when "a handful of resolute newspaper women"—that is, the wives and female assistants of male editors and publishers—clamored for a league of their own. Their first meeting in Traverse City, with assistance from the local Ladies' Library Association, resulted in its founding. At first it was limited to journalists, but the membership was expanded to female "literary workers," thus welcoming authors such as Johnson into the fold.[5]

A leading compendium on Michigan literature reveals that her first literary works appeared in periodicals and were collected in *Agnes Grant's Education*, published in 1902—"with several later editions." The University of North Carolina–Greensboro includes the cover of the first in its rare book collection, detailing its grayish-olive calico-texture cloth with flowering stems in white, gilt lettering, and a "border of black thick rule between gilt thin rules; spine lettered and ruled in gilt." Some expense went into its production, appropriate given the author's apparent popularity. The same occurred for another of her novels, *Madeline: The Island Girl*, which "went through several editions from 1907 to 1923."[6] The book's setting was a significant feature, with its natural attributes playing a key role such as with a picnic near "Sugar-Loaf Rock" that sought to invoke First People lore. Photographs—perhaps taken by the author—show several sites. It also contains a historical surprise, in which a native Virginian seeks to escape having to choose sides in the American Civil War:

> When the civil war broke out, Richard Lawrence found himself in an anomalous position. He could not raise his hand against his country's flag, and he

> believed the North to be in the right. Still the beautiful Southland was his home; he loved it too well to wage war against it.
>
> There was but one way open before him. He left his home, the residence of many generations of Lawrences. After spending some time in travel, in 1863 he settled at Mackinac Island.[7]

Books about the picturesque and historic isle are not scarce. Some have become classics, such as Iona Fuller's *The Loon Feather*.[8] Others have lasting power because of movie adaptation, the best example being *Somewhere in Time*.[9] Constance Fenimore Woolson's *Anne*, another first novel set on the island, first appeared full-length in 1882.[10]

Hope Daring has only a mention on a cemetery tablet. She had ceased writing by the 1940 Census, when she responded "no" to the question about being employed. Just a decade before, she had specified her occupation as author of books and short stories. Aside from brief mentions in author anthologies, her life's work is forgotten. Perhaps it deserved nothing more. But this real-life Anna did dare.

Selected Works

Agnes Grant's Education (1902)
An Abundant Harvest (1904)
Madeline: The Island Girl (1907)
Father John; or, Ruth Webster's Quest (1907)
The Woods in the Home (1927)

Belle Kanaris Maniates

A Studiously Cheerful Woman

September 1861–November 13, 1931

Born in Marshall, long-time Lansing resident

Born when the United States was tearing itself apart in the Civil War, Belle Maniates was of distinguished Greek heritage. Newspaper stories relate how her physician father became the elected city recorder of Marshall. Her mother was a descendant of an American officer in the Revolutionary War. Wanting to act as a patriot in the fashion of his ancestors, Dr. Maniates volunteered for service in the Civil War. But he died before mustering into the 6th Michigan Infantry Regiment in June 1861. Widowed in her early thirties, Martha Arabelle ("Belle") Becker became family breadwinner through employment at the local post office and as a public school teacher.[1] The younger Belle never knew her father and did not see her mother purely as a stay-at-home mom.

Perhaps this forced example became the springboard for the daughter's vision for life. Belle never married. She began to support her mother's finances by age twenty, teaching school while living in the family home in Jackson. She apparently moved to Detroit for a U.S. government job before taking a State public sector post in Lansing, first as a clerk in the auditor-general's office. She next took a position in the State military department as aide to its director. Her first published work focused on one of the five regiments mustered into service in 1898 during the Spanish-American War. She thus became the first self-identified Greek American author.

Belle's government position provided subject matter for her first novel, *David Dunne: A Romance of the Middle West*. The main character first appeared in a widow's household; he became an orphan with his mother's sudden death. Taken into a kind household, one day he was delighted to receive a dozen classic books with his name on the flyleaf of each. He had an aptitude for reading and studying, laying the groundwork for a career in law that began optimistically when he won acquittal based on his conviction that the client was innocent. More success propelled him to the State House as the youngest member, then to a foreign consul position that enabled his authorship of a best-selling novel. Such fame brought him back home and elevation to the position of speaker of the House, then to governor—and to marriage, fulfilling the "romance" aspect of the subtitle. Faced with a difficult decision, Dunne took his childhood protector on a tour of the State Capitol that reached "the room where in glass cases reposed the old, unfurled battle flags" of the Civil War—paralleling how Michigan's regimental banners were installed in the 1879 Capitol. The older man was allowed "with trembling hands" to take out his regiment's flag, "gazed at it in silence, and then restored it carefully to its place." The scene underscored the integrity of both men, and the story closed with an embrace between mentor and the governor's betrothed.

A promotional piece by publisher Rand McNally emphasized the book as "a charming love story . . . with genuine and exquisite pathos." But it was *Amarilly of Clothes-Line Alley* that struck gold—the Hollywood version. Categorized as "a bit of light character fiction," the story of a lower-class but noble working woman perfectly fit the vision of producer Adolph Zukor, a founder of Paramount Pictures, for his main female star, Mary Pickford. The sixty-seven-minute movie (available online) was summarized as "a comedy drama full of wholesome philosophy." Success bred more acquisitions: a short story became the 1918 silent movie *Mirandy Smiles* starring Sparta, Michigan, native Vivian Martin. Two more books became motion pictures, and several short stories were made into stage productions. Her main theme—"homespun"—brought notoriety among the "well-known writers of clever little love stories for ten minutes' reading." The appearance in 1917 of *Our Next Door Neighbors* (with characters of Greek extraction) prompted this summary:

> Miss Maniates does not attempt heavy plots or long thought out and unreasonable characters. Instead her writing is characterized by a personality which sees humor in the ordinary and commonplace situations so frequently occurring in the human relationships. And she writes of these little comedies in a whimsical vein that is very entertaining.

The "young and cheerful Michigan author" had made her mark.[2]

Belle's writing style never involved pre-planning the plot. She wrote longhand, being carried as the muse inspired her, since using a typewriter "makes sentences short and choppy." Writing after hours, she believed, resulted in a better product as a labor of love.[3] Eight years before her death, Maniates left government employment. She devoted her remaining time to study and writing, withdrawing from the social circles she had frequented, becoming a recluse in the house, still standing, at 314 N. Walnut Street. She was eulogized as "a very studious woman" who was interred in the family plot in Marshall's Oakridge Cemetery.

Two of her books have been recently republished by Hastings College Press. Dr. Patricia Oman of Hastings College explains: "In the early part of the century, the teens and '20s, the Midwest was a stand-in for the country as a whole. The Midwest, by the end of the 20th century, became 'fly-over country.' Also, young adult novels with a female protagonist fell out of popularity."[4] Stories by a female mid-Michigander—sufficiently interesting enough for Hollywood repeatedly to call—lost favor.

Belle Maniates did not follow the conventional female path of her time. Many main characters in her stories were women. During the era of the war to end all wars, her written words took readers, and moviegoers, on heart-warming journeys of love and lift. She needed this creative outlet: in 1906, fiancé John Ford North died in Tucson, Arizona, while forty-five-year-old Belle was en route to complete their marriage license. She escorted his remains home via the Grand Trunk Railway,[5] arriving at the depot (still standing) in REO town and to a quarter-century of aloneness. Little wonder, then, that she devoted her contemplative talent to fictionalized happy endings.

Selected Works

Souvenir of the Thirty-Fifth Michigan Volunteer Infantry (1898)
David Dunne: A Romance of the Middle West (1912)
Amarilly of Clothes-Line Alley (1915)
Mildew Manse (1916)
Amarilly in Love (1917)
Little Boy Bear (1917)
Our Next Door Neighbors (1917)
Penny of Top Hill Trail (1919)
Sand Holler (1920)

James Milford Merrill

For Nickels and Dimes

October 15, 1847–April 1, 1936

Born in Muskegon, lived in and wrote about West Michigan locales

William T. Bartwick. Victor O. Endall. Dayton Mulgrove. Wendal Parrish. Morris Redwing. E. Alden Wicks. Will Winch. And, most apt, Old Timer. Pen names, all under which a prolific storyteller wrote for some of the most popular affordable publications of the late nineteenth century including *The House of Beadle & Adams.*[1] The genre was the "dime novel," an inexpensive paperbound book easily affordable and eminently readable. Many authors appeared under a pseudonym in order to heighten the mystery and maintain their anonymity for books seen by critics as lacking in quality. James Milford Merrill used all of these fictional identities in his craft—and perhaps more that remain to be discovered.

Born in Muskegon, Merrill moved when four years old with his family up the Muskegon River to rural Bridgetown Township. Before long, while he worked at his father's mill store after school, he fashioned written sketches, some of which were published. After a year at the Ypsilanti State Normal School and marrying, he lived in Sparta and Bridgetown and continued writing. In the 1880 Federal Census, he, wife Elizabeth, and two-year-old son Raymond were residents of Newaygo County engaged in farming. His parents, Isaac and Augusta, were tallied on the same census page, also engaged in agriculture.[2] James and Elizabeth had moved south to Ashland Township by 1900, still engaged in farming. He spent the last years of his life in Grandville and was buried in the Parkview Cemetery in Grant beside his wife and son.[3]

The setting in *Cloudwood; or, The Daughter of the Wilderness* was the fictional "little village of Wilton, which was built on the left bank of the river M——." It featured "startling" incidents "among the wilds of early

Michigan." Merrill proudly admitted his authorship of *Starr's American Novels* No. 66, not yet assuming the cloak of a nom de plume. It was a bit of a potboiler with the wooing of two "maidens," a tall and uncouth character named "Big Buck," and several plot twists. At the end of the ninety pages, the main characters are "all prosperous, happy, and enjoying life as well as mortals well can" for the "10 cts."[4] of investment. Because of her need and love for adventure, one of the young women in the story turns out to be Cloudwood—a reputed horse thief—with an alternate identity as Ralph Ernstein, a dashing young man who, in disguise, purports to wed her own cousin. A contemporaneous publication of a Michigan female soldier's story might have served as inspiration.[5] After all, five years from the end of the American Civil War, and under the pen of an author who led a conventional rural life, *Cloudwood* would not have sold many copies had it been an attempt to shatter nineteenth-century gender roles with twenty-first-century sensibilities. Its four reprintings seem to prove that point.

Regardless, Merrill wrote many more stories in this genre, among them one in the "Catalogue Pocket Edition of the War Library" series of historical fiction: volume 1, number 8, entitled *A Night in Dixie; or, Kilpatrick's Ride to Richmond: A Startling Tale of a Famous Raid* (New York: Novelist Pub. Co., 1883). Some stories appeared in *The Michigan Tradesman*, a weekly business journal in Grand Rapids. A "right-to-work" paean dedicated to his friend Almon Gilbert of Grand Rapids as "the best Workingman I know, and the Workingman I know best" was an early twentieth-century effort.[6] The opening chapter was entitled "Homeward Bound," presenting these first words:

> A more beautiful sky could not well be imagined—a rare May day such as few opening seasons grant to poor mortality.
>
> A steamer was plowing the waters of one of our great lakes, with the sunlight kissing the foam-ripples which bubble and dance aside from the vessel's prow as she forges ahead over the unruffled bosom of the inland sea.[7]

Fictional settings included Lake City, Grandburg, Villadale, Hilldale Academy, "a small fruit farm" named Oak Ridge, and others that were distinctly Michigan sounding—as well as a nearby big city pronounced, and spelled, "Shecargo." The underlying message was put this way: "Business cannot be run these days without the consent of the labor unions" but "Capital has equal rights with labor."[8] Merrill harkened back to his innocent youth:

> I call to mind a few years since, when I was a boy and my father operated a large sawmill in the Michigan pine country. There were no labor unions in those days; in fact, we had never heard of anything of the kind in the woods. Father's men were honest, intelligent fellows in the main, and were treated as equals by their employer, who was himself an educated, self-respecting New Englander. Had any danger threatened my father from outside, every man of his crew would have fought for him to the last breath. He paid them fair wages and strikes and lockouts were unknown.[9]

Two friends parted at the end of the book, one for the foreign land of Hawaii, the other deciding not to "expatriate" himself and remain a Michigander.

A few years later, Merrill's name appeared in a *Who's Who* publication, with "author" accompanied by "fruit-grower."[10] He apparently found both occupations productive. It would not be until the 1960s when the United Farm Workers formed; by contrast, the Michigan Farmers Union has represented family farmers since its founding in 1932. By then, Merrill, eighty-five years old, had moved in with a sister after losing his wife ten years prior. Son Raymond had died the same year after serving as reporter for the *Grand Rapids Herald* and editor at the newspaper at Sault Ste. Marie.

Perhaps his last published short story was *The Boy Woodsman; or, The Mill Guard*, published during the First World War. Its author was identified as "Milford Merrill" when it appeared in the *Chicago Ledger*, a "story paper" focusing on rural readership. Episode 1 appeared in the April 14 edition, à la Charles Dickens.[11] Although a conventional frontier story of lumbermen and natives, it also possessed certain attributes that removed it from the realm of stereotype. Amos Rand, the "boy woodsman," had many Indian friends and dealt honestly with them. The narrator, by contrast, employed typically paternalistic terms. The setting was "the Muskegon at Cedar Pond," and the morality play required investment in further five-cent issues before its conclusion. Merrill still had the formula down, with his compensation for the piece still only a modest supplement to agricultural earnings.

Whether the storyteller fully appreciated the magnificence of the mighty Muskegon is an open question. Merrill more than once used it in his fiction, suggesting something more than mere familiarity. Like Merrill, fruit grower–*cum*–creative writer, the river once provided boatloads of patrons with enjoyment before almost being consigned to the rubbish heap of history.[12]

Selected Works

Cloudwood; or, The Daughter of the Wilderness (1871)

Jane Bernice Macklem Murfin (Crisp)

From Quincy Town to Tinseltown

October 27, 1884–August 10, 1955
Born and raised in Quincy, lived in Sault Ste. Marie,
attended college in East Lansing, married and resided in Detroit

Ask about Quincy to a Michigander who knows geography, and the discussion will likely center on the iconic mine shaft house on the Keweenaw Peninsula. Mention it to an antiques collector, and you'll hear about a village that participates in Michigan's Longest Garage Sale on the US 12 Heritage Trail. Only a resident would be aware its name derives from a New England town known as the City of Presidents after the two Adamses.[1] The Midwest town was "a beautiful country village with bright prospects."[2]

No one will cite the Lower Peninsula community of 1,500 as the birthplace and childhood home of one of the great pioneers in American films. When Jane Bernice Macklem was born on Monday, October 27, 1884, its population had reached 1,094. Her father James was a sewing machine salesman and part-time deputy sheriff; her mother Henrietta was a milliner and homemaker for their four daughters and a son.[3]

American females would not get the vote until 1920, but opportunities were beginning to widen. A "Women's Program" had been established at the Michigan State Agricultural College in East Lansing in 1896; the recently established Themian Society offered a women-only social organization devoted to literary studies. In 1901, the Women's Building opened to provide a haven for its residents:

> Each room came fully furnished with a bedstead, mattress, dresser, washstand, two chairs, washbowl and pitcher, and a closet and would cost about ten to twelve dollars a term. The building itself contained a kitchen laboratory,

small dining-room for classes in cooking, parlors on the second floor, large dining room on the third floor, a two-story gymnasium on the ground and first floors, music rooms, waiting and reception rooms, toilet and bath rooms, laundry rooms, and living rooms.[4]

Constructed of a wooden frame and Lake Superior sandstone exterior,[5] it provided independent living for Jane, listed in the 1903–1904 college directory as "Macklen" with a major in "Sp"—"Special" studies.[6] The October 6, 1903, *M.A.C. Record* identified her as "Macklem, J Bernice, w, Sault Ste Marie."[7] The 1900 Federal Census reveals her employment as stenographer while residing with older unmarried sister Ida, a schoolteacher.[8] The 1904 graduation booklet included the "Society Roll" for the Themians, and, among the Class of 1907, appeared "Bernice Macklan."[9]

On April 23, 1907, Jane and thirty-two-year-old lawyer James Orin Murfin Jr. obtained a marriage license in Wayne County for their wedding the following day. He became a Circuit Judge the next spring, and they rented a Jefferson Avenue residence in 1910. Jane was listed in the census without occupation.[10] The couple received mention in the 1911 Detroit *Blue Book*, living on the fourth floor of The Pasadena luxury apartments at 2170 East Jefferson Avenue and amenable to receiving guests on Fridays. James held membership in a number of clubs and organizations while Jane was listed for three: the College Club of Detroit, the Fine Arts Society, and the Franklin Street Settlement Association (a social service organization in line with the Hull House in Chicago).[11]

They appeared a decade later in a similar social register but with different addresses. James lived on Van Dyke; Jane's entry: "Murfin Mrs James M (Jane Macklem) . . . New York."[12] They had divorced eleven years to the date of the wedding. James Murfin was the complainant. The reason for granting his uncontested petition: "desertion."[13]

The *Ladies Home Journal* for November 1917 held the key. On a page headed "Going Girls: The Who's Who of the Women of To-Morrow" appeared a piece entitled "These Two Girls Work Profitably Together—One Writes a Play, the Other Acts It." Two actresses of the same first name had met in New York City "three years ago," both of whom had come to the stage around 1904. Jane Cowl felt pigeonholed in emotional roles where she was "terribly tired of sobbing her emotions three hours each night." The other Jane—last "name Macklem—gave up the stage for domesticity as the wife of Judge James O. Murfin, of Detroit." In 1914, Cowl had a suggestion for "her girl friend:"

"Why don't you write a nonsob play for me?" That began it. Mrs. Jane Murfin went back to Detroit and set to work. By telegraph, letter, and long-distance telephone, she and Miss Cowl keep in touch daily, each doing a share in the self-set task. Such collaboration had never been dreamed of before and possibly won't be believed now, but it's absolutely true. *Lilac Time* was the result. Then followed *Daybreak*, and a third play with Jane Cowl in the leading part will shortly be presented. Jane Cowl doesn't have to sob anymore, and Jane Murfin doesn't have to ask the Judge for a new limousine.[14]

Mrs. Murfin's image had appeared in the June 4, 1914, *Detroit Times*, accompanying an article headed "Artists and Professionals Join in Entertainments for Animal Welfare League." It described her as a member of The Players and Theater Arts Club and she was to act a character in a scene from *Madame X*, the drama authored by Alexandre Bisson in 1908.[15] Was she, like the protagonist in the play, thrown out of her home by an angry husband? Perhaps their estrangement arose from diverging life goals and interests. Jane wanted to bring her talent to Broadway; James wanted to practice law and to fish, according to a journal of the "North Shore Club."[16]

Lilac Time debuted in 1917 and ran for 176 performances, reviewed by the *New York Times* as "a fragrant title that carried with it the promise of a gentle, Springtime romance."[17] *Daybreak* featured "smart dialogue" but a "terribly messy" plot.[18] Their third effort, *Information Please*, appeared in 1918 but without much notice. Under the name Allan Langdon Martin, the Janes collaborated on *Smilin' Through*, a romantic three-act comedy opening in 1919 that had longer staying power. Set in an English country garden, the play took on issues of love and loss, concluding with the encouraging line that people who suffered would "go smilin' through the years if they knew what they'd find at the end of the road." A publicity release summarized the work as "the story of a woman who, the victim of a bullet in the hands of one of her lovers on the night of her wedding to the man she loves, promises that she will come back to him. . . . A comedy-drama with a smile and a tear, it has all of the quaint, whimsical Irish sentiment without sentimentality."[19] It was made into a film in 1922 and remade twice, by major studio MGM in 1932 and 1941.

In the 1920 Census, living in Manhattan near Forty-Ninth Street, Fifth Avenue, and Madison Avenue, Jane Murfin listed her marital status as divorced and her occupation as "author."[20] Well-known American theater critic Robert Burns Mantle's 1919 article entitled "Milady Writes a Play" said it was "a new era for the woman playwright." He noted that Jane Murfin had recently joined "the scenario staff of the Famous Players-Lasky people," a motion-picture enterprise launched by two film pioneers who went on to found Paramount Pictures. Mantle expanded: "Those who have gone from the stage to the screen, playwrights of the caliber of . . . Jane Murfin, frankly admit that the salary and not the work attracted them, and that sooner or later they expect to return to the other field."[21]

According to the Women Film Pioneers project at the Columbia University Libraries, Murfin's first solo motion-picture script, *Marie, Ltd.*, was written and produced in 1919 by Select Pictures Corporation in New York. After several middling West Coast projects, she achieved Hollywood success for a continuing series of films featuring her German Shepherd named Strongheart. The dog came from Laurence Trimble, a trainer and director for Vitagraph Studios. She wrote, and he directed, a series of outdoor adventure films starring the canine as hero: *The Silent Call* (1921), *Brawn of the North* (1922), *The Love Master* (1924), and *White Fang* (1925), an adaptation of the Jack London novel. These plus *North Star* (1925) and *The Return of Boston Blackie* (1927) were silent films. All contributed to making Strongheart into the first major canine film star, preceding Rin Tin Tin, Lassie, Toto, and Beethoven. Because "potentially this dog's earning capacity runs close to $1,000,000 a year,"[22] he received good care:

> Murfin was so devoted to Strongheart she even wrote a 1924 editorial for the *Los Angeles Times* discussing the importance of treating animals well on set, and mentioning the Trimble-Murfin Productions' habit of hiring someone from the Animal Defense League to oversee the making of the film, ensuring that no animals would be harmed.[23]

For RKO Radio Pictures' first singing, talking, and dancing picture—the 1929 film *Street Girl*—Murfin wrote the screenplay. It was based on the story "Scandals of Broadway: The Viennese Charmer" by W. Carey Wonderly, published in the March 1928 issue of *Young's Realistic Stories* magazine.

On August 15, 1932, Murfin wed one of the mid-century's great character actors, Donald Crisp—who would later star in a Lassie movie—in the Ventura Baptist Church.[24] The couple divorced in 1944 after Jane sued for desertion on the occasion of their tenth wedding anniversary. He did not contest the petition, and they resolved on a property settlement.[25]

Murfin's film career was lengthy and successful. According to one commentator, "the film that really established Murfin's career" was *Way Back Home* in 1931, starring Bette Davis.[26] She received an Academy Award nomination in 1932 as co-writer on the script of *What Price Hollywood?*, directed by George Cukor (losing to Frances Marion for *The Champ*). Cukor directed several pictures for which Murfin wrote the script. She was screenwriter for *The Runaway Bride* (1930), *Little Women* and *Double Harness* (1933), *Alice Adams* (1935), *The Women* (1939), *Northwest Passage* and *Pride and Prejudice* (1940),[27] and *Andy Hardy's Private Secretary* (1941). In 1936, she earned over $92,000 from Samuel Goldwyn, Inc., more than director Howard Hawks or actor Joel McCrea.[28] A revealing newspaper blurb deemed her "probably Hollywood's busiest screen writer" after taking her first vacation in three years. It was going to be special: "Miss Murfin will sail her 90-foot yacht to the Aleutian Islands, spending more than two months on the trip."[29] She was "one of the most prolific" and "one of the most reliable" screenwriters of the 1920s and 1930s.[30]

Some of her sixty-nine efforts came straight from imagination, but others had roots in the social undercurrents of the era.[31] An interview in 1930 about the most recent script suggested a storyline grounded in marital issues, perhaps her own:

> It is principally about [wives] . . . who have reached that stage in their lives where love is dead—or at least, they think it is. If there is a theme in it, it is that marriage should be based on friendship . . . not love. . . . I believe women are tired of plays in which their men hop around where fancy wills, then trot back home to be forgiven. Modern life is not like that. Women come home to be forgiven, too, once in a while.[32]

The script for *The Life of Vergie Winters* in 1934 embroiled her in a censorship dispute, given that the story went deep into adultery, politics, and crime. The title character and a member of Congress carried on a twenty-year affair, resulting in murder at the hands of his wife. A dying confession sprang Vergie from her jail cell, and she found a home with her daughter, their love child, where they lived happily ever after. The movie nearly was not made, given changes mandated by the censor at the Motion Picture Producers and Distributors of America. The U.S. Catholic Church placed the flick on its "films to be boycotted" list.[33]

The Women presents the viewer with an interesting puzzle. Based on the Clare Booth Luce play,[34] the movie version incorporates the characters and much of the dialogue but adds more: the cast is doubled in size, the opening scene and others feature canines, the dialogue pacing is rapid-fire, "another lecture on the modern woman" is a retort to criticism, and the main character asserts that she is content to be a woman. At the end, the estranged wife and husband appear as equals—it is pride that keeps them apart—and both must move toward the other to achieve reconciliation. Parsing out Murfin's contribution as co-writer is difficult, but her life experience suggests powerfully that it was not limited to introducing dogs into the production.

Murfin's role in Hollywood did not stop at the creative side of the business. She became a founding member of the Screenwriters' Guild in 1921, and in 1933 she was one of the key activists behind the formation of a more effective successor organization. She was nearly elected its vice president. Murfin supported charitable efforts well into the 1940s.[35] She had pledged $50,000 in bonds according to an article at the World War II midpoint, more at that time than Bob Hope.[36] Her obituary listed service on various boards, including the Academy of Motion Picture Arts and Sciences.

Her last credited screen work was the year her second marriage ended. In 1950, she worked as talent scout for a large agency.[37] Her death, lamented Crisp, "was a great loss to me. . . . We had always discussed our work together."[38] The funeral services were private, per direction by the nephews and nieces who survived her.[39] The gravestone in Valhalla Memorial Park, North Hollywood, identifies her as Jane Murfin Crisp, and it bears the inscription "still 'smilin' through,'" citing the first writing success that provided film industry recognition.[40]

None of the press clippings or other publicity after 1917 mentioned her Michigan origins. None revealed her first marriage to a prominent Michigan barrister or her Michigan roots in the fine arts. It is the rare source that speaks of her upbringing in Quincy. She was of pioneer stock, and she became a pioneer in an American film industry that would captivate the world. She had her hand in over sixty films, she was a producer who championed strong female roles, and she "may be one of the most prolific but least known writers of the 1920s and '30s."[41]

Prematurely dead at age seventy, Murfin is not completely gone. In 2008, a remake of *The Women* was released. Clare Booth Luce was listed as author of the play in the credits, which stated that this movie was based on "the 1939 motion picture" co-scripted "by Anita Loos and Jane Murfin." Credited as lyricist for several songs, one of her poetic passages was set to music ("Turn to the Lord") by composer Martin Broones. The words of the Quincy native live on, perhaps no more curiously than in a lullaby sweetly sung by Doris Day:

> In my arms I'll hold you tight
> Snug and warm through the night
> And I'll tell the evening star
> Just how wonderful you are
>
> Then in dreams we'll drift away
> Far from all the cares of day
> Till the morning shadows creep
> Sleep, my sleepy baby, sleep

Clara Eleanor Dillingham (Pierson)

At Home in Nature

March 11, 1868–1952

Born in Coldwater; lived in Alma, Stanton, and

Grand Rapids; with her husband, built a summer home in Omena

It was a world where four pre-teen boys could wander off, with their parents' permission and unescorted, for a day of fishing. And where animals of the woods, the meadow, and the pond co-existed peacefully.

It was the world Clara Dillingham Pierson created for thousands of children. Beginning in 1897, Pierson was the author of popular works for children that gave wildlife human characteristics while educating young readers about the outdoors, making the natural world safe and welcoming.

The roots of this world view took hold after Clara planted her first garden as a child. The little girl saw her first mouse. It seemed harmless, even welcome. "I have always had a friendly feeling toward mice and trap them with regret," she wrote in her unpublished memoir.[1]

The same kitchen into which mice fled was the site of her introduction to literature. It was not the simple, sweet tales she read early on that most stood out to Clara in adulthood, but Meddlesome Mattie because of her "sad end." Mattie played with matches despite parental admonitions and set fire to herself.[2]

After early years in the state of New York, Clara spent most of her youth in Coldwater, where her father, through family connections, obtained a job at a carriage manufacturer. A sickly child, Clara was homeschooled by her mother for several years.

Clara's interest in outdoor life was fanned by her father, a former Civil War officer who pointed out subtle features in the woods and fields around their home.

Thanks to a doting librarian, Eugenia Pruden, Clara soon coupled her love of the outdoors with a love of books. The librarian even introduced young Clara to books written for grownups. Although religious faith did not take hold in her childhood, the author-to-be learned to appreciate the Book of Common Prayer whose authors "knew the needs of the human heart."[3]

Originally hoping to become a doctor or architect—she contributed to the design of the Branch County Courthouse in Coldwater—Clara was nudged in another direction in her twenties by a New England minister who encouraged her to write stories. Meanwhile, she learned the teaching of kindergarten at a Chicago training school.

At twenty-six, Clara married hardware merchant John W. S. Pierson of Stanton; the couple inhabited a house made from one of her designs. Still standing in 2025, the house features four Georgian pillars on the front portico, a library and living room each with a fireplace, two sun porches, large arches at the top of the stairs to the second floor, and a writer's room.[4]

The writer would soon be making use of that room. In 1895, Clara submitted a story in a prize competition administered by publisher David C. Cook. A tale set in slums like those she had observed in Chicago, *The Top Floor Mission* came in second out of 488 entries and warranted a check worth $30. Not long after, she sent a manuscript containing nineteen nature stories to the publisher E. P. Dutton and miraculously, this unsolicited creation by an unknown was snatched up within a week. The power and charm of Clara's writing would now guide her work.

Writing proved a critical means of self-renewal in 1900 when her son John Lincoln was born but lived only a few days. Mentioning the infant's death in her memoir and then stoically never returning to the subject, she wrote, "I returned home thankful that there was a beloved work calling me to my desk, or rather, just calling me."[5]

A fateful moment came on Clara and John's 1896 trip to Traverse City in blazing heat. A friend suggested they travel up Grand Traverse Bay to Omena to catch a cooling breeze. While there, the couple encountered a developer and immediately believed they had found the property that would become their summer refuge. When a Grand Rapids minister with whom they traveled on the return steamer down the bay sang the praises of Omena as a summer resort, the deal was clinched.

Charmed by the location on the shores of the bay, the couple, on the spot, bought a right of first refusal on a lot within a new development. The property deal was based on the author's expected book royalties. The lot became theirs.

Clara designed a summer cottage that was completed in 1898. She remembered the second morning after taking occupancy:

> The trees, all newly freshened by the copious rain, stood motionless in stately dignity; Grand Traverse Bay was a gently dimpling sheet of blue and gold, ten miles wide in front of the cottage and showing no farther shoreline in northerly and southerly directions; squirrels and chipmunks frisked about and the birds were singing their madrigals of joy, the veeries leading.[6]

In summer, the cottage became her writing studio as well as her family's escape. She spent the first and last two weeks of her stay concentrating on writing, the intervening time belonging to the whole family. The cottage was named Pencroft instead of the suggestion by Clara's mother that it be named Typewriterhurst in recognition of the means of the author's creations.

Clara's stories began as tales for her kindergarten students, and by 1897 she said it seemed wise to collect and

> send them out to a wider circle of boys and girls. . . . In selecting the tiny creatures of field and garden for the characters in this book, I have remembered with pleasure the way in which my loyal pupils befriended stray crickets and grasshoppers, their intense appreciation of the new realm of fancy and observation, and the eagerness and attention with which they sought Mother Nature.[7]

She wrote her nature series—five books about "people" of the meadow, forest, farm, pond, and night—in a five-year span ending in 1902.

Typical of Pierson's nature writing for children is the opening of *Among the Meadow People*:

> As the warm August days came, Mr. Yellow Butterfly wriggled and pushed in his snug little brown house, and wished he could get out to see the world. He remembered the days when he was a fuzzy little caterpillar, crawling slowly over grass and leaves, and he remembered how beautiful the sky and the flowers all were. Then he thought of the new wings which had been growing from his back, and he tried to move them, just to see how it would feel. He had

> only six legs since his wings grew, and he missed all the sticky feet which he had to give up when he began to change into a butterfly. The more he thought about it the more he squirmed . . . The thin dark brown wrapper around him popped open, and out he went. Poor Mr. Butterfly! He found his wings so wet and crinkled that they wouldn't work at all, so he had to sit quietly in the sunshine all day drying them. And just as they got big, and smooth, and dry, it grew dark, and Mr. Butterfly had to crawl under a leaf to sleep.[8]

The book's twenty chapters include "The Contented Earthworms," "Mr. Green Frog and His Visitors," "A Gossiping Fly," and "The Katydid's Quarrel." The closing chapter is "The Last Party of the Season." At summer's end, the wildlife of the meadow readies for fall: "When it grew dark, the Fireflies' lights shone like tiny stars, and the dancing went on until all were tired and ready to sing together the last song of the summer, for on the morrow they would go to rest."[9]

In her second book in the nature series, *Among the Forest People*, Pierson responded to a key question young readers of the first book had asked:

> I have been asked if I am acquainted with the little creatures about whom I tell you, and I want you to know that I am very well acquainted indeed. Perhaps the Ground Hog is my oldest friend among the forest people, just as the Tree Frog is among those of the meadow. Some of the things about which I shall tell you, I have seen for myself, and the other stories have come to me in another way. I was there when the swaggering Crow drove the Hens off the barnyard fence, and I was quite as much worried about the Mourning Doves' nest as were Mrs. Goldfinch and Mrs. Oriole.[10]

Clara's nature studies books, costing a healthy $1.25 in 1901 (over $45 in 2025 dollars) were exquisitely illustrated by F. C. Gordon.[11] The combination of words and sketches enraptured children. This was, in part, due to Clara and John's adoption of two sons, Harold and John, who served both as a source of material and an audience for first drafts. They and the family cat, Silvertip, provided fodder for Clara's books.

Pencroft also became the stage for a series of four books Clara wrote, including *Three Little Millers* in 1901. The book describes simple summer delights and gently learned life lessons. When his parents invite a girl named Lucinda recovering from illness to join the family at a campfire barbecue, one of the Miller boys, Ralph, sulks at the thought of sharing food with her. When he sees how her inclusion in the feast lifts Lucinda's spirits, he passes up frosted cakes and suggests they be given to the girl.

Pierson's books reached mass audiences. Critics approved of the works as appropriate for young children. "A thoroughly charming book for the little people," said one, "which grown folks can read also, with many a chuckle at its slyly insinuated 'morals.'"[12]

But the books would never have succeeded if they lacked strong storytelling. Of *Among the Night People*, a *Buffalo Commercial* critic wrote, "there is only one reason why mothers and big sisters need hesitate to buy this bewitching book—if once they read it to the youngsters, they will be made to read it over and over again until they know it by heart, and never a word will their delighted little listeners allow them to alter or skip."[13]

Clara's love of nature was deep and unequivocal. A granddaughter said that Clara would tiptoe into the kitchen late at night to feed mice that came into her house and would even coax them with bits of cheese.

Stories involving domesticated animals, like *Tales of a Poultry Farm*, also won critical praise. Their purpose, "to amuse the children and instil [*sic*] into them at the same time a sort of fellowship with the barnyard fowls," was well-served by Pierson's writing, said the *New York Times*.[14]

After fifteen years of fruitless inquiries from her publisher about another manuscript, Clara produced a book. When published several years later, *Living with Our Children* was described by the *Buffalo News* as "short essays on principles of child training in a servantless house." But it was not what the publisher had wanted. "I can find one thousand people who can write acceptably to one who can write acceptably for children," Clara recalled the publisher's representative writing. "One who can write so well for them should continue to do that."[15]

Clara responded enthusiastically. In the summer of 1922 at Penhurst, she wrote "in negligee" from 4 a.m. to 7 a.m., dispensed with household duties, and returned to her craft for another three hours. The result was *Plow Stories*, a series of tales with the plow serving as a measure of human development. The *Minneapolis Tribune* called it a "real romance which can leave reader young or old enthralled until the end of the book is reached."[16] It was Clara's final book.

Clara and her husband spent their final years in Grand Rapids after moving there in 1930. At her death in 1952, Pierson had an estate worth over $1.5 million in 2023 dollars.[17] Her success could not be measured in revenue from her abundant writing; rather, its measure is the number of young minds whose curiosity Pierson stoked and whose hearts came to know and appreciate the variety of the natural world as well as the safety of a happy family home.

Selected Works

Among the People series

Among the Meadow People (1897)
Among the Forest People (1898)
Among the Farmyard People (1899)
Among the Pond People (1901)
Among the Night People (1902)

The Millers series

Three Little Millers: A Story of the Boys and Girls of Pencroft (1905)
The Millers at Pencroft (1906)
The Millers and Their Playmates (1907)
The Millers and Their New Home (1908)

Other books

Dooryard Stories (1903)
Tales of a Poultry Farm (1904)
Plow Stories (1923)
Living with Our Children: A Book of Little Essays for Mothers (1923)

Rose Hartwick Thorpe

The Poem Heard 'Round the World

July 18, 1850–July 19, 1939

Authored her famous poem as a high schooler in Litchfield, Michigan

While many artists are remembered primarily for a single work, not many compose that work at age sixteen. Rose Hartwick took her distinction a level higher: she authored her poem's first draft in one burst of energy on her school slate during an evening when her math homework bored her.

She did so surreptitiously. Her practical parents did not want Rose to waste her time on "idle dreams and restless rhymes," she wrote long afterward in the *Ladies Home Journal*. But when her mother read the verses, she insisted that Rose write them down on something more durable than a chalked school slate.

Rose continued to tinker with the poem, *Curfew Must Not Ring Tonight*, even as she began providing other verses to the *Detroit Commercial Advertiser*, which published them without compensating the author (except through a free subscription). She was pleased simply to share her art with a large audience.

One day, ill, unable to compose something fresh for the newspaper, she dug up *Curfew* and mailed it with an apologetic note to the editor. She said it might not warrant publishing. To the contrary, when the editor read the poem, he at once "wrote me a lengthy letter of congratulation and praise, in which he predicted the popularity for the verses that they have since enjoyed." In fact, within weeks the poem was the equivalent of a modern runaway bestseller. Rose was shocked. "The poem seemed at once to attract public attention, and raised me from a shy, obscure country girl into the public notice."[1]

What was it that moved a newspaper editor so—and soon, thousands of readers around the world, including Queen Victoria?[2] It was a ten-stanza tale of romance and a woman's bravery. Set in England during the time of Oliver Cromwell, the poem dramatizes young Nessie's determination to save the life of her lover, who is imprisoned and to be executed on trumped-up charges when the curfew bell rings—the community signal at 8 p.m. every evening proclaiming end of the day. Bessie implores the sexton to prevent the ringing of the bell, and when he refuses, she climbs to the top of the bell tower and, with her hands, prevents the bell from ringing. Moved by her daring, Cromwell issues a pardon to her lover, Basil Underwood.

English scholars would later find evidence of the story's general accuracy. A young woman had saved her lover from hanging in Chertsey parish at about the time of Cromwell, the early 1700s. *Curfew Must Not Ring Tonight* began:

> England's sun was slowly setting o'er the hill-tops far away,
> Filling all the land with beauty at the close of one sad day;
> And its last rays kissed the forehead of a man and maiden fair—
> He with steps so slow and weary; she with sunny, floating hair:
> He with bowed head, sad and thoughtful, she, with lips all cold and white,
> Struggling to keep back the murmur, "Curfew must not ring to-night!"[3]

The twenty-year-old Rose never thought to copyright this work, and it immediately entered the public domain. She said a half century later that while she never made a cent off *Curfew*, it had brought her a "wide circle of admiring friends," whom she treasured. It also won her an honorary degree in 1883 from Hillsdale College, whose president predicted, "You have written a poem that will never permit the name of its author to die while the English language is spoken."[4]The poem would become source material for three silent movies and a play. It was also the inspiration for an eight-foot bell that honors Hartwick in Litchfield, where she lived for twenty years.

A measure of the poem's impact in its day are the rhetorical questions posed in 1916 by a writer who documented the composition of *Curfew*:

> Who is there that has not read *Curfew Must Not Ring Tonight*? Or, if he has not read it, has not heard it quoted or referred to as familiarly as household words? It has been translated into scores of tongues. It has been recited in every school, lyceum and pulpit in the English-speaking world.

> And, strange to say, this world-popular ballad was not written by a master of English, one who had already won his laurels, but by a 16-year-old school-girl, devoid of any education save that afforded by the little red schoolhouse of the American country side, and gained in a home where books were as rare, scarce and precious as jewels and diamonds, and far more treasured.[5]

Rose's youthful heart had throbbed to the pulse of a world far away from rural Hillsdale County, where her family moved in 1861. Receiving a book of Byron's poems when she was fifteen, Rose was soon immersed in the world his romance created. It took just one more match to light the combustible mix of imagination and language. Borrowed from a neighbor, this was the September 1865 edition of the periodical *Peterson's*, which featured the story "Love and Loyalty," the tinder for her poem. Less than two years later, she chalked the first draft of *Curfew*.

It turned out that nothing Rose wrote in the sixty-nine years that remained to her after publication of her signature poem rivaled it. She achieved modest notice for *The Soldier's Reprieve, Remember the Alamo* and *In a Mining Town*.[6] She continued writing for several decades on topics as varied as temperance and stories for boys and girls. But her early poem anchored her in the public mind and in the minds of other writers such as Lucy Maud Montgomery, who cited it in her classic novel as if everyone knew of it.[7] Looking back seventy years in 1939, one writer said the poem "for a generation was on the lips of lovers in England and America."[8]

Upon her death, it was *Curfew Must Not Ring Tonight* for which she was remembered in her *New York Times* obituary. Rose wouldn't have minded. "I have my reward in the knowledge that the world appreciated the story I told," she once said.[9]

Selected Works

Ringing Ballads (1887)
Fred's Dark Days (1881)
Nina Bruce; or, A Girl's Influence (1886)
Temperance Poems (1887)
The Chester Girls (1887)

The Year's Best Days for Boys and Girls (1888)
As Others See Us, or, The Rules and Customs of Refined Homes and Polite Society . . . : Also Complete Self Instruction in Physical Culture for Both Ladies and Gentlemen (1896)
White Lady of La Jolla (1904)
The Poetical Works of Rose Hartwick Thorpe (1913)

Southwest Michigan

Muhammad Ali

Of the GOAT and the River

January 17, 1942–June 3, 2016
Lived in Berrien County

At the height of his sports fame, the great pugilist and world figure Muhammad Ali, born in Louisville, Kentucky, on January 17, 1942, seemed timeless. On August 8, 1975, "a sun-splashed day," he fought an exhibition match at Filstrup Field in Benton Harbor against sparring partners, "regaling crowds with swagger and showmanship."[1] It was a year after "the Greatest" defeated Joe Frazier in the "Rumble in the Jungle" and before his victory in the rematch known as "Thrilla in Manila." He earned millions and had houses in Chicago, Los Angeles, Miami, and New Jersey. He retired from boxing to a home acquired that summer of 1975 on a horseshoe bend of the meandering St. Joseph River. The river rises near Hillsdale, disappearing into Lake Michigan at the Berrien County shore.

The eighty-some-acre estate featured extensive lawns, trees, and gardens. After an associate of gangster Al Capone reportedly lived there in the 1920s, it had functioned as a church sanitarium for mental and physical healing. The carriage house became Ali's office when he moved in, and there he composed a best-selling memoir. One sentence began: "When I am at home in Michigan. . . ."

Astonishingly, the self-described "Greatest" (his first championship was at age twenty-two; his last when he was thirty-eight), Olympic gold medalist (age eighteen), Vietnam War conscientious objector (sustained by the U.S. Supreme Court), and recipient of the Presidential Medal of Freedom (2005) had defied convention yet again by making his home in the lower southwest portion of the Great Lakes State. Here, where no one could hound him, began his confrontation with a diagnosis that became public in 1998: Parkinson's syndrome.

Among the farms and fields of author/horticulturist Liberty Hyde Bailey, of old-time villages named for clear waters, and of modern-day vineyards, Ali found refuge. The peaceful retreat nurtured a body that had been a punching bag and a mind that had fought prejudice and political opposition. The pastoral setting refreshed him and fostered reflection that imbued his retrospective:

> When I am at home in Michigan, I like to take walks around my farm and observe the beauty of nature. One morning, while I was walking, I came across a trail of ants. As I took a closer look, I noticed that the ants were heading somewhere. . . . As I watched them, I was reminded of how great God is. There are signs all around us, most of which go unnoticed, but when we do pay attention to the little things, we witness how even the smallest of creatures have challenges and obstacles to overcome, and then our own don't seem insurmountable.[2]

Ali had also found community. He supported the baseball team of his adopted son Assad's school in Niles. He bought prom tickets for underprivileged children. He quietly donated funds to local philanthropies. He was seen around town, frequently on a walk to get an ice cream—his voice, once exuberant, quieted.

Arizona became his residence once the disease took hold. He died on June 3, 2016, in his eighth decade. The Michigan estate sold three years later. A farm along a Michigan river was not Ali's only residence, but it held him for a lengthy stay and fulfilled the lyric: "A River sings a beautiful song. It says, Come, rest here by my side."[3] Near a painting by his father mounted on the wall over the desk in the carriage house, he authored *Reflections*.[4] The work stands as a testament to tranquility following years of strife.

Selected Works

The Greatest: My Own Story (1975)
The Soul of a Butterfly: Reflections on Life's Journey (2004)

Lyman Frank Baum

Macatawa's Man

May 15, 1856–May 6, 1919

Owned a summer writing cottage on Lake Michigan

NO OUTLET, says the yellow-and-black sign heading westbound on 146th Avenue after its junction with 66th Street. The message helps recall a scene toward the climax of the 1939 classic motion picture *The Wizard of Oz*, as Dorothy and her colleagues are trapped by hostile forces within a turret high along a battlement in a castle inhabited by evil personified. The avenue soon makes a left turn and becomes Audubon Road, an appropriate designation given the proximity to two major nature preserves, Dune Pines and Castle Park. Together, they protect nearly four hundred feet of undeveloped Lake Michigan shoreline in a designated Critical Dune Area and more than fifty acres of lakeshore habitat. The rationale for the first-named forested site is obvious. The second requires investigation.

Inquiry is hampered for those of conscience, for Audubon becomes a private road, owned and patrolled by an association. It cannot be too private, however, for online mappings take the virtual visitor west on the road, past charming houses and vegetation-covered ridges raised up by sand and wind. Another sign, more ominous, appears at a junction, but curiosity drives one to see up close an unusual yellow brick structure exhibiting a turret, crenels, and merlons. Vintage postcards show its other sides and refer to it as "The Castle Near Macatawa, Mich." According to one indefatigable writer of "lost Michigan" places, it was built in 1876 by a Chicago businessman.[1] Other sources cite construction by a different man of Chicago commerce in the 1890s.

In 1899, a Chicago publisher issued a book of poems for children by a Chicago writer and a Chicago illustrator. The volume's sales enabled the author, Lyman Frank Baum, to take up temporary residence at a cottage near the meeting point of Macatawa Lake and Lake Michigan, on the south shore of the inlet. After a visit that summer, the Baums rented a cottage there for two summers before acquiring property in 1902 and naming their house "The Sign of the Goose," for *Father Goose: His Book* had finally brought success to the hopeful writer.[2] Baum commuted to Chicago by vessel, returning on the Saturday 2 p.m. boat to arrive by dinner.[3] The navigation light that would become a Michigan icon was then only a small square wooden structure erected in 1872. Not until 1907 did the Holland Harbor South Pierhead Lighthouse, with its gabled roofline and fire-engine red hue, replace the light atop a metal pole in a protective cage. Those several years had enlarged the Baum family's fortunes after publication of a fantasy book in fall 1900 hit the jackpot and spawned best-selling sequels.

The Wonderful Wizard of Oz, published by the Hill Company with Denslow's illustrations, sold ten thousand copies in its first run, ultimately outlasting copyright protection in mid-century after several millions were bought. *The Marvelous Land of Oz* appeared in 1904, followed by a dozen more books and several short stories. In 1939, Metro-Goldwyn-Mayer made *Oz* into a movie that became a cinema classic.

Michigan served as inspiration for the storyline, according to some sources. Local city fathers and mothers in nearby towns have held festivals grounded on the notion. Perhaps the "Castle Near Macatawa" inspired the witch's lair and the yellow brick road. The accuracy of the claim cannot be asserted beyond a reasonable doubt. In his son's biography, Baum took inspiration not from Michigan but from events and imagination inspired within his own Chicago home, commencing in 1898.[4] Since he finished the manuscript in October 1899, after spending several years developing its characters and themes, tying the classic work to the east side of the Big Lake is problematic.[5]

Nothing is doubtful about another of Baum's fictional works. The cover of *Tamawaca Folks* exhibits a sailing vessel on a shoreless waterway carried by a strong wind under a puffy clouded sky. Resemblance to an excursion off the beach on the great lake is obviously intended. The author maintains in the introduction that:

> Tamawaca exists, and is as beautiful as I have described it. I chose it as the scene of my story because I once passed an entire summer there and was

fascinated by its incomparable charm. The middle West has no spot that can compete with it in loveliness.[6]

The site is, obviously, where Baum's cottage lay. In Chapter 1, an exhausted lawyer looks for a quiet and pleasant summer resort. A friend gives him counsel:

> "Why, any of the Lake Michigan resorts are desirable—Tamawaca, Bay View, Charlevoix or Petoskey. I've been to Tamawaca a couple of summers myself, and like it immensely. It isn't so fashionable as Charlevoix and Petoskey, but it is the most beautiful place I have ever seen, bar none."
>
> "What's there?" enquired Jarrod, listlessly.
>
> "Lake Michigan, to begin with; and Tamawaca Pool, which is really a lovely inland lake. You'll find there good fishing and bathing, a noble forest running down to the water's edge, pretty cottages nestled among the trees, lots of ozone, and quiet till you can't rest."
>
> "Eh?"
>
> "I mean quiet so you can rest."
>
> "It sounds promising," said Jarrod. "Guess I'll go. My wife remarked yesterday we ought to escape the summer's heat on the children's account. This idea will please her—and it pleases me. I used to fish when I was a boy. And hunt. How's the hotel, Brush?
>
> "Bad as possible. Take a cottage. That's the only way to enjoy life."
>
> Upon arrival, Jarrod is guided to his summer house: "A few paces more brought them to a magnificent view of the great inland sea, and soon they emerged upon a broad beach lapped by the rolling waves of grand old Michigan." Restoration began immediately:
>
> Jarrod's eyes sparkled. It was beautiful at this point, he was forced to admit, and the cool breath of the breeze that swept over the waters sent an exhilarating vigor to the bottom of his lungs and brought a sudden glow to his cheek.

Macatawa Park itself was established in 1881 as a pleasure resort. The Macatawa Park Cottagers' Association has governed the private community on the peninsula bordering the Holland channel ever since. Some historical cottages from the turn of the nineteenth century still exist, but the Baums' is gone thanks to fires in the 1920s. An 1899 photo album, recently discovered, provides images of the places and people that once inhabited the lakefront.[7]

Any debate over the inspiration for Oz seems misplaced given this 1907 book, but perhaps its attribution to John Estes Cooke caused confusion. Cooke was a nom de plume, one of several imagined identities that Baum employed in his vast trove of works, and nearly identical to an author of American Civil War (for the South) experience. Cooke wrote of how the semi-imaginary location along the inland sea was a "little heaven upon earth." Although the Baums enjoyed a pattern of living that included summers at Macatawa, the California sunshine drew them to make their final home at "Ozcot," in Hollywood, in 1910.[8] The author died there in 1919. Two decades later came the feature film that bestowed immortality to Baum and his imaginary land. It may also be that the Lake Michigan location inspired aspects of the sequels. For example, *The Marvelous Land of Oz* (July 1904) included an encounter with a ferryman, a lack of money for a ticket, and a resourceful alternative. A ferry once ran from the interurban station at Jenison Park near Macatawa across the bay.

Baum wrote the twenty-five thousand words of *Tamawaca Folks* directly from personal experience. He called it "the most original and wonderful place in all the world" and "an imitation paradise." He wrote *Ozma of Oz* in summer 1906 on the "broad veranda at the back of the house" that "looked down through trees to the lake." Here, he "often wrote, edited, and read," and the "sound of the typewriter must have clattered through the woods."[9] His days on Michigan's lower west freshwater coast did affect him, deeply. Reportedly, his last words to a heartsick wife were, "Now we can cross the Shifting Sands."[10] Was he referring to some place in Oz? Or did he have in mind, as a final vision of a place far away, how the wind off the Big Lake continually contours neighboring ridges and slopes in ever creative ways? Perhaps. After The Sign of the Goose burned, the remnants disappeared over time under the rolling surface of the great blue waters of the bordering freshwater sea.[11]

Selected Works

Tamawaca Folks: A Summer Comedy (1907)
To Macatawa (1907)

Ben East

Conservation Curmudgeon

July 18, 1898–August 1, 1990
Born and lived much of his life in Holly, outdoor writer for *Grand Rapids Press*, championed fish and game conservation and protection of special natural features in Michigan

Once upon a time—until roughly 1970—there was no such thing in common parlance as the term "environmental protection." Instead, there was conservation, understood to be the careful husbanding of natural resources such as fish and game and their habitat to allow recreational and other use not just in the present, but for generations. The operative word for this approach was "use," not preservation alone.

In this same era, when the echo of the indiscriminate industrial ax still reverberated disturbingly in the memories of many—when the slaughter of the forest primeval of the three upper Great Lakes states had left behind killer forest fires and a denuded economy—some of the loudest voices calling for a new and better way were outdoor writers.

Often found in the sports sections of newspapers, outdoor writers were typically free of the constraints binding other reporters, serving up as much opinion as information. And the opinion was often raw. It had to be, these writers thought, to challenge the corruption of government processes that had stolen the people's natural resource legacy.

In short, the typical outdoor writer was a curmudgeon, telling adventure stories of the hunt for the big bear or the cast for the big fish, but also mocking politicians and crusading for the prudent use of natural resources. And if any of these writers could be considered a classic specimen, it was Michigan's Ben East.

East spent his childhood in the Holly area, where there were plenty of lakes and forests for the outdoor-driven child to roam. He was the only kid in grade school who knew how to kill and skin a skunk without being engulfed in its odor. He gave the oil to mothers, who used it as a remedy for the croup. "Give a kid a teaspoon of skunk oil and his throat would open right up," East told outdoor writer Frank Mainville.[1]

During an initial stint as a public school teacher, East began peddling stories. His first, he recalled, was one about a farm collie and a mink entitled "Buff and the White-Throated Killer."[2] He "shot high" and sent it to the *Saturday Evening Post*, from which he received encouragement and successive rejection slips.

He eventually had more luck selling stories to the *Detroit News*. In 1926, he was given a golden opportunity to edit the outdoor page of the *Grand Rapids Press*. It was a superb podium from which to extol Michigan's wealth of natural resources and to war with those who would exploit them without thought of the public good or of future generations. He would remain in the post for twenty years.[3] He wrote over one thousand articles during a long career.[4]

His efforts to call attention to the need for conserving Michigan's special natural places involved a little derring-do. He generated headlines in 1931 when he was part of the first team to reach Isle Royale in the winter by airplane.[5] While there, he assisted in a survey of the island's moose herd and added to a growing collection of outdoors films that he would show to audiences far from the North in an attempt to persuade them of nature's spectacular qualities.

East also chose winter to popularize the cause of protecting Tahquamenon Falls. He organized a six-man expedition that snowshoed approximately fifty miles round trip on the Tahquamenon River to capture the first winter photographs of the falls. The campaign he helped foster culminated in the establishment of a state park encompassing the waterfalls in 1947.

East was not a preservationist. In a 1938 speech to the Sault Ste. Marie Chamber of Commerce, he urged Upper Peninsula leaders to inventory and develop their natural resources and to lure tourists. "You haven't even scratched the surface of the chances that are yours," he said. In 1961, he told the West Michigan Tourist Council to step up its efforts to develop and promote outdoor recreation in part for the economic benefits it would bring. He announced his opposition to the creation of a national park at Sleeping

Bear Dunes in the same talk, saying he disapproved of the use of eminent domain to take private land for the park.[6]

But there were places that deserved special status, he knew. East's love affair with the Porcupine Mountains began on a fishing trip in the late 1930s. He marveled:

> That was my first trip into the heart of the Porcupine Mountains, there on the south shore of Superior a few miles east of the Wisconsin-Michigan border. I had done a little prowling around their edges and I knew they were the highest and most picturesque mountain range, north of the Ohio, between the Black Hills of Dakota and Adirondacks of New York. I knew, too, that they were a beautiful region, still covered with virgin forest. But up to now I had not even dreamed what they were really like.[7]

When short-sighted politics warped state conservation decision-making, East employed his columns to outrage the public and bring to bear its weight. Outdoor writer Dave Richey described him as being like "a little banty rooster that dominated a barnyard; he didn't care whose toes he stomped because he cared only for the wise use of our natural resources and would fight anyone who disagreed."[8]

Such advocacy promoted him to the national stage. Beginning in 1946, East held a succession of positions at *Outdoor Life*, a nationally circulated magazine whose primary audience at the time was sportsmen. Rising to the position of senior outdoor editor, he wrote hundreds of stories and mentored younger outdoor writers. He won a reputation as one of America's leading conservation champions.

That image, and East's uncompromising opposition to conservation policy that surrendered to politics, resulted in the rejection by the Michigan State Senate of his 1953 gubernatorial appointment to the Michigan Conservation Commission. The commission was the body in state government with legal authority to set fish and game seasons, acquire and manage parklands, and choose the director of the state Department of Conservation. Governor G. Mennen Williams, who had named East to the post as a political Independent, complained that the Senate's unexplained failure to approve the pick of the outdoor writer "demonstrated that some people are determined to inject politics into conservation."[9]

It also proved East's assessment of that warfare: "The people I fought against never had a kind word for me. By the time we were finished with a battle, everyone was bloodied and beat. Simply put, I lived down most of the animosity I created by outliving most of my opponents."[10]

Ordinary citizens flocked to hear the nationally recognized preacher of conservation. Touring widely, he drew large crowds in small towns and mammoth crowds in cities. East's showing of a film about the Arctic and lecture on conservation attracted a crowd of 5,300 (of which 3,500 had to sit in an overflow room) in Knoxville, Kentucky, in 1950. Two East presentations one night in Flint attracted a total audience of fourteen thousand. After a presentation in St. Joseph, Michigan, the local newspaper said that East "thrilled 1,200 people" with a movie and lecture in 1942.[11]

East, described as "almost legendary among members of the sporting fraternity" by the Knoxville *News-Sentinel*, administered the conservation pledge to the large crowd: "I give my pledge as an American to save and faithfully to defend from waste the natural resources of my country—its soils and minerals, its forests, waters and wildlife."

After retiring from the magazine, he continued to fulfill his pledge by writing eight books in a late burst of creativity beginning at age sixty-seven, holed up in an old family cabin on Big School Lot Lake near Holly. He told a reporter when he was seventy-seven that he was generating three to four thousand words a day.

East's books were not stilted conservation policy analyses but instead works of the outdoor (often hunting) adventure genre characteristic of outdoor writers of the period. *Narrow Escapes and Wilderness Adventures* tells twenty-one stories "about humans who suffered pain and fear, hunger, freezing and exhaustion; ordinary persons confronting the ultimate, frightened but swallowing their fear, knowing the odds but refusing to die." *Ben East's Hunting Book* won praise as "one of the most fascinating volumes this reporter has ever come across," said *Traverse City Record-Eagle* outdoor writer Gordon Charles."[12]

One of the stories in the book, "Frozen Terror," is a tale of survival against all odds. Lew Sweet, an ice fisherman, is blown far from shore by a Lake Michigan blizzard, drifting on an ice floe many miles to the lake's archipelago. He becomes the object of a nationally publicized rescue mission but is given up for dead after five days. Through sheer stubbornness, Sweet makes it back to shore—barely.

A rescue plane flies overhead but fails to spot Sweet. "Most men would have lost heart then and there," East writes, "but Lew had been through too much to give up at that point. Back in the living quarters [of a lighthouse abandoned for the winter] he sat down and went stoically on with the job of administering first aid to his feet. 'It don't hurt to freeze,' he related later with a dry grin, 'but it sure hurts like hell to thaw out.'"

A catastrophic stroke stilled East's pen in 1980. He died ten years later. But his name lived on in the Michigan United Conservation Clubs' annual Ben East Award, which recognizes distinguished conservation reporting in Michigan.

He left his own epitaph in a newspaper interview. Describing himself as a crusading journalist, he said, "If I felt an issue needed my editorial efforts, I fought by putting my teeth in it like a bulldog. I would ride herd on a problem until it was brought to a satisfactory conclusion." Bulldog or banty rooster, Ben East was one of a kind among the clan of fierce outdoor writers.

Selected Works

Narrow Escapes and Wilderness Adventures (1960)
Survival: 23 True Sportsmen's Adventures (1967)
Danger! Explosive True Adventures of the Great Outdoors (1970)
The Silence of the North (co-author, 1972)
The Ben East Hunting Book (1974)
The Last Eagle: The Story of Khan (1974)
This Was the North (1975)
Bears: A Veteran Outdoorsman's Account of the Most Fascinating and Dangerous Animals in North America (1977)
Frozen Terror (1979)
Danger in the Air (1979)
Trapped in Devil's Hole (1979)
Desperate Search (1979)
Forty Days Lost (1979)
Mistaken Journey (1979)

Edna Ferber

A Note

It would indeed seem lovely to include a chapter, in a book about authors inspired by Michigan, on this award-winning writer. Born in Kalamazoo on August 15, 1885, Ferber began writing for compensation upon high school graduation in 1902. Her portfolio included two novels made into epic motion pictures, *Show Boat* (Garden City: Doubleday, Page and Co., 1926) and *Giant* (Garden City: Doubleday and Co., 1952). *So Big* (New York: Grosset and Dunlap, 1924) received the 1925 Pulitzer Prize for fiction. Some sources incorrectly place it in Michigan—the location is a Dutch suburb of Chicago. A plaque on an apartment building in Manhattan, where she died in 1968, states: "Ferber's fiction is distinguished by larger-than-life stories, strong female characters, and distinctive renderings of American settings."

Not one principal setting, however, was within the Great Lakes State. Her first autobiography acknowledged how Michigan provided no inspiration, for she was too young to have rooted memories of the place: "Being little more than a baby when we left Kalamazoo, I remember very little about it, but certain things there are which I do recall clearly."[1]

Those certain things were a little boy whose name inspired her to call him Monkey Mitt, and she dressed in his clothes as a source of amusement to the neighborhood. The family doctor, to whom she would stick out her tongue. A willow rocker. A lullaby entitled "Champagne Charlie" (perhaps a garbled memory). And the kids' classic tune "Ten Little Indians."[2] All of which could have been encountered practically anywhere on the planet. Her parents agreed upon a plan to move (back) to Chicago when Edna was eight, which she found vastly more exciting than Kalamazoo, a town name "so improbable-sounding."[3] Iowa also became their residence. Perhaps writing *Come and Get It* during a week's stay in Ironwood reflected the state of her birth.[4] Alas: the novel was set in Wisconsin with comparatively little emphasis on Michigan. Perhaps the plan changed after encountering a

Nazi-sympathizing lumber baron during her sojourn. Prejudice had already attacked her Jewishness in Ottumwa.[5]

Her death in 1968 enabled election to the Chicago Literary Hall of Fame, an honorary degree from Columbia University, and inclusion in a U.S. postage stamp series unveiled in Appleton, Wisconsin. The three places were her favorite stomping grounds.

Bessie Ray Hoover

Writer to the Very End

September 28, 1874–December 30, 1953
Born in Berrien County, lived and taught school in
St. Joseph, lived in Benton Harbor and Kalamazoo

No one really noticed when a seventy-nine-year-old who regularly wrote for magazines passed away in Manhattan just before New Year's Eve 1953. The borough's population, after all, approached two million—hers was just one of many lives that appeared inconsequential. An only child, never married, born and raised in the Midwest, renting an apartment far north in the Grinnell residences at 800 Riverside Drive and West 157th, the ambit of her influence did not extend to the *New York Times*. In her native Michigan, no one appeared to have taken notice either. When a few later bibliographies noticed her work, they lacked critical aspects of her story. One listed her birth year with a question mark and left blank the date of death. Another reported her birth in St. Joseph in 1874 and profession as a college teacher. Like one of her fictional characters, however, Bessie Ray Hoover had carved out an unconventional path and lived her dream of being a writer first and foremost.[1]

If noted at all, Hoover's main output is a trilogy of Berrien County–based novels.[2] Each took its setting and characters largely from that region of Southwest Michigan, noted most for its agricultural heritage and picturesque Great Lake shoreline. The first two were published by a New York house; the final volume appeared in 1922 out of Boston. Entitled *Rolling Acres*, the book's setting was a "fine farm" denoted by a large two-story pillared house made of stone on a gravel way edged by Lombardy poplars. A wide shaded lawn filled in the space down to Hollywood Road. As the novel commenced, a warm September evening breeze caused the front yard fountain to extend its spray onto pink flower borders. The bucolic scene was interrupted by a family dispute, the centerpiece of the story. Its creator took inspiration from her neighborhood, something extolled by the local press under a headline of "Bess Hoover Scores Another Literary Triumph in New Book."[3]

Bessie grew up (and likely was born) on a ten-acre farm on the east side of Lincoln, north of Glenlord Road.[4] Her father, Alphonso V. "Hover," age thirty-eight in 1880, gave his occupation as fruit farmer while wife Etta, thirty-one, was keeping house. Both New York State natives, they had married in Berrien Springs on March 1, 1870, a year after Alphonso had moved to the county. It was in that state's voluntary infantry (112th regiment) that he had enlisted in August 1862, then transferred to the U.S. Signal Corps to serve out the entirety of the Civil War.[5] Mr. Hover did not confine himself to farming. He ran for supervisor of Lincoln Township and served on the local school board.

The couple's only child began her professional life in 1891 when a local paper reported her as among the teachers in St. Joseph. Her eighteenth birthday had yet to arrive, but she had the capability to instruct. She attended the Berrien County Teachers Institute in August of that year. She received a teaching certificate for grade three in 1897.

Her father had died in 1893 of cancer, leaving the survivors to take care of each other. They at first stayed near his grave in Riverview Cemetery, St. Joseph. In 1900, they lived at 300 Church Street—Etta a widow, Bessie answering the census taker's question about occupation with "school teacher." That year, she supported a local theater by participating in the chorus. But she had another passion—after the first two novels appeared in 1909–1910, Bessie provided a biography for a "who's who" list, saying that she had been a "writer since 1900." In 1901, she had worked as a reporter for the Benton Harbor *Herald-Palladium*. She also gave her occupation as "author," not educator. One humorous morality story, authored by Bessie and published in 1906 in *Everybody's Magazine* and entitled "Wayside Ambrosia,"[6] had links to the House of David. This Berrien religious community was famed for its prize-winning farms, amusement park featuring miniature trains, ice cream parlor, zoo, and baseball teams. In 1907, two stories—one entitled "Bill's Budzbanowsky"—appeared in the periodical. Another, "When Cupid Delayed Dinner," made another magazine. A national survey publication listed a total of twenty-seven magazine articles she wrote just in the 1907–1914 span.[7]

What became her first novel, *Pa Flickinger's Folks*, saw the light of day in *Harper's Monthly Magazine* for June–November 1908 under the titles "The Anniversary Present" and "Mr. Flickinger's Vacation." The table of contents listed them as among "Introductory Stories," suggesting her debut on a well-known national stage.[8] A national review gave this summary:

> A story of Ma and Pa Flickinger and their family, types of ordinary working people in every day life. The author convincingly portrays the fun they get out of life, the philosophical way in which they look upon all hardships when influenced by their belief that every one is fitted for his burdens and all things come right.[9]

The author must have been thrilled with the positive estimation given her first full work by the most prominent newspaper in her parents' home state:

> There isn't any doubt that Miss Hoover writes of these people with full knowledge of the class of which they are types, nor that the book is a faithful portrayal of the life with which it is concerned.[10]

The sequel, *Opal*, was a character in and thus grew out of the first book with *Harper's*. The same national review gave this summary:

> Opal Flickinger had been thru the high school and longed to be a lady. This she found difficult in the face of a distressing family who would eat off oil cloth to save table linen and insisted on keeping the coffee pot on the floor to save the oil cloth. But Seftie Woods, a well-to-do young farmer, weathered the storms caused by a mischief making cousin, a rival, and worse than all by ma, who felt that as Opal had got her education she had oughter use it and teach school. In spite of everything a pretty romance budded and bloomed in a setting grotesquely squalid and amid the alarming frankness of the family's humorous comments.[11]

One analyst described this second effort as "a novel of the 'new woman'" who strikes out on her own in contravention of "old nineteenth-century strictures about women's roles."[12]

In 1900, Bessie answered the census taker's question about occupation with school teacher. Two decades later, her answer was "author." Single still, she lived with her widowed mother at 604 Central Avenue in St. Joseph, a two-story Victorian-style house that remains standing. A decade later, she lived in rented quarters on South Rose in Kalamazoo, working as "writer," a move made to be near her mother in the final months. The *St. Joseph Herald-Press* reported in October how she had paid a visit to a friend, referring to her as a "well-known writer, whose stories feature this locality."[13] By 1940, she had made the great leap and lived on Hamilton Place in Manhattan while working as a writer. At the age of seventy-five in 1950, she continued to answer the census as "writer, in the magazine business," living on Riverside Drive.

She died in Manhattan on December 30, 1953, having been a resident of the Big Apple for a quarter century. All her major acknowledged writing took place while in Michigan before the move back East, whence her parents had come. Those works took their essence from her home state, in a region that has rarely been the subject of other than a sporadic effort. If all her work could be discovered, it likely would place Hoover among the Great Lakes State's most prolific writers.[14]

Selected Works

Pa Flickinger's Folks (1909)
Opal (1910)
Rolling Acres (1922)

Isabella Van Wagenen/Sojourner Truth

Greatest Black Woman of the 1800s

Circa 1800–November 26, 1883
Lived in Harmonia and Battle Creek, where she was buried

In 1850, the American Civil War was a decade off yet seemed near. The year marked yet another compromise between Northern and Southern sectional leadership to hold together the Union of free and slave states. Two years later, the presidential election was a battleground for seven separate political parties. The Whig party's national convention endured fifty-three ballots before settling on a nominee. The Democratic party required forty-nine rounds. Voter turnout was low, despite intense campaigning for their support. The state of the nation appeared more fragmented than at any point in its less than four-score years.

Into the swirling cultural maelstrom came the *Narrative of Sojourner Truth: A Northern Slave, Emancipated from Bodily Servitude by the State of New York, in 1828*. Its title page informed readers that the volume had been "printed for the author"—a suggestion that the narrator lacked literacy and resources—and that she had "not been able to see a single proof-sheet" of the work.[1] In truth, the credited author had not written or narrated, in the strictest sense, the words contained in the hundred or so pages of type. It had been penned for her, based on her oral accounts, by Olive Gilbert, a fellow member of the Northampton Association for Education and Industry. Gilbert was an abolitionist, as was William Lloyd Garrison, a renowned and reviled figure, who secured his printer for the work and later added a preface. The book was a financial success, prompting republication overseas. An 1855 edition contained an introduction by Harriet Beecher Stowe, author of *Uncle Tom's Cabin*.

Subsequent editions revised and extended the original. In 1875, the author was gifted with the plates that had been used to print prior iterations. A new version was issued containing editorial changes to the text, an updated biography, and elimination of an appendix credited to another. An excerpt from Truth's scrapbook entitled "Book of Life" was included. Further versions appeared in 1878, 1881, and 1884, the last being issued posthumously.[2]

All four post–Civil War editions originated from Michigan, specifically from the Battle Creek area, because of Truth's relocation there in 1857–1858. The onset of that war brought her life's story into sharp focus. She was, among her peers in efforts at social change, among the most quoted. She would be awarded title of "the most notable and highly regarded African American woman in the nineteenth century,"[3] more so than contemporaries such as Harriet Tubman, Elizabeth Keckley, or Mary Bowser.

Born into slavery in New York State most likely in 1797, Isabella had a "master" named Johannis Hardenbergh, a Revolutionary War officer of Dutch origin. When nine years old, the girl was sold for $100 to the Neelys, then to the Schrivers, then to John and Sally Dumont. After years of separation from family, as well as abuse producing a permanent injury to her right hand, Isabella walked away to freedom in 1826, a year before New York law would have declared her free. She moved in with and took the last name of Isaac and Maria Van Wagenen. Only a baby came with her; her other children by two enslaved African Americans remained in bondage. On June 1, 1843, she took the name Sojourner Truth and moved to Massachusetts where she began public appearances on the abolition circuit. In October 1856, she spoke in Battle Creek at the annual meeting of the Michigan Progressive Friends. Several members, including Frances Titus, became friends, prompting Truth to acquire a lot in Harmonia on July 28, 1857, and build a home there.[4]

Harmonia was platted in 1850–1855 by two Quakers (or Friends) who had become Spiritualists. In the southwestern corner of Bedford Township in Calhoun County, west of Battle Creek, the village was to be the home of a seminary and other buildings and homes that would nurture a spiritual community.[5] Living in Harmonia provided Truth with greater accessibility to the hospitable audiences of the Midwest for her touring and lectures.[6] In the 1860 Census, her home in Harmonia included daughter Elizabeth Banks and grandsons James Caldwell and "Sammy" Banks. The village never thrived, and a destructive tornado on August 4, 1862, accelerated its demise.[7] Truth moved to 38 College Street in Battle Creek; it was her home when she died on May 23, 1883.

Truth apparently never learned to read, so she relied primarily on memory for learning. She never exhibited the "mock southern dialect" ascribed to the enslaved, having lived her whole life in the North.[8] Instead, she was "a Dutch-speaking child" who "took pride in speaking correct English" as an adult and in refutation of bias against the capabilities of the formerly enslaved.[9] She collaborated with Titus—"her neighbor, friend, and informal business manager"—on the "augmented" edition of her book, published in 1875, that incorporated Truth's scrapbooks under the heading "Book of Life."[10] The original had been just over one hundred pages, plus a preface, an appendix, and "certificates of character" that were not of her creation. The later editions added a "part second" full of post-1850 chronicles.

It also included the remarks of activist Frances D. Gage of Truth at the 1851 Women's Rights Convention in Akron, Ohio. That account was rendered in dialect, beginning with: "Well, chilern, whar dar is so much racket dar must be something out o' kilter," and it became widely known by the title "Ain't I a Woman?" But the best and, it should be accepted as, accurate version sounded much different:

> May I say a few words? I want to say a few words about this matter. I am a woman's rights [*sic*]. I have as much muscle as any man, and can do as much work as any man. I have plowed and reaped and husked and chopped and mowed, and can any man do more than that? I have heard much about the sexes being equal; I can carry as much as any man, and can eat as much too, if I can get it. I am as strong as any man that is now. As for intellect, all I can say is, if a woman have a pint, and a man a quart—why can't she have her little pint full? You need not be afraid to give us our rights for fear we will take too much—for we can't take more than our pint'll hold. The poor men seem to be all in confusion, and don't know what to do. Why children, if you have woman's [*sic*] rights, give it to her and you will feel better. You will have your own rights, and they won't be so much trouble. I can't read, but I can hear. I have heard the Bible and have learned that Eve caused man to sin. Well, if woman upset the world, do give her a chance to set it right side up again. The Lady has spoken about Jesus, how he never spurned woman from him, and she was right. When Lazarus died, Mary and Martha came to him with faith and love and besought him to raise their brother. And Jesus wept—and Lazarus came forth. And how came Jesus into the world? Through God who

created him and the woman who bore him. Man, where is your part? But the women are coming up [—] blessed be God and a few of the men are coming up with them. But man is in a tight place, the poor slave is on him, woman is coming on him, he is surely between a hawk and a buzzard.[11]

Her delivery left an indelible impression: "Those only can appreciate it who saw her powerful form, her whole-souled, earnest gestures, and listened to her strong and truthful tones."[12]

Other portions of the longer edition also gave her dialect as anything but "mock Southern." The volume began with her employment of the King's English—more accurately, the syntax of educated Americans: "Sojourner Truth once remarked, in reply to an allusion to the late Horace Greeley, 'You call him a self-made man; well, I am a self-made woman.'"[13]

In 1862, when opponents to abolition threatened to burn the meeting house where she was to speak, Truth replied, "Then I will speak upon the ashes." She delivered her speech, and the rendition in the book contained no idioms within the "mock Southern" dialect. Perhaps, to be charitable, some listeners mistook her Dutch-speaking upbringing for what they understood to be the dialect of the enslaved people of the South.

The 1884 book included a memorial chapter. Among its stories was an "Incident at Georgetown" within the District of Columbia. Having encountered a "Jim Crow" streetcar designated for persons of color while they were excluded from all others, she sought to exercise her hard-won rights:

Not long after this, Sojourner, having occasion to ride, signaled the car, but neither conductor nor driver noticed her. Soon another followed, and she raised her hand again, but they also turned away. She then gave three tremendous yelps, "I want to ride! I *want to ride*! I WANT TO RIDE!"

Consternation seized the passing crowd—people, carriages, and go-carts of every description stood still. The car was effectually blocked up, and before it could move on, Sojourner had jumped aboard. Then there arose a great shout from the crowd, "Ha ha ha! She has beaten him." The angry conductor told her to go forward where the horses were, or he would put her out. Quietly seating herself, she informed him that she was a passenger. "Go forward where the horses are, or I will throw you out," he said in a menacing voice.[14] She told him that she was neither a Marylander nor a Virginian to fear his threats but was from the Empire State of New York and knew the laws as well as he did.

> Several soldiers were in the car, and when other passengers came in, they related the circumstance and said, "You ought to have heard that old woman talk to the conductor." Sojourner rode farther than she needed to go; for a ride was so rare a privilege that she determined to make the most of it. She left the car feeling very happy, and said, "Bless God! I have had a ride."[15]

Nearly a century before Rosa Parks's famous refusal to obey Jim Crow in a public transit vehicle, her Michigan predecessor set a precedent as one of the first freedom riders.[16]

Truth's spiritual beliefs provided her with profound strength. The *Narrative* republished this account of her conversion (without stigmatized language):

> About a year previous to my emancipation, I ran away from my master, and went to live with Mr. Wagner; it was here that a change first came over my heart, and I felt that I was a sinner. I prayed to God, and he answered my prayers, and I have experienced his blessings. I said, I really believe I am a sinner, and that Jesus died for me. I had never been to church, and never heard any one say this. I believe my only sin consisted in wishing harm to the white folks; but now I love everybody.[17]

Presumably, the expanded version met the author's complete approval. Had she never learned to read and write, after nearly six decades of freedom? She proudly sold her books as earnest authors do.[18] She was reported in 1871 as confessing, "I can't read a book, but I can read de people," but the article stereotyped her speech.[19] One biographer concluded that she "wrote herself into history" through dictation, lectures, and life.[20] When she visited the office of a Battle Creek newspaper "to subscribe for the *Journal*," was it so someone else could read it to her? A letter of hers to the editor of the *New York Tribune* began: "Seeing an item in your paper about me . . ." It also appeared to bear her signature. A letter in 1870 from the compiler of the 1850 edition spoke of Truth having "so little book-education"—little, but not *none*.[21] If nothing else, she can be accredited as a lyricist for having contributed to a paean to the men of the First Michigan Colored Regiment.

Truth died early in the morning on November 26, 1883, at her Battle Creek home. On November 28, her funeral was held at the Congregational-Presbyterian Church, with prominent citizens of Battle Creek acting as pallbearers. The building was packed. Burial was deservedly in Oak Hill Cemetery, the traditional site for community leaders and notables. For three decades, she had widely traveled, lectured, advocated.

A late nineteenth-century album of history and information about Calhoun County included her story. Although it repeated both misinformation and myth, its opening message demonstrated an awareness of Truth's position in American history:

> This volume would certainly fall short of its mission if we omitted the mention of one so well and favorably known as Sojourner Truth, whose slave name was Isabella. Nor is her fame confined to the limits of Calhoun County or the State of Michigan, where she so long resided and where she ended her days, but wherever the English language is spoken, wherever freedom and justice rule with mighty sway, there her name is spoken and revered.[22]

The people of Battle Creek did not forget her, though commemoration did take time. The first marker was dedicated as part of the Stone History Tower in Monument Park in 1935. In 1976, the State of Michigan honored community wishes by designating the Interstate 194 spur as the Sojourner Truth Downtown Parkway. In 1987, the State Bar of Michigan unveiled one of its "Michigan Legal Milestones" bronze plaques in a local bar ceremony in the Battle Creek Hall of Justice. To mark the bicentennial of her birth, a larger-than-life bronze sculpture was installed in Monument Park accompanied by various signage.

"May her legacy live on," is the message on one of the plaques surrounding the statue. Her words, unfiltered by paternalism and prejudice, are worthy of being revered. Among them are the lyrics she created for "The Valiant Soldiers," the first Michigan Regiment of colored soldiers, to be sung to the tune of "John Brown's Body." It was sung by her in Detroit and Washington, D.C.

> We are the valiant soldiers who've 'listed for the war;
> We are fighting for the Union, we are fighting for the law;
> We can shoot a rebel farther than a white man ever saw,
> As we go marching on.

Chorus.—
Glory, glory, hallelujah! Glory, glory, hallelujah!
Glory, glory, hallelujah, as we go marching on.

Look there above the center, where the flag is waving bright;
We are going out of slavery, we are bound for freedom's light;
We mean to show Jeff Davis how the Africans can fight,
As we go marching on.—Cho.

We are done with hoeing cotton, we are done with hoeing corn;
We are colored Yankee soldiers as sure as you are born.
When massa hears us shouting, he will think 'tis Gabriel's horn,
As we go marching on.—Cho.

They will have to pay us wages, the wages of their sin;
They will have to bow their foreheads to their colored kith and kin;
They will have to give us house-room, or the roof will tumble in,
As we go marching on.—Cho.

We hear the proclamation, massa, hush it as you will;
The birds will sing it to us, hopping on the cotton hill;
The possum up the gum tree couldn't keep it still,
As he went climbing on.—Cho.

Father Abraham has spoken, and the message has been sent;
The prison doors have opened, and out the prisoners went
To join the sable army of African descent,
As we go marching on.—Cho.[23]

Northern Lower Michigan

David Salzer Broder

Community Over Celebrity

September 11, 1929–March 9, 2011
Wrote from Beaver Island summer home

The month and date of David Salzer Broder's birth would later have great significance to his country, but it was the year that meant everything with the arrival of the Great Depression. Despite the woeful economy, a highlight of his youth was carefree summer stays in a family cottage near a sand dune along the northern Indiana shore.

At the University of Chicago, Broder met Ann Creighton Collar. Marriage would bless them with nearly sixty years together and four sons. They made their home in Arlington, Virginia, as David's journalism career took him to the *Congressional Quarterly*, then the *Washington Star*, followed by the national capital desk at the *New York Times*, and, for the final forty-two years, the *Washington Post* as lead political reporter. He won the Pulitzer Prize in 1972 for political commentary. Ann became a political activist, member and chair of the local board of education, philanthropist and supporter of the arts (herself an artist), and supporter of outreach to the homeless. Her 2016 obituary revealed the driving force: "Ann never lost touch with her Midwestern roots."

Their mutual rootedness in the heartland was nurtured by a family tradition. Every summer after school ended, Ann made all the preparations before piling everyone into the Broder van for the long first day's drive. They always stayed at the same Toledo motel, then continued on the following day to Charlevoix in time for the afternoon ferry and a two-hour excursion to Beaver Island.

The marital connection to "the Emerald Isle" began while they were dating in 1949, and it was where they honeymooned. It reached farther back through the Collar family. An aunt to Ann's mother, Helen Hoffman Collar experienced severe summertime allergies that drove her parents' search for a haven far enough north where the air would be purer. In 1915, on the first visit to Beaver Island, its Lake Michigan breezes proved so conducive that the family acquired a shoreline property and built a rustic cottage on the northwestern tip. Sublime views of Garden, Trout, and Whiskey Islands and unrivaled summer sunsets validated the decision. Over time, Helen became the community's unofficial historian, preserving the family stories of its residents, a history rich with the Indigenous people who trapped and fished there, the French who learned of its bounty from their trading partners, the colony of a religious sect who made it a haven, and the influx of Irish—the last providing its Emerald Isle nickname.

For the reporter, known for flannel shirts and reliance on a trusty Royal typewriter, writing from and about the island came naturally. Despite a thirty-mile distance from the mainland, Beaver Island boasted museums, churches, a chamber of commerce, a historical society, restaurants, shops, and a medical facility, with a pace for its inhabitants that aided perspective. It had enough civilization to teach important lessons. Border's inaugural column extolled how it "displays, in microcosm, the qualities America must somehow recover if it is to survive as a nation." Survival would depend, he wrote, on "cooperation and improvisation," two qualities found in abundance among the small coterie of island denizens.[1]

That initial piece was dated September 1, 1970, reflecting a classic end-of-summer topic: the return of children to school. The sense of neighborliness enabled Beaver Island to hold onto its attractiveness as a year-round place to live. Broder lamented how America was becoming ever more sharply divided, how those divisions were choking out a sense of belonging to each other, and how a lack of leadership was threatening the nation's very existence by failing to inspire unity and sacrifice. Beaver Islanders, by contrast, were showing the way.

Some island columns were lighthearted. Broder recommended that President Gerald R. Ford initiate his new administration with a simple strategy: knock off for summer, not do much until into the fall, and give the nation a sorely needed respite from the rigors of the Watergate scandal. Each summer on the island showed how beneficial vacation time was. He predicted a successful campaign for Ford in 1976 if Great Lakes water levels continued to fall as they had during the summer of 1975, but the tide carried the Michigander's fortunes away.

Such location specifics were found in each piece: "the chain-activated switch on the bathroom light" in the cabin; "shaking the beach sand" out of books enjoyed during summer reading; passages about "boys who, as lads, learned to skip stones" across the great blue water; "wind-tossed Lake Michigan swells"; "formal" attire that really meant T-shirts and shoes; "frostbite symptoms" attached to swimming "in the extension of the Arctic Sea called the top of Lake Michigan"; "a deck on which to sun after a swim"; whether to immediately eat "the fresh-picked apples and blackberries after a swim or bake them into pies"; "building a marvelous fire ring out of beach rocks for the marshmallow roast"; "hikes to search out raspberries or loons"; and the "sense of remoteness from the over-hyped." Joyful were "muddy slogs in search of exotic plants."

On a beach walk, Broder concluded that "the legacy we inherited is worth struggling to preserve" on the green and pleasant island, since Beaver Island "is a fabled place, shrouded in the mists of northern Lake Michigan." A column devoted to jazz, among America's great contributions to culture, made sense when penned in a place where the music of the lake played for those with ears to hear.[2] Local scenes, shops, and people all found their way into these bulletins from the beachfront.

Great Depression, World War II, totalitarianism, Vietnam, racial division, Wall Street calamities, 9/11. These American experiences and their political response all passed through Broder's typewriter and into print for readers to ponder. One op-ed began: "Someday, we will learn. When it's September and important issues cry out for attention, but we seem consumed by trivia—watch out." He also lamented "the psychological damage to an electorate already struggling to maintain any optimism about the country and its future."[3]

His final column was written from Washington in some despair over the state of the national government. A rare bit of good news had come in the form of a Congressional action plan to help save those "incomparable resources" appropriately referred to as Great Lakes. A longing for this special place brought Broder again and again to find renewal on its freshwater shores. Neither Nantucket nor Martha's Vineyard nor Kennebunkport would suffice. Beaver Island held far superior attributes, and it was where he experienced sustaining simple joys:

> Happily, some things do not change. It is still a place where you can look up and down a magnificent sweep of beach on a sunny midafternoon and not see

> another soul, where deer and fox and wild turkeys become your neighbors, where the sunset over Indian Point never loses its beauty, where the Big Dipper seems to wheel directly overhead and, occasionally, the northern lights mount their awesome display.
>
> There is something about the combination of sand and water that delights children of all ages.

He hoped that enlightened public policy would enable more generations to experience that delight. Though a journalist, he eschewed neutrality when it came to this issue: "Like everyone who comes under Lake Michigan's spell, I love it."[4]

The state of the nation remains as divided as Broder lamented in 1970. Some say more so. Perhaps it is time for another Midwest-based conference, not on Mackinac but on Beaver Island, where leaders can come together and reach "a unified policy statement" on how to fulfill stewardship responsibilities.[5] Broder would have predicted good things from their stay on the Emerald Isle.

Selected Works

The Beaver Island Columns (2012)

Johnston "Jack" Davis Kerkhoff

Home (Bitter) Sweet Home

November 1, 1900–May 2, 1958

Spent childhood in Traverse City, wrote memoir of stay in Traverse City State Hospital

On the first page of his final book, author Jack Kerkhoff explains why his Traverse City stay in the winter of 1950–1951 was not joyous:

> So this is my homecoming. This is my return to the town where I spent the happiest days of my youth . . . so this is my return to Traverse City, Michigan. Not to the sprawling white house on Washington Street, which all of us loved, but to the Traverse City State Hospital, in other days bluntly called the insane asylum.[1]

Significantly, the author is not being hauled to the hospital; he is committing himself voluntarily, despondent after the death of his wife and older daughter. The narrative tracks the author's slow, hard-won recovery in a surprisingly benevolent institution and documents the humanity of the men and women housed in the hospital.[2]

Before all this happened, Jack Kerkhoff enjoyed a childhood in the Traverse City region that grew more luminous in retrospect as his adulthood darkened. Young Jack and his family lived for a time on a farm eighteen miles outside of Traverse City. Thanksgiving was a cherished holiday, his mother and grandmother spending days preparing the holiday feast. "There always seemed to be visiting relatives from faraway places with presents and exciting stories. But there were no stories after Thanksgiving dinner; everyone sprawled in easy chairs and groaned or fell asleep."[3] These were heartwarming memories of a Midwestern childhood.

After the family moved into town, the author remembered hamburgers and banana splits following high school dances, and he joined his classmates in going to Liberty Loan rallies and "damned the Kaiser without knowing why.[4]"

But another childhood memory intrudes on his thoughts as he is driven to the state hospital in November 1949—the fear and distaste his circle of boys felt toward the hospital in their neighborhood. "How many times I had scampered up that driveway with my gang, fearful yet curious. How many times we had wandered outside the bleak, tower-topped buildings that had iron bars at the windows, and shouted at the men and women behind the bars and giggled over the obscenities they tossed back at us."[5] More than three decades later, the author checks into the same facility, believing it to offer the best opportunity for regaining sanity.

Kerkhoff's chosen profession was journalism, where he excelled. Beginning at the hometown *Traverse City Record-Eagle*, he reported for the *Detroit News*, *Philadelphia Record*, *New York Journal-American*, *New York Post*, and the *Grand Rapids Herald*. His stories spanned the distance from an analysis of the conviction of Bruno Hauptmann for the kidnapping and death of the baby of Charles and Anne Lindbergh to a piece enraging the people of Tappahannock, Virginia, which he described as a "town where nothing happens . . . living with the ghosts of the past."[6] He noted that the only life he saw on the village's main street was a swayback horse and mangy chickens. The newspaper's management dispatched a rewrite man to the village to assuage the townspeople with a new article.[7]

Kerkhoff attracted headlines himself. In February 1937, a Michigan judge jailed him for contempt of court after he refused to provide information about an article in which he reported on the alleged brutal beating of a union sympathizer. He was released after a night behind bars.[8] In 1943, gathering material for an article, he was called into action to assist in the delivery of a baby in a tourist camp. "Not if I can help it," he said when asked whether he would do it again.

Kerkhoff's first book, *Traitor! Traitor!*, about the Dreyfus affair won respectful but not glowing reviews when published in 1930.[9] His second, a "romantic biography" of Aaron Burr, struck some critics as an oddity while others praised it.[10] Of these books, Kerkhoff tells the state hospital treatment team, "Good reviews, but I regret to say that I was unable to retire on the proceeds."[11]

Tragedy stalked Kerkhoff in the 1940s. First, his wife, Eleanor, in 1940 died at thirty-eight in New York City. Her death notice described her as a poet and author. In 1948, his twenty-five-year-old daughter died, beginning a downward journey for Kerkhoff. The path, which included two suicide attempts, ultimately led to the state hospital.

The price of a stay at the hospital was cheap, $2.40 a day for a bed, state-issued clothes, and food. Accordingly, the accommodations were spartan: a screened window, a small bed, a small chest of drawers, a chair, and a throw rug.

Kerkhoff soon discovered kindred troubled spirits, some of whom aroused his empathy and some who became friends. One man was nicknamed "Heil Hitler" in accordance with the two words he uttered frequently. Another was convinced that Kerkhoff was "the inspector" who could defend him from electrocution for his sins. Others drew these nicknames: Boy Blue for the color of his slacks and shorts; the Financier, who imagined he was making a killing from gambling; and the Brat, Curly, and Willie.

In one memorable adventure, the author climbs into his car with three fellow patients. Not having the key to the car until he leaves the hospital, he takes them on a virtual drive, stepping on the gas, turning the steering wheel, and heading down imaginary roads. "I felt a wave of tenderness for the three of them. And then a wave of hopelessness, for I could do nothing for them. Nothing more than I was doing now, sitting in a motionless automobile and pretending as we used to pretend on the Farm in a horseless buggy."[12]

A doomed love affair developed between patient Suzy and Kerkhoff—doomed because Kerkhoff would get out, but Suzy, for reasons that were not quite clear, expected a lifetime stay at the state hospital. As his forty-five days in the hospital came to a close, Kerkhoff felt balance and a renewed vitality.

The hospital staff—physicians, nurses, attendants, and support workers—were almost uniformly compassionate and concerned about the welfare of their wards. Several of the support workers knew Kerkhoff from his childhood in Traverse City and treated him warmly. When Kerkhoff was interviewed by his treatment team, the physicians treated him respectfully and gently. They emerged as heroes just as the patients did.

Kerkhoff's life ended just six years after the publication of his state hospital memoir, *How Thin the Veil* under ambiguous circumstances. Moving in 1957 to Imperial Beach, California, to live with his surviving daughter and son-in-law, he journeyed into Tijuana the following spring.[13]

There, on May 2, 1958, he was found dead in his hotel room. The Chula Vista newspaper said there was no evidence of violence in the room, but his empty wallet was found on the roof of the hotel.[14]

Kerkhoff's 1952 book, however, had a second life. Mission Point Press of Traverse City heard of it and learned the original publisher had let the copyright lapse, leaving it in the public domain. The press decided to resurrect it in 2016. The press sends the Commons—a shopping, retail, and living space redeveloped out of the old state hospital buildings and grounds—a monthly donation based on sales. The revenues boost a non-profit heritage fund set aside for expanding knowledge about the hospital.

Kerkhoff's best epitaph was a review of *How Thin the Veil* by F. A. Behymer in the *St. Louis Post-Dispatch*: "There is much in a state hospital that is not lovely, and Mr. Kerkhoff has not been one to try to make it lovely. But there is much, too, that is human and therefore lovable, as he reveals, without romanticizing. It could be that the recovery of the author was due to the [15]compassion that he found in the rending of the veil."

How Thin the Veil continues to offer hope to those struggling with their mental health, showing that recovery is often possible, that dignity is each person's right, and that despite stereotypes suggesting otherwise, some public institutions of the mid-twentieth century cared humanely for the mentally ill.

Selected Works

Traitor! Traitor! The Tragedy of Alfred Dreyfus (1930)
Aaron Burr: A Romantic Biography (1931)
How Thin the Veil: A Memoir of 45 Days in the Traverse City State Hospital (1952, republished 2016)

Larry Woiwode

Michigan's Dakota Bard

October 30, 1941–April 28, 2022

Set his first novel in Michigan, the land of relatives

When it comes to the work of author Larry Woiwode, knowledgeable readers are more likely to think of the sky-mirroring wide horizons of North Dakota than of the intimate forest presence of northern Michigan. Woiwode indeed was the longtime poet laureate of North Dakota and the architect of several novels set on the prairies. But before all that, there was his first published novel. Set in a fictional Northport, *What I'm Going to Do, I Think*, won warm praise from many critics.

One of nine children, Larry moved with his family from North Dakota to Forest City, Illinois, after the economic conditions of the Dust Bowl cost his parents Everett and Audrey the family farm. He graduated from the University of Illinois. But his imagination lingered behind. It would flourish in the landscapes of his birth state. At his death, the *New York Times* characterized Woiwode as "the author of expansive novels, short stories, poems and essays, mostly planted in the American West."[1]

Yet his first novel was set in a lodge on Lake Michigan. Larry and his wife Carole spent their honeymoon in a similar environment, near Northport, Michigan. Under the headline "Lost Innocents in Hemingway Country," Webster Schott praised Woiwode's debut in the *New York Times*, declaring it a "touching, sometimes deeply moving novel about youth growing up to the pain of loss, the puzzle of love, and the sense of despair lying near the surface of modern consciousness." Published in 1969, the novel won the William Faulkner Foundation prize for the most notable first novel of the year.

The book was written in part during an emotional firestorm in the Woiwodes' marriage. Carole moved out of their home for more than a year with the couple's first child. Larry endured a nervous breakdown. But the two reconciled and remained married for the rest of his life.

More than the backdrop of the novel originated in Michigan. Larry's cousin, Thomas Woiwode, recalled sitting at a table with other family members, including the author, as he discussed his work in progress on a visit to his Southeast Michigan relatives. These included Tom's sister Mary Ellen and brother James Christopher, known as Chris by most. Thomas Woiwode recalled,

> During the visit, and over dinner at the kitchen table, Larry would lament the names he had given the characters in his yet-to-be-published novel. . He didn't think the names he currently had for the characters connected well, to the characters themselves or to each other. He was concerned that their names didn't evoke the kind of sympathy or interest the reader should have for the characters. It was clearly affecting the way he thought about the nearly final product. . . . When the novel was published, the names of the characters were . . . Chris and Ellen.[2]

Shortly after the delivery of his first novel, the Woiwodes moved to New York, where Robert De Niro became his "drinking buddy," according to his *Times* obituary. His new residence put him close to the offices of the *New Yorker*, which regularly published Woiwode.

Woiwode's first novel was well-liked; the second won raves. Published in 1975, *Beyond the Bedroom Wall*, a tale of four generations of a North Dakota farm family, earned comparisons to Dickens, Melville, and Tolstoy.

In 1978, Larry and Carole bought a 160-acre North Dakota farm near the town of Mott. They raised grain crops, hay, and quarter horses. Farm life was not easy. Besides the grueling physical labor involved, danger was often at hand. Woiwode suffered three broken ribs, a compressed spine, and a near-severed right arm in a hay baler accident. Despite these challenges, Larry worked in a writing office in the barn.

When he died in 2022, few noted the author's ties to Michigan, and even fewer knew Michigan was the fertile soil from which the names of the leading characters of his first novel were harvested.

Selected Works

What I'm Going to Do, I Think (1969)
Beyond the Bedroom Wall (1975)
Even Tide (1977)
Poppa John (1981)
Born Brothers (1988)
Neumiller Stories (1989)
Indian Affairs (1992)
Silent Passengers: Stories (1993)
Acts (1993)
What I Think I Did: A Season of Survival in Two Acts (2000)
Aristocrat of the West: The Story of Harold Schafer (2000)
A Step from Death (2008)
Words Made Fresh: Essays on Literature and Culture (2011)
The Invention of Lefse (2011)
Words for Readers and Writers (2013)
The Dignity of Grace: A Life of Sister Thomas Welder (2021)
A Legacy of Passion: The Scheel Family Story (2022)

Upper Peninsula

Charlotte Armstrong

Underground Discoveries

May 2, 1905–July 18, 1969
Born in Vulcan

What makes a seemingly conventional person—a mother and homemaker born in a small Michigan town—into a celebrated author of mystery and suspense fiction with a body count? (One discussion of her work was headlined, "The Place Fairly Teems with Corpses."[1]) In her own case, Michigan's Charlotte Armstrong provides a clue from childhood memory:

> Above the dam, crossing the river from Michigan to Wisconsin, there was a footbridge, a suspension bridge, narrow, with 2 cables for handrails. It was my father's delight to walk us out to the middle of this airy thing and stand there, with the falls roaring beneath us, and bounce so that the flimsy thing under our feet jumped and swayed. He wasn't afraid. He thought it was fun. I guess it was fun, in a terrifying sort of way, to swing between Michigan and Wisconsin.[2]

The young Charlotte, who adored her father, learned from him the thrill of apparent danger that is safely experienced, much the way readers of her twenty-six novels, three novellas and more than seventy short stories would.

But there was real danger in the Michigan community in which Charlotte grew up. Named after Vulcan, the Roman god of fire, the town, like its neighbors, was an iron ore mining community in which the risk of a calamitous accident was ever present. Between the 1890s and 1950s, twelve iron ore mining accidents in Michigan killed 161 miners, with hundreds more injured.[3]

Charlotte Armstrong was Vulcan-born to Clara and Frank Armstrong in 1905. Frank was chief engineer for the Penn Iron Mining Company.[4]

A primary task for Frank was promoting safety in the high-risk industry. According to his grandson, Frank invented machines that blasted coal with greater safety for the miners than traditional explosives.

Charlotte grew up in "a house built into and hanging onto the edge of a hill," close enough to the mine to hear all night what she called "the hiss and rattle and long, loud snorting sounds of the steam shovels loading ore" onto railroad cars. "And there were the whistles hooting shifts—blowing time (all day, all night)."[5]

The contrast between the natural beauty of the Upper Peninsula and the world of the miner moved Charlotte. In her novel *The Trouble in Thor*, based on her childhood, she describes a land "hilly and woodsy [that] smells of pine."[6] But the town itself yields up different sights: "great pipelines, tarred and black, running through woods and fields . . . men going to work in the evening with their full dinner pails."

Despite this evidence, Armstrong writes, "perhaps you would not know that this is a violent place; that under the pretty little town, each day, each night there was risk, and bold struggle, and sometimes death, and always danger."[7]

Two other influences shaped Charlotte's sensibilities. Her father loved puzzles, often taking matches or pennies out of his pockets, laying them on a table, and performing little tricks. She loved to read, devouring the Sherlock Holmes canon at age eleven.[8]

By her own account, Charlotte felt protected and loved in her childhood. She was also attracted early on to writing as self-expression. In 1959, she told the *Green Bay Press-Gazette*, "I wanted to write about as soon as I could read. Earned my first cents aged 11. I wrote a play, cast it, directed it, produced it in a neighbor's barn (playing the star role, naturally, myself). Admission one cent, with profits evenly divided among us all."[9]

Charlotte's high school graduating class consisted of eight students. Her son said, "My mother often told the story, with some degree of pride and a little bit of embarrassment, of how she voted for herself as class president, not considered cricket in those days. She was outed when she won the election unanimously."[10]

After high school, Charlotte's education continued at a college preparatory school, Ferry Hall, outside Chicago. She then attended the University of Wisconsin for two years, finally transferring to Barnard College in New York and graduating in 1925. She had dreams of becoming an author.

Charlotte's first job after graduating from Barnard was in the classified ad department of the *New York Times*, "where telephones rang all day." There she met another aspiring writer, Joseph (Jack) Lewi, whom she married on January 21, 1928.

As the marriage matured and children arrived, demands on Charlotte increased. She did find time to write poetry, and the *New Yorker* published one of her creations. This only whetted her appetite to write. She composed plays, taking advantage of the two hours each afternoon when her infant son napped. (She gave birth to two sons and a daughter.)[11]

Her first play never made it beyond Cape Cod summer theater. Her second reached Broadway but flopped.[12] The third, she said, "got raves in Philadelphia but went down with a great crash on Broadway." From the experience, Charlotte said, she salvaged two things: a fondness for rewriting and a decision to write novels instead of plays.

According to one newspaper account, Charlotte was confined to bed with sickness and read every suspense and mystery novel in the local library, declaring, "Hell, I can write one of these."[13] For whatever reason, she went on to prove she could during a successful writing career.

She began acquiring notice from suspense readers and critics alike with her first work of significance, *Lay on MacDuff*. Well received, it created a recurring character, MacDougall Duff, a professor whose sideline was solving crimes. But Charlotte proved more diverse, moving on to fiction without a formula.

Her commercial breakthrough was *The Unsuspected*, which not only sold well, but was picked up by Warner Brothers.[14] The *Lexington Herald-Leader* said "it mounts in excitement in every paragraph, every page, to a terrific climax. It is indeed hair-raising drama."[15] It became a film directed by Michael Curtiz and starring Claude Rains, a winning pair from the film *Casablanca*.

The Unsuspected was controversial to a degree, opening deliberately with a spoiler: the killer is revealed almost immediately. The suspense was not in divining the murderer, but in the cat-and-mouse game of how the murderer was identified. Regardless, critics hailed the book as well crafted and suspenseful.

The commercial success of the book and sale of the movie rights enabled Charlotte and her family to move to Southern California, taking up residence in Glendale. Charlotte lived there for the remainder of her life, turning out book after book and earning a reputation as one of America's great suspense authors. Readers and critics continued to remark on the contrast between the charming author and her dark subjects. "Miss Armstrong poses suitably as the smiler with a knife: she is a cheerful-looking woman who has written some of the most edgy and gripping psychological thrillers of our time," wrote critic Robert Weaver.[16]

A second Armstrong book, *Mischief*, became a movie starring Richard Widmark and Marilyn Monroe under the title *Don't Bother to Knock*. Its premise is an apparently typical teenage babysitter whose insanity is initially concealed. Critic and author Anthony Boucher praised the book as "surely one of the finest pure terror-suspense stories ever written."[17]

As she saw it, Charlotte never again wrote a "whodunit." She told a reporter that her 1956 novel, *A Dram of Poison*, "has no crime, no violence and no villains. . . . I find I kill off fewer and fewer characters all the time."[18] She considered her works thereafter to be suspense books. *A Dram of Poison* won the 1956 Edgar Allan Poe Award of the Mystery Writers of America. Coward-McCann published all her books, while *Ellery Queen's Mystery Magazine*, the *Saturday Evening Post* and *Argosy* published the bulk of her short stories.

Her novel set in a community not unlike her childhood home, *The Trouble in Thor*, appeared under the pen name Jo Valentine in 1953. In the story, after workers die in a mining accident, a character asks why such tragedy is accepted as inevitable:

> She thought of the ore that would yet be torn out of the earth, and come up, and fall into the cars, and ride the long water, and meet, in the mills, the fires and the manipulations of men, until it was iron. And then steel, which men demanded, men would have it, so they would get it. . . . She sighed and picked up a pancake turner to slip under the eggs and the bacon. Its thin steel shaft and its supple blade were strong and handy.[19]

Charlotte died at age sixty-four. Her passing was noted nationally. The *New York Times* said, "For her readers, Miss Armstrong was an established witch who conjured terrifying suspense and conjured agonizing uncertainties to plague them."[20] Summing up her career, a critic noted her unique ability to endow her characters—murderers, would-be murderers, victims, and lookers-on—with a depth and dimension rare in the goose-pimple world of suspense fiction.[21] Readers and critics who rediscover her forgotten works see Charlotte as part of a notable current in American literature—the emergence of female mystery and suspense authors in the 1940s and 1950s.

In 2008, residents of Norway, Michigan—near her birthplace—sponsored a well-attended three-day Charlotte Armstrong Festival that focused on her youth in the area. With the help of Norway's Jake Menghini Museum, her children published Charlotte's biography of her father, *I Knew a Fellow Six Feet High*, a loving tribute. They also brought out a collection of writings by the author and her family, *Charlotte Armstrong: A Master Storyteller Remembered.*

Despite sometimes bridling at being tagged a suspense writer, Charlotte defended the genre with spirit:

> Devotees of the suspense story know that they can be good or bad and they come in variety. People who never read them tend to call them all "mere escape." I wonder if these people find reading a task and cannot read for fun. Or think that they ought not? If they suppose a suspense novel to be easy to do and therefore somehow "cheap," they should try to do one. The form is related to and has the stricture of drama. Therefore it has form, which not every novelist bothers about. The fact is, they are stories, and storytelling is an old human delight that began in the caves in antiquity.[22]

Selected Works

The Happiest Days (1939)
Ring Around Elizabeth (1941)
Lay On, Mac Duff! (1942)
The Case of the Weird Sisters (1943)
The Innocent Flower (also known as *Death Filled the Glass*, 1945)
Fatal Lady (1950)
Mischief (1950)
The Black-Eyed Stranger (1952)
Catch-as-Catch-Can (also known as *Walk Out on Death*, 1953)
The Trouble in Thor (as Jo Valentine; also known as *And Sometimes Death*, 1953)
The Better to Eat You (also known as *Murder's Nest*, 1954)
A Gun Is a Nervous Thing (1955)
The Dream Walker (also known as *Alibi for Murder*, 1955)
A Dram of Poison (1956)
And Already Lost . . . (1957)

The Albatross (1957)
Incident at a Corner (1957)
Something Blue (1959)
The Seventeen Widows of San Souci (1959)
The Girl with a Secret (1959)
The Ring in the Fish (1959)
Then Came Two Women (1962)
The One-Faced Girl (1963)
The Mark of the Hand (1963)
The Witch's House (1963)
Who's Been Sitting in My Chair? (1963)
A Little Less Than Kind (1964)
Run—If You Can (1964)
The Turret Room (1965)
Dream of Fair Woman (1966)
I See You (1966)
The Gift Shop (1966)
Lemon in the Basket (1967)
The Balloon Man (1968)
Seven Seats to the Moon (1969)
The Protege (1970)
Night Call and Other Stories of Suspense (2014)

William Chalmers Covert

In the Cathedral of Creation

October 4, 1864–February 4, 1942

Lived five years in Saginaw, wrote two meditations on the Upper Peninsula

He was born a Hoosier, began service as an ordained minister in Minnesota, died in Pennsylvania, and was buried in central New York. How came the Reverend Covert to be included in an anthology of Michigan writing? He did live and serve in the Great Lakes State, but only for a five-year period from 1900 to 1905. And why this off-piste chapter on a limited and seemingly religious literary output; why did it commence with a pair of books on the upper state's charms?

William Chalmers Covert was born in the town of Franklin, not far from Indianapolis, during the American Civil War. His life extended into three more: the two World Wars and the Spanish-American conflict of the 1890s. The First World War caused him to write in encouragement of a renewed effort to carry the Christian message into the world after the horror and carnage of the European conflict. Before then, however, he had begun his authorship with a book about a place hardly anyone has written about—much less given treatment in a novel.

Covert was highly educated at several Presbyterian institutions of higher learning, obtaining first a bachelor's degree from Hanover College along the right bank of the Ohio River in 1885, followed by a master's in 1888. He attended the church's seminary in Chicago and obtained the requisite degree in 1888, followed by a Doctor of Divinity from Hanover in 1905, and then what appear to be three honorary degrees: Hanover, Doctor of Letters, 1933; Blackburn College in Carlinville, Illinois, Doctor of Laws, 1917; and Waynesburg College, Waynesburg, Pennsylvania, Doctor of Sacred Theology, 1924. He began his ecclesiastical career in St. Paul, Minnesota, serving until 1900, took up positions in Chicago from 1905 to 1924, then moved to the Philadelphia area to work for his church in various capacities until death. He also served as vice chairman of the Save the Children Federation, a charity organized in 1932 to aid children in the Appalachian region during the Great Depression.

For an interval of only five years, 1900–1905, he served in Michigan, occupying the pastoral role at the First Presbyterian Church in Saginaw, founded in 1838 as the first church in the Saginaw Valley.[1] Both books on Michigan were written during his Chicago pastorate. In the latter, he acknowledged "deep personal debt to intimate companions whose fellowship has enriched forest joys."[2] One name: lumber baron Clark Lombard Ring (1861–1933), who with his wife Lizzie Merrill (1862–1912) built a classic red brick Georgian Revival house in Saginaw, donated by their daughter to the City to become the home of Saginaw Art Museum. Another owned a yacht moored in a marina on Lake Michigan. He had friends in high places.

None of this background explains why Covert chose the far western reaches of the U.P. for his first book or the novel for his inaugural genre. He neared the half-century mark in age; perhaps the milestone gave him enough impetus. Perhaps semi-autobiographical, the book nevertheless employs for its narrator the grandson of a "patriarch" who had pronounced at birth the baby would become a minister, who upon growing up "spent years dodging" the vocation. After a quarter-century, the vicar had become employed at a parish "hidden deep in the pine forests lying along the south shore of Lake Superior" near the town of Ontonagon. Here, "in the shadows of the green woods . . . amidst the beauty and purity of the vast pine forest and under the clean skies of the North," the newly minted "sky pilot" confronted evil. The book, then, proves to be a straightforward morality play.

The rough setting is an important counterpoint to the good-versus-bad plot. The era is of the plaid flannel–shirted lumberjack, before the railroad came, just as farmers were beginning to stake their claims, when the "village herd" of cows roamed freely, and the only unspoiled aspect was nature's. It is inherently holy, full of beauty, and the "unbroken forest" is itself a wholly unmarred component, with "the amber waters of the Ontonagon" symbolizing how nature involves color but not corruption. Covert nailed it home: "Heaven stooped close to earth in that forest, and the solitude was full of fellowship." The first glimpse of the big water inspires this:

> We stopped on the brow of the hill and swept with our eyes the vast widths of Lake Superior, glowing in the reddened tints of the sun just at setting. The disk of fire lay on the water and lighted the whole expanse with a glory that made my heart think of the molten sea in Revelation. Over the shoulder of the high point that ran far out into the lake above Silver Creek, twenty miles away, there was uplifted the banner of a blood-red cloud, which went streaming far up into the sky, while upon the bits of clouds flying below there fell a wealth of beauty that drew upon every color of the prism.

Later, our narrator reports how the lake-fed air was "fresh and sweet," frequently "pine-laden," how "the stars had a color and brilliancy they never wear except in the North, and specially when they shine down through the dark corridors of the woods," and that "the sky seemed a million miles high." Trout swim their way into the story. There is a lighthouse, of course, but it is up the shoreline at Ten Mile Point. Winter comes early, and it is brutal. The prose may not achieve immortality, and neither would a mention of warfare among the Indigenous people to the exclusion of their typical pursuits. The history of the town, and of nearby Greenland and Rockland, is rendered inaccurately, though the manufacturing facility run by the Diamond Match Company did exist.

Instead of civilization, the vicar finds a kind of wild west. The Glory in the title is a woman, last name Garvin, not something ephemeral. She had absconded from her home in Detroit only to find the north woods inhospitable to the innocent. The melodrama proceeds to a conclusion that the reader can expect, with love triumphant—except that it includes the conversion of a saloon into a public hall where "books and papers, lots of 'em," replace occupations of ill repute. The Superior surf murmurs "sweet and low" as the story closes, with the wind "whispering through the needles of the white pines."[3]

This conventional tale of falling away and redemption in the backwoods of the nineteenth century is novel only in its selection of Ontonagon for the host community. The name is said to derive from the Ojibwe term for a bowl, characterized by the mouth of the river of that name, and a town did begin to assemble in 1843, but it is much older and found on a map of the Jesuit order sketched in 1672.[4] Its fame largely derived from a massive boulder of native copper that was appropriated by the federal government in 1843; more recently the community attracted attention from an ill-fated attempt at a state-sponsored vessel construction that went bust.

Not nearly as famous as the Keweenaw Peninsula, not at all accessible to the communities along US-2, the village has seen a few "up" periods and many "down" ones. The public school district is the oldest in the U.P., dating from just before the Civil War. It proudly opened a commodious three-story high school in 1912, so designated by its headstone above the entrance, joined in 1938 by a two-story addition for elementary students. Interior walls were lined with ceramic tiles displaying "whimsical figures" and "a linoleum floor inlaid with storybook characters" enlivened the kindergarten room.[5] The building, added to the National Register of Historic Places on May 25, 2011, sits today unused at 301 Greenland Road. All classes meet elsewhere.

If Covert made his way to the town, he apparently never traveled much to its west. Here lies the Porcupine Mountains, one of Michigan's grandest natural sites, home to the well-named Lake of the Clouds. He mentioned the Ontonagon River but without distinction, failing to record the several picturesque waterfalls that mark its transit to Lake Superior. In March 1992 it received designation as a National Wild and Scenic River. The area is a flourishing outdoor recreation locale, and the North Country Trail—far longer (4,800 miles, equivalent to walking from Detroit to Rome, Italy) than the Appalachian (2,200 miles), Pacific Crest (2,653 miles), or Continental Divide (3,000 miles) counterparts—is a major resource. In the spring, the winter melt overflows the containment lake and rushes through a sluice on the Victoria Dam, producing a prodigious cascade. Nearby, Old Victoria is a preserved mining settlement that has been added to the Keweenaw National Historic Park. Where the wild river meets the often wild lake, a historic lighthouse stands—the other structure in the town that merits a mention in the anthology of great Michigan buildings.[6]

Covert's companion work was essentially a collection of rather brief essays or meditations. It contained little dialogue, the main feature being the author's monologue into the ear of the reader. Fly fishing is involved, and a water course referenced in the title is the Au Sable: "the finest trout stream in the Middle West." The dunes characterizing much of the eastern shore of Lake Michigan are extolled. Other places are covered beyond the Great Lakes State, including along the north shore of Superior. Nearly all content applies to the northern Michigan experience.

One book was dedicated to his wife, the other to his children. The pastor cared much about family; perhaps he could have been more sensitive to those who had lived and enjoyed the land and the waters long before Europeans came. Still, "God's free out-of-doors" appealed to the middle-aged cleric enough to inspire him to write and publish two efforts. The divine outside the church doors appealed to Covert, mandating that he put before the world his interpretations. Open your eyes and ears and heart, he urged. Annually, from out of the desolations of winter, the earth becomes clothed with life and loveliness, he wrote. Should not our own lives bring glory?[7]

Selected Works

Glory of the Pines: A Tale of the Ontonagon (1914)
Wild Woods and Waterways (1915)

Edward Everett Hale

Superior Country

April 3, 1822–June 10, 1909

Authored a classic short story with Michigan connections and a middling Michigan novel

"When people ask, 'Who was Edward Everett Hale?' the usual literary answer is, 'The author of The Man Without a Country.'" So begins the introduction to the 1960 version of the classic work, penned by Van Wyck Brooks, an award-winning American biographer and literary critic who is himself now unknown.[1]

Readers might ask, "Why is Hale, a New Englander his whole life, included in this series?" The answer is complicated but possesses interesting Michigan connections.

First published in the December 1863 edition of *The Atlantic*,[2] then in book form in 1865, then in numerous editions, *The Man Without a Country* has become an American classic. It was authored in the dark summer of 1863 when the outcome of the War of the American Rebellion remained uncertain. Two years had elapsed in the bloodiest and costliest conflict in the nation's history, involving a titanic struggle between two halves of the country over its very soul. Within a year of publication, over a half-million copies were in print. The author explained in the 1905 school edition—for the story had become an instructional resource—its basic appeal. He had conceived of it to show Americans "what a terrible thing it would be if we had not a country," and the forlorn outcome resonated with those who loved the Union. Although another similar crisis was unlikely, Hale believed, the moral of his story could promote good citizenship and national loyalty by teaching students that "all the time they are receiving blessings from that country, and all the time they have duties to that country."[3]

Hale's rosy view of America's future is best exemplified by his statement of faith, comparing the world of 1865 to forty years later:

> Men are nearer unity—they are nearer to being one—than they were then.
>
> Thus, at that moment each tribe in unknown America was at war with each other tribe. At this moment there is not one hostile weapon used by one American against another, from Cape Bathurst at the north to the southern point of Patagonia.[4]

The author's death four years later mercifully preceded the ensanguined wars of that brutal century, along with much other inhumanity.

Hale was of the New England elite, a nephew of orator Edward Everett, who delivered a long-winded speech before Lincoln's famed Gettysburg Address, and grandnephew of Nathan Hale, the Revolutionary War hero executed as a spy by the British. The latter gained immortality for his dying words, "I regret I have but one life to give for my country." Born in Boston, educated at Harvard (entering at age thirteen), Edward became a long-time pastor of a congregational church in the city. Retiring from that ministry,[5] he became chaplain of the U.S. Senate. Hale was a social reformer, philanthropist, and member of the U.S. Sanitary Commission, a civilian aid society operating during the Civil War. His wife Emily Baldwin Perkins was related to equal rights activists Harriet Beecher Stowe, Henry Ward Beecher, and Lyman Beecher.

Such provenance suggests privilege, which could bring naivety to life's seamiest sides. A pastoral role can also make one privy to the worst of human thought and behavior. Hale's story had its foundation in a real-life national crisis, a horribly brutal civil war brought on by the crime of human bondage. The barbarities of slavery in the United States had been portrayed in Stowe's *Uncle Tom's Cabin: or, Life Among the Lowly*, a best-selling novel first published in Boston in 1851. The book was also published out of Cleveland, Ohio, and that state became the setting in May 1863 of proceedings charging former congressman Clement C. Vallandigham for undermining the Union war effort. The Ohioan's speeches attacked emancipation, a Union policy goal, for prosecuting "a war for the freedom of the blacks and the enslavement of the whites." His defense admitted opposition to "a war for the abolition of slavery" in the name of maintaining the U.S. Constitution as it was.[6]

Convicted, and denied freedom via habeas corpus, Vallandigham was exiled behind Confederate lines.

This case set the example for Hale's piece, first published in the December 1863 issue of *The Atlantic*. By then, Vallandigham was operating out of Windsor, across the Detroit River, as the Democratic Party candidate in the fall election for governor of Ohio. A delegation of Detroiters traveled across to show their support for his campaign.[7] Major Union victories at Gettysburg, Vicksburg, and Chattanooga altered the political dynamics by the end of the year, and a little over fifteen months remained before the Confederacy's collapse. Even then, whether the American nation would become united again remained an open question.

Of all possible settings, Hale began his fictional account of treasonous sentiment in a Michigan locale. Written in first person, the narrator commences his reminiscence on Mackinac Island: "I was stranded at the old Mission House in Mackinaw, waiting for a Lake-Superior steamer which did not choose to come." The narrator was a U.S. Navy veteran and thereby knew the identity of Philip Nolan, "the man without a country." But why locate the opening of the story on the Great Lakes? And at this structure? And use the "aw" format rather than "ac"?

There is, indeed, a "Mission House" where Lakes Michigan and Huron connect. One of the earliest structures on Mackinac Island, fashioned in 1825 of wood and covered with clapboard siding, its purpose was to house families under the auspices of the Mission Church led by Presbyterian minister William Montague Ferry. The 1830 church building, the oldest standing in Michigan, remains where Lake Shore Drive (M-185) meets Mission Street and remains a wedding venue. The "house" also stands, just to the east near Franks Street and the Mission Point Resort lobby entrance. Part of the Mackinac Island State Park, it is not open to the public. In 1845, it was converted into a hotel and continued in that function well into the twentieth century.

So, Hale had his history right even if spelling it inaccurately. He did base the story on research: "I had to make as careful study as I could of the history of the acquisition of Louisiana by the United States." He made Nolan a protégé of Aaron Burr, third vice president of the United States, and connected with a plan to found a separate country out of U.S. territory acquired by the 1803 Louisiana Purchase orchestrated by President Thomas Jefferson. Brought up on charges of aiding and abetting Burr, the impetuous Nolan erupted with

"D—n the United States! I wish I may never hear of the United States again!" Jefferson confirmed Nolan's sentence of exile aboard U.S. naval vessels, never to be allowed to set foot on its soil or hear about its affairs again.[8]

The third president had many connections with Michigan. Jefferson proposed the name that became Michigan. He laid out the township square method of organizing land once it would be procured or seized from the Indigenous people who lived on it. He was the brains behind the Northwest Ordinances, which forever barred slavery from the five-state territory around the Great Lakes—this from a slaveholder, but one who had penned the immortal precept that "all men are created equal" and endowed with inalienable rights. French Louisiana permitted its own form of chattel slavery. The U.S. Constitution did not prohibit slavery but referred to it by a euphemism—"persons held to service"—and authorized banning the slave trade as of 1808, which Congress did effective the first day permitted.[9]

Hale involved Nolan in a scene where his ship encountered a slave trader and its prisoners were released from their shackles. He knew Portuguese, so was asked to translate a vital message: "Tell them they are free." Returning to his self-imposed cell, Nolan urged the narrator never to abandon his country and, "no matter what happens to you, no matter who flatters you or who abuses you, never look at another flag, never let a night pass but you pray God to bless that flag."[10]

Before Nolan died aboard ship on May 11, 1863, before the battlefield triumphs that helped secure the future of the United States, he sought to understand how that flag bore representation of thirty-four states:

> "Tell me their names," he said, and he pointed to the stars on the flag. "The last I know is Ohio. My father lived in Kentucky. But I have guessed Michigan and Indiana and Mississippi—that was where Fort Adams is, they make twenty. But where are your other fourteen? You have not cut up any of the old ones, I hope?"[11]

Nolan also asked who was in command of his old western army, and the correspondent replied, "a very gallant officer named Grant." Ulysses S. Grant had been stationed in Detroit before the Civil War, and the house where he and his wife Julia lived still stands not far from where it once did.

Hale also used Michigan in another work. In *How They Lived in Hampton*, he had a character speak about the benefits of home-grown food, as opposed to that purchased at a lower price from a more distant location. "Suppose that every egg in the omelet you ate to-night had been bought in Michigan," the person posited, and the honey "had been brought from Detroit."[12] A state known once for its agricultural output, instead of manufacturing, provided the appropriate setting.

Another incredibly odd connection exists. Hero Nathan Hale graduated from Yale College in 1772 with classmate William Hull. The American Revolution reunited them in service to a new nation dedicated to the proposition of human equality. Hale was caught in the act of spying and sentenced to death at age twenty-one. A British engineer who witnessed Hale's execution carried a message under a flag of truce and told Hull about his colleague's last words. His remains were never found; there is no accurate likeness of him. It was Hull whose memoirs publicized the story and helped send his classmate into immortality.[13] Hull became the first territorial governor of Michigan, serving from 1805 to 1813. He is known today for the ignominious surrender of Detroit to the British during the War of 1812, for which he was court-martialed. He died at age seventy-two, still attempting to recover from the disgrace.

Contrary to assertions that Hale never set foot in Michigan, he visited on at least one occasion. In June 1898, he presented a lecture on the naval battles of the American Revolution at the Unitarian Church on Woodward. The *Detroit Free Press* of June 24 cited his 1863 short piece as "the story that gained him world wide fame" in its publicity about the talk.[14]

And what of the other effort? Described as "one of the poorer of his fifty volumes," *Ups and Downs: An Every-Day Novel* included mentions of Ann Arbor, Detroit, Dexter, and Marshall, along with a fictitious rural town in the southern tier of counties named Duquesne.[15]

The Mission House has a complicated storyline. Founded in 1823 by the American Board of Commissioners for Foreign Missions, it provided residential learning to students of Indigenous heritage in both Christianity and western culture. In doing so, it pursued assimilation rather than respect for native traditions—even in the case of "Metis," children of Indian and Euro-American parents. Yet this organization also opposed Indian removal, promoted women's status in society, and castigated slavery. The structure transitioned to a hotel, then in the mid-twentieth century became home to an American branch of the Moral Re-Armament movement, which sought to avert another world war. The structure has been home both to idealism and insensitivity.

Brooks's 1960 introduction maintained that the classic tragedy "remains the monument by which [Hale] is remembered, 'a sensation story,' he called it, 'with a national moral' . . . and nearly a hundred years later it is a classic that almost everybody knows and that every child has read." For an American child of the Baby Boomer generation, the story's accessibility came at the measly price of fifteen cents in a *Classics Illustrated* comic book version. On its cover, a young man in a bright red coat holds an officer's sword as he directs a gun crew in action against an enemy sailing vessel, an eye-catching lure if there ever was one. The volume was Number 63 in the series "featuring stories by the world's greatest authors." Hale's classic in comics form had its first publication in 1949 and a revised edition in 1962, and like all others remained in print and at bookshops and newspaper retailers for years after. Some ten million were sold annually between 1941 and 1962. For the children of a Michigan university professor who made Sunday excursions to obtain the hefty *New York Times*—and were blessed to make occasional purchases—the *CI* version became loved and well worn.[16]

Much has happened to undermine the story's fame and Brooks's assertion in the succeeding six decades. During recent presidential elections, celebrities have vowed to alienate themselves by moving to another country in the event of a victory by the candidate they disfavor. Yet a modern Michigan author based a novella on Hale's "obscure" story, finding it inspirational.[17] Patriotism, human rights, and spirituality are universal themes that defy time and generational changes. The story of "a heart-wounded man" who never married, never had children, never reunited with family, and had his demise published obscurely in a newspaper read on the grounds of a Mackinac Island hotel has power.

The question remains: Why Mackinac? Perhaps the geographical fact that it was the farthest point north within the United States was plausible for the story. Perhaps it was a bit exotic, so far away from New England, up where the winter ice landlocks the island and ships need to be careful of storms and shores. Perhaps it was the melodic sounding name, mack-in-aw, the last syllable contrary in pronunciation to the spelling.

Perhaps to Hale, like nearly everyone who ever thinks of the Great Lakes, it was an iconic place on pure waters near a boundary to another country, the perfect setting to launch an iconic story of rooted life.

Selected Works

Ups and Downs: An Every-Day Novel (1873)
The Man Without a Country and Other Tales (1882)

James Thomas Harrison

Word Weaver

December 11, 1937–March 26, 2016

Born in Grayling, Haslett High School and Michigan State University graduate, lived in Reed City, Kingsley, and near Lake Leelanau and at Grand Marais

Perhaps no writer associated with Michigan better fits the concept that underlies these *Ink Trails* volumes than did Jim Harrison. In 1980, while your three co-authors were experiencing our own new beginnings in the Great Lakes State, Harrison began to inhabit a cabin near Grand Marais specifically as a writing retreat far from Hollywood, where several of his works would be converted into major films, with all the fame and inquisitive attention attendant to such good fortune. He'd already been to other parts of America and to Africa and could have decided to locate his author's den anywhere. Rural Northern Michigan above the Bridge was chosen. It was the best site for inspiration over the next two dozen years for the man who claimed to be distinctly a rural Northern Midwesterner.

Tragedy befell Harrison in his childhood: his sister and father, a Michigan State University assistant professor, were killed in a traffic accident near Mount Pleasant in 1962. In his childhood, the boy lost the sight in his left eye when a girl stuck a bottle in his face during a quarrel. On the other hand, at MSU he had met Linda May King. They married on October 10, 1959. Her death in 2015 ended their love affair of over a half-century.

The journals of his wife's great-grandfather, a mining engineer named William Ludlow, had served as inspiration for *Legends of the Fall*, one of Harrison's most popular works. The major motion picture made from it in 1994, starring Brad Pitt and Anthony Hopkins, became the door into Harrison's works for many who had never heard of him. The film's payday liberated the author to create the poetry and fiction of his choosing.

Like many a fiction author, his work got mistaken for autobiography. Much of it was grim, overtly masculine, and coarse. But "Jim was down to earth—literally and figuratively," said a literary expert and friend. "I think that often wasn't seen because he was caught up in being the macho hunter, fisherman. But that wasn't Jim. He was kind, gentle—and would do anything for anyone."[1] Harrison's literary assistant echoed that perspective: "Family was Jim's life."[2] Another friend eulogized him: "Jim Harrison was one of the most generous men I ever knew. He lent countless thousands to dozens of less fortunate friends who needed help; he seldom if ever got paid back and that didn't stop him."[3]

Harrison hired his assistant by virtue of having met her when she was a server during his regular visits to the Blue Bird, a restaurant in Leland. She bought one of his books at Horizon Books in Traverse City in order to understand the frequent patron. Her interest in his writing differentiated the college student from other seasonal workers. The Harrisons hired her to watch their place while they traveled.

Joyce Harrington Bahle became so trusted that she was tasked with accompanying Linda Harrison on an excursion to find a haven in the Upper Peninsula for Jim's writing. When they purchased the property on the Sucker River, he had nothing to do with it other than point them beyond the Mackinac Bridge. Bahle began to type his handwritten drafts and incorporate his changes into new manuscripts. For four decades she worked with him to bring his work into print, becoming friend and confidant.[4]

In 1968, not long into his career, Harrison and fellow Michigan poet and friend Dan Gerber launched a Michigan literary journal entitled *Sumac*. Novelist Thomas McGuane came aboard the next year. Though short-lived, the periodical rapidly rose to notice as a magazine chock-full of good and intriguing writing grounded in the heartland of America: the Midwest. Its base was Fremont, Gerber's hometown, with a satellite at Lake Leelanau. An anthology remains in print.[5] Harrison's contributions to heartland fiction and poetry won him the Mark Twain Award from the Society for the Study of Midwestern Literature.[6]

McGuane was the unlikely connection between Harrison and musician Jimmy Buffett. As Buffett's landlord in his Key West place, McGuane introduced them and fostered a connection between two artists who enjoyed big game fishing. They collaborated on a 1973 fly-fishing documentary, *Tarpon*, with Buffett writing the soundtrack while Harrison, McGuane, and Richard Brautigan wrote the script.[7]

When a summer concert ended in Detroit, Buffett "would escape" to Harrison's Lake Leelanau place. They shared an "unforgettable drive across country, just the two of us in his Ford Cortina, taking turns at the wheel, as we crossed the heartland from Montana back to Michigan, sharing our vision of America to each other and the cows we passed along the way." Buffett's Harrison eulogy ended with "*adiòs mi hermano*"—farewell, my brother.[8]

In a travel section piece published in the *New York Times* on December 1, 2013, Harrison wrote sentimentally about the Upper Peninsula. It was far from his first paean in the East Coast opinion leader. It contained a lament, since he no longer owned the "fairly remote cabin off a two-track road where when you try to sleep at night you hear a river flowing, probably the best sound on earth." The use of "fairly remote" is intriguing; its address off East Highway 58 (Alger County Road) placed it three miles from the center of Grand Marais. The town exhibits several aspects of civilization, including a museum and historic structure on the National Register of Historic Places,[9] a retro diner, and a lighthouse keeper's cottage, situated on a bay that forms a harbor of refuge with marina and docks. Less than a thousand square feet, the two-bedroom cottage is within a stone's throw of the Sucker River and a short walk to the Superior shoreline. In other words, it was as remote as a writer needed it to be.

In novels like the late-in-life *True North* and *Returning to Earth*, Harrison evoked the complicated heritage of Michigan. The protagonist descends from an Eastern family that built its wealth from the extraction of the upper state's minerals and timber, leaving waste and poverty for the locals. He seeks to reconcile with his family's past and escape its corruption.

Although best known to the general reading public as a fiction writer, Harrison was a well-regarded poet as well. One evocatively named poem, "Northern Michigan," sought to paint a picture of abandonment:

> On this back road the land
> has the juice taken out of it:
>
> stump fences surround nothing
> worth their tearing down
>
> by a deserted filling station
> a Veedol sign, the rusted hulk

of a Frazer, "live bait"
on battered tin.

A barn
with half a tobacco ad
owns the greenness of a manure
pile

a half-moon on a privy door
a rope swinging from an elm. A

collapsed henhouse, a pump
with the handle up

the orchard with wild tangled branches.

Perhaps the only verse in poetry touching on a creek off the Manistee River talks of the land-locked region south of Grand Traverse Bay and comes from "Lisle's River":

Dust followed our car like a dry brown cloud.
At the river we swam, then in the canoe passed
downstream toward Manton; the current carried us
through cedar swamps, hot fields of marsh grass
where deer watched us and the killdeer shrieked.

If anyone has heard of Luther, Michigan, they can place it in a non-verse reminiscence entitled "Early Fishing" about a boy's trip when only age ten with his father: "we were off in the car, a '47 Chevy two-tone, blue and beige, for the Pine River about an hour's distance up through Luther, the two-track off the county road so he gunned it."

It is difficult not to feel sympathy in "Drinking Song" for the narrator after "she left me," when all of his poems "were born dead":

I left when it was still dark and walked on the path to the
river, the Yellow Dog, where I spent the day fishing and drinking. . . .

In the river was a trout, and I was on the bank, my heart in my
chest, clouds above, she was in NY forever and I, fishing and drinking.

The shack along the Sucker River inspired the poem "Grand Marais," published in 2011:

The wind came up so strongly at midnight
the cabin creaked in its joints and between
the logs, the tin roof hummed and shuddered
and in the woods you could hear the dead
trees called widow-makers falling
with staccato crashes, and by 3 a.m.
the thunderous roar of Lake Superior miles away.

Another verse, from "Dead Man's Float," clearly originated from near the region of Grand Sable Dunes:

Once I heard wolves in full moonlight.
A huge storm visited the cabin, also green northern lights.
The sky split open in the west.

That stanza named the title piece to one of his last books. Its first poem was entitled "Where is Jim Harrison?" and contained a curious self-reflection:

He believes in the Resurrection mostly
because he was never taught how not to.

A religious Jim Harrison? When a teenager, he had found religion at a revival meeting. It led him to preach at youth gatherings. A major newspaper, reporting on his death, referred to him as "charismatic." In Christian spheres, the term denotes the influence of the Spirit of God. A true and generous friend, a devoted and loving husband and father, a hard-working professional: all embody the virtues of the Midwest he cherished. Lines invoke the prophet Isaiah, "Christ's wounds,"[10] Jesus by name; one poem was entitled "Homily."

While still in the prime of working, Harrison donated his papers to Grand Valley State University in Allendale, where they remain largely open to researchers. He knew time was running short, and he chose a Michigan institution as a repository for the artifacts of his craft. Poetry published in 2016 revealed a deep sense of mortality: one poem hearkened back sixty-eight years:

> Yesterday I was seven in the woods,
> a bandage covering my blind eye,
> in a bedroll Mother made me
> so I could sleep out in the woods
> far from people.[11]

And in "Death Again," Harrison came face-to-face with the impending close, advising not to get romantic or dismal about it but to take it in stride, likening it to a day in Northern Michigan:

> it's mostly a placid
> lake at dawn, mist rising, a solitary loon
> call, and staring into the still, opaque water.
> We'll know as children again all that we are
> destined to know, that the water is cold
> and deep, and the sun penetrates only so far.[12]

His heart gave out in its seventy-eighth year while he was at his desk, pen in hand, working. Accolades poured in. Some got him right. The writer who had been misleadingly compared to Hemingway for his muscular themes had outlived his fellow Michigander in several ways. Ever since the age of fourteen, he had "been a slave to language."[13] Only mortality in its ultimate form could free him. As for Michigan and Jim Harrison, they never let each other go.

Aldo Leopold

Habitat for Humility

January 11, 1887–April 21, 1948
Summer visitor in his childhood to family's cottage on Marquette Island in Les Cheneaux Islands; conveyed importance of conservation in writings about game management and land protection in the Upper Peninsula

If the child is father to the man, then conservationist and writer Aldo Leopold was raised by a boy playing among the rocks, trees, and craggy shores of Marquette Island, part of the thirty-six-island Les Cheneaux chain ornamenting fourteen miles of Lake Huron on the southeast coast of Michigan's Upper Peninsula.[1] The island was the closest thing to wilderness Leopold would know until his adult years as a professional wildlife biologist. The summer retreat of his family for years, the island provided a sharp contrast to the settled land of northeast Iowa where the Leopolds made their permanent home.

In the 1890s, the family took August trips to the island. "The train ride from Chicago to Mackinaw City took all night," writes Leopold's biographer, Curt Meine.[2]

> When the family awoke and looked out the windows, they found themselves in the recently cutover northwoods. Young scrub forests of jack pine, aspen, and paper birch grew up in the lands where the slash fires had burned. On the farmsteads that dotted the gaunt landscape, farmers fenced their fields not with barbed wire, but with the massive, upturned stumps of the old white pines.[3]

The island had not escaped development. There were tennis courts, a golf course, and a clubhouse, but there was also good fishing for smallmouth bass, pike, and brook trout. There was a view of the Upper Peninsula mainland and the north country beyond. Leopold sometimes rode with his father to the mainland to hunt ruffed grouse and to fish for trout. He dreamed of finding a river beyond the northern horizon and paddling a canoe to the faraway, mysterious sub-Arctic north.

His interest in the outdoors persisted into adulthood. Graduating from Yale Forestry School in 1909, he began his natural resources career working for the U.S. Forest Service in Arizona and New Mexico before moving to the Madison, Wisconsin, Forest Service lab. He eventually became the first appointed professor of game management at the University of Wisconsin and research director of the university's arboretum.[4] In that position he authored *Game Management*, a text that guided wildlife professionals for decades. The book opens thus:

> We of the industrial age boast of our control over nature. Plant or animal, star or atom, wind or river—there is no force in earth or sky which we will not shortly harness to build "the good life" for ourselves.
>
> But what is the good life? Is all this glut of power to be used for only bread-and-butter ends? Man cannot live by bread, or Fords, alone. Are we too poor in purse or spirit to apply some of it to keep the land pleasant to see, and good to live in?[5]

His time in the Southwest led to an epiphany. Originally assigned to eradicate bears, wolves, and mountain lions to control livestock losses on area ranches, Leopold came to see something besides a threat to domesticated animals, a glimpse of something ancient and wild. After fatally shooting a wolf, Leopold approached the animal to see "a fierce green fire dying in her eyes. . . . I realized then, and have known ever since, that there was something new to me in those eyes—something known only to her and to the mountain."[6] Before long, he was proposing the first designated wilderness preserve on national forest lands.

In Wisconsin, he purchased eighty acres, some of it fronting the Wisconsin River. The land had been cut over during the state's logging boom, devastated by fire and overtaxed by a dairy herd, a scarred land that he hoped to heal. It was in this sand district that his careful observation led to a series of essays collected in the posthumously published *Sand County Almanac*. The book has become a bible of sorts for conservationists and environmentalists.

His thinking moved humankind from master of the environment to a place in the web of life. "In short," he wrote in an often-quoted passage of *A Sand County Almanac*, "a land ethic changes the role of Homo sapiens from conqueror of the land-community to plain member and citizen of it. It implies respect for his fellow-members, and also respect for the community as such."[7] Other quotes from *A Sand County Almanac* reverberate through the decades:

> One of the penalties of an ecological education is that one lives alone in a world of wounds. Much of the damage inflicted on land is quite invisible to laymen.
>
> There are two spiritual dangers in not owning a farm. One is the danger of supposing that breakfast comes from the grocery, and the other that heat comes from the furnace.
>
> To those devoid of imagination a blank place on the map is a useless waste; to others, the most valuable part.

Leopold's approach to writing was thoughtful and painstaking. The website of the foundation established in his name reports:

> [Leopold] almost always wrote with pencil on yellow lined paper. After finishing an article or essay he would put it in his "cooling drawer" for several days or weeks, then ask various friends or students for a critical reading, rework it, and have it typed on yellow paper for further criticism and revision. A paper might go through several typed yellow drafts before it was finally considered finished and the order given, "Go to white." Even then it might be further revised.[8]

In addition to summers in his youth on Marquette Island, Leopold had other ties to Michigan. His 1938 plan for the land of the private Huron Mountain Club, west of Marquette, was an innovative attempt to undertake landscape-level thinking.[9] Listing wilderness recreation first among the land's values, he suggested protection of undeveloped areas of the preserve, serving as a baseline for scientific study. "All earth-sciences must, in the long run, learn how to use land by referring to unused land as a base-datum or starting point. . . . It is clear, then, that the Club has not only a unique property but a large opportunity for public service in science and conservation."[10]

In 1944 and 1945, Leopold cheered on efforts by Michigan officials to create the Porcupine Mountains State Park in the western Upper Peninsula, protecting hardwood forests that had largely escaped the industrial ax. When a timber company proposed to log much of the proposed park, Leopold urged preservation, writing in the periodical *Outdoor America* that the land was "a symbol. It portrays a chapter in national history which we should not be allowed to forget. When we abolish the last sample of the Great Uncut, we are, in a sense, burning books. . . . To preserve a remnant of decent forest for public education is surely a proper function of government, regardless of one's view on the moot question of large-scale timber production."[11] The state used the long-standing tool of eminent domain to include private parcels in the park.

Michigan celebrates the Leopold legacy, which is globally recognized, with an annual Aldo Leopold festival in Hessel, an Aldo Leopold Park and Preserve on Marquette Island and a State historical marker on the island.[12] The marker puts Leopold's legacy in perspective: "As prolific author, researcher and educator whose works still influence the field, Aldo Leopold is widely considered to be a founder of the conservationist movement in America."

Selected Works

Report on a Game Survey of the North Central States (1931)
Game Management (1933)
A Sand County Almanac (1949)
Round River: From the Journals of Aldo Leopold (1953)
A Sand County Almanac and Other Writings on Ecology and Conservation (2013)

John Bartlow Martin

Mesmerized by the U.P.

August 4, 1915–January 3, 1987
Author and diplomat whose first book celebrated Michigan's
Upper Peninsula and who built a cabin near Herman

Before he was a diplomat, John Bartlow Martin was an advisor to a presidential candidate. Before that, he was a notable author. And on his way to becoming a notable author, he chose the Upper Peninsula as the subject of his premiere title.[1] This began a love affair with place that lasted the rest of his life.

Call It North Country, published in 1944 and still in print, captured the vivid beauty of the peninsula's lands and waters—but also the singular characters to whom those places were home. One elderly U.P. eccentric he described was given to lengthy orations to audiences of one: "I talk to myself for two good reasons," the man told Martin. "Number one, I like to hear a sensible man talk. Number two, I like to talk to a sensible man."[2]

"This book is about the Upper Peninsula of Michigan, a section of the wilderness country, but mostly it is about some of its people," Martin said near the opening of the book. "Some of the people who pioneered it with bateaux and snowshoes and dog teams and some of the people who live in it now."[3]

Call It North Country told the story of U.P. development, from timber harvest to mining to shipping and finally to tourism, through a focus on individuals in each industry. It was well reviewed by the Upper Peninsula's media. The *Escanaba Daily Press* said it was "an admirable piece of Americana, rich in dramatic incident, racy in its interpretation of the resourceful people who live on this tough land, yet fundamentally sober and sympathetic in the study of their plight."[4] The book remains in print in a 1986 edition by Wayne State University Press.

Martin's path to the U.P. began in Hamilton, Ohio, where he was born. Martin moved with his family to Indianapolis, graduating from high school at sixteen. He acquired a journalism degree from DePauw University and set out as a reporter, eventually contributing award-winning articles on crime, poverty, and other subjects to periodicals like *Harper's* and *Atlantic Monthly* before writing his U.P. book. The book germinated in his mind after he and his wife spent their honeymoon near Michigamme in 1940.

Martin's career as an author of books ranged in subjects from true crime and prison reform to the monumental two-volume biography of his friend Adlai Stevenson, governor of Illinois and two-time unsuccessful candidate for the presidency. Martin also participated in and sometimes advised Democratic presidential candidates into the 1980s. President John F. Kennedy appointed him ambassador to the Dominican Republic, a post he occupied between 1962 and 1964.[5]

Although Martin went far afield in his diplomatic and political journeys, the Upper Peninsula remained close to his heart. In 1964 Martin and his wife, Fran, purchased a 180-acre site on 87-acre Smith Lake outside of Herman, Michigan. The area was and is remote, tucked into a lightly populated reach between Michigamme and L'Anse.

They had a cabin (or camp, as such structures were called in the Upper Peninsula) built atop a granite cliff sixty feet above the lake. It had indoor plumbing, abundant square footage and a mammoth fireplace built out of fifty tons of native rock. Martin left the trees on his land untouched, even if they blocked the view of the lake from the cabin. "If you want to see the lake," Martin said, "go get in the boat and see it." At the cabin, Martin wrote, tried his hand at carpentry, and enjoyed the sauna.[6]

Martin quickly became possessive of his beloved Upper Peninsula, writing just three years after *Call It North Country*:

> I wrote [in the book] that the region was at least fifty years behind the times, a bypassed pioneer island in the stream of civilization, the last Midwest wilderness, where the leading industries are still iron mining and logging, not tourists; where you burn kerosene, not electricity; where only one highway goes through the woods; where you sleep in "camps," not "cottages" (a holdover term from the great white pine days of the logging camps). Well, if you want to see it this way, you had better look fast. Even next year may be too late.[7]

He complained of a post-war rush to the northland, "with girls in shorts on the porches of resorts, with speed boats, night clubs, and slot machines everywhere. The tourists are coming."[8]

Fortunately for Martin and many others, the predicted ruin of the U.P. landscape and the homogenization of its characters has not happened. The author found refuge there until the end of his life.

Selected Works

Call It North Country: The Story of Upper Michigan (1944)
Butcher's Dozen and Other Murders (1950)
Why Did They Kill? (1953)
Break Down the Walls: American Prisons: Present, Past, and Future (1954)
Overtaken by Events: The Dominican Crisis from the Fall Of Trujillo to the Civil War (1966)
Adlai Stevenson of Illinois (1976)
Adlai Stevenson and the World: The Life of Adlai E. Stevenson (1977)
It Seems Like Only Yesterday: Memoirs of Writing, Presidential Politics and the Diplomatic Life (1986)

John Moody

A Riddle Wrapped in a Mystery Inside an Enigma

May 2, 1868–February 16, 1958
Only work of fiction set in the Upper Peninsula's
rugged, wild, pristine western highlands

A recently published catalog about books poses challenging questions: What is the cultural value of a particular bound volume of pages and words; why should it be "looked after" on behalf of future generations; "is it a book whose loss to posterity" would matter; if it has lasting value, "where does that value reside?"[1]

The Library of Congress is engaged in a program to digitize little-known works, enabling wider readership and potentially saving them from becoming lost to posterity.[2] The LOC website gives little justification for such decisions, other than to confirm each book "can be made openly available"—that is, copyright protection has expired. One recent upload dates from the early twentieth century, a novel of two hundred pages or so, written by Thomas Enright. Research fails to disclose information about any such individual, suggesting a pen name was employed and eliminating the author's identity as the cause of the library's action. Perhaps the scarcity of the publication served as the essential reason. It is not available at any Michigan library, nor through the Michigan eLibrary (MeL), and a search of several collegiate databases does not turn up copies. So, too, is a search unavailing through the next two likeliest, given the settings and the author: neither the Chicago nor the New York public libraries list a copy in their collections. Neither does the Harvard, Bodleian Libraries of the University of Oxford, nor the HathiTrust digital library—or other online sources.

Perhaps its literary qualities establish merit for inclusion. It appears to have garnered only three reviews, and it was omitted from one national survey.[3] The first appeared in the Sioux Falls, South Dakota, *Argus-Leader* on July 31, 1909, when that city numbered fewer than fifteen thousand inhabitants: "true lovers of nature" will enjoy this book. More promising was notice in the *San Francisco Chronicle* of August 1, 1909, judging it "a distinctly American story." The "hero," John Douglass, is jaded by financial dealings in railroads and "weary of all that the world offers him." On his doctor's advice, he takes a train to "the great forest belt on the border line between Wisconsin and Michigan." Here, Douglass finds paradise, healing, and love. The *Chronicle* could only identify the author as "a writer unknown to fame."

The third review appeared in a publication that occasionally included such a feature within its pages, no matter how it would seem a waste of space. In its November 1909 edition, Vol. 5, No. 1, *The Ticker and Investment Digest*—focused on and issuing from Wall Street—praised the author who "shows a literary touch," using "straight-forward and well chosen English." Most important, though, is the flow: "the story grips the reader from the first chapter" involving "the struggle for wealth, of a great wrong and its punishment, and a happy termination." Curious, though, the item was for sale by the *Ticker*'s publisher. Is there an additional clue in the book's sponsor, "The Gibson Publishing Company" of New York, with office addresses variously at 15 William Street and the Corn Exchange Bank Building in Manhattan, at 185 Jackson Boulevard in Chicago, and 5 Laurence Poutney Hill, London—all home to financial institutions? Other of the firm's volumes bore authorship by Thomas Gibson, with such alluring titles as *The Pitfalls of Speculation* (1906) and *Daily Average Prices (Thomas Gibson's Figures): Daily Volume of Transactions* (1910). *Simple Principles of Investment* (1919) came from a major publisher.[4] Was "Enright" the nom de plume of T. Gibson?

Yes, says a modern-day investment advisor whose firm has an online library website with over 2,500 titles.[5] We are told here that "Thomas Enright was the pen name used by Thomas Gibson. This was the only financial novel written by Gibson and very scarce." So who is he?

Before addressing that question, why go down this rabbit hole in a Michigan-centric book? Because two sources attribute the LOC's uploaded title to the Great Lakes State. Most recent: Grand Valley State University's online collection of "Decorated Publishers' Bindings" includes the front cover sourced to "Michigan Novels Collection. PS3509.N57 K54 1909."[6] Earlier: Clarence Andrews's "A Bibliography of the Literature and Lore, Together With Historical Materials, of the Upper Peninsula of Michigan" in *The Great*

Lakes Review referred to the work as "a novel set in the Western UP."[7] How far west? Has there ever been a novel centered on Michigan just east of longitude 90 west?

When young and largely ignorant of our U.P. heritage, trips to its far western end bemused us. The family station wagon drove through two towns with curious names: Bruce's Crossing and Watersmeet.[8] It was rugged country where a Travelodge or Howard Johnson was unlikely and as far-fetched as a private homeowner renting to total strangers. Cheese curds may have been in vogue, but not on our menu. A giant Hiawatha statue appeared in 1964. A trip in 1978 from Chicago for a visit to a grandparent there in Ironwood took her along to Lake of the Clouds in the Porcupine Mountains. We did not know about the Paulding Light as adolescents, only skirted the fried-clam shape of Lake Gogebic on M-28 as passengers, and were unaware that the upper state holds all but one of Michigan's three hundred waterfalls. If asked, we would have confessed a lack of knowledge about one of the most photographed of those natural features, Bond Falls. Spreading one hundred feet across the middle branch of the Ontonagon River, named for its last private landowner, it is accessed off US-45, the two-lane that connects those two curiously named towns. Did the "Bond" waterfall have a connection for Enright/Gibson, who was familiar with trading in bonds of another sort?[9]

According to research by a person connected with a major university, and for whom the author's identity has been an intensive pursuit, the answer can be affirmative. Both names were intended as cloaks, for none other than John Moody—according to the University of Notre Dame's Donna McClelland—of Moody's Investors Service fame is the real person behind the novel. Born in 1868, which various sites attribute as the birth date of the author (whatever his name), Moody's life is a story unto itself. Never graduating college, he began his professional career as a journalist before joining a major Wall Street firm and for a decade rising through its ranks. In 1900, he issued a *Manual of Corporate Securities* that sold thousands of copies, thanks to its provision of statistics about investment vehicles and the management of their issuers, and made him wealthy. He launched the Elizabeth Printing and Publishing Company, source of *The Evening Times* of New Jersey.[10] Moody's bond ratings have long been the key determinant for investment houses. The company once hailed its founder for holding "a strong entrepreneurial drive and a firm belief about the needs of the investment community—as well as considerable journalistic talent." With the market crash of 1907, he was forced to sell his manual business but returned in 1909 with a new publication that analyzed security values of railroads. It provided the first rating system of public market securities, regularly expanded its coverage, and by 1924 covered nearly all of the U.S. bond market.[11] It became the bible of bond ratings.

John Moody experienced a crisis just before attaining forty years of age—which is the age of the novel's John Douglass, who makes a million dollars and then loses half of it, betrayed by a more cunning and less ethical dealer.[12] Moody castigated himself for his mistakes, having not earlier found out that "two and two make four, and not six, or eight, or ten." His "house of cards collapsed," and all his commercial interests fell in ruin at his feet. He went out to Block Island, beyond the eastern tip of Long Island, and took stock one Sunday morning as sunlight made the sea "waters glisten and shine" with "his face in his hands." He disdained despair, though, and formed a plan to begin again.[13] From the ashes arose a more solid career; his little family and his devoted wife would be the prime beneficiaries. He owed an unpayable debt to his loving wife, but he would endeavor to make repayments on the pleasurable obligation.[14]

Is Moody the true author of *The King of Nobody's Island*? Would he have wasted time investing in this scarce volume, a novel that incorporates romance, fishing, canoeing, and other less capitalistic themes? In some respects, the work bears a striking similarity to *Superior Shores*, also set in Chicago and locations west of Marquette, with a protagonist whose fealty to the dollar brings conflict in the course of the story where the central character is Michigan's natural beauty.[15] Certainly, Moody's prodigious capacity for working long hours enabled extracurricular efforts like writing a novel. He admitted to being "a great reader of books" and having a "writing bent." The latter led him early on to "dream of a literary life," to sell a juvenile short story at seventeen and jump deeper into publishing, eventually to write his manual—inspired by his early successes.

But is Michigan the true setting? It does not appear that Moody ever visited any part of the Great Lakes State. He built a summer home for his family, but it was located in the Catskill foothills in New York State. Indeed, the Manitowish Waters Historical Society of Wisconsin has laid claim to *Nobody's Island* as being situated in the Badger State. The novel mentions Crooked Lake, and the society points to a body of water by that name connected to Wisconsin's Mamie Lake as part of the proof that Moody/Gibson/Enright located the story south of the border.

But another such body of water exists just northwest of the termination point for Douglass in the novel, then known as "State Line," changed to Land O'Lakes in 1948. He is the only passenger to step off onto the station platform, so remote is this destination. He joins up with a guide who has one parent of full native heritage who takes him as their first stop on a longer journey to Crooked Lake—"an easy trip, three short portages." The author can't have meant in Wisconsin, for the body of water with that name is miles in the wrong direction and without easy portaging. By contrast, the Crooked Lake in Watersmeet Township, Michigan, is less than five miles from the depot as the crow flies. Here they stay for a week in a cabin of a hospitable resident, and "Jack" makes plans to stay longer, finally "about decided to enter the Ontonagon River" when he embarks on something different. They strike out for "Lost Lake"—not far from "Harrison's Lake"—where, so the story goes, Douglass will find the love of his life, who will save his life and then agree to join theirs together forever.[16] Harrison's Lake? Again, the wrong direction and much farther away if in the Badger State.

Did Moody know about this territory from his railroad research? His autobiography acknowledges the late nineteenth-century battle between rail companies to obtain a Chicago landing right.[17] The official Wisconsin rail map for 1900 shows the Chicago and Northwestern Railway's station at State Line. But the line continues north—to Watersmeet, platted in 1884 by the Milwaukee, Lake Shore and Western Railway.[18] The town is on the middle branch of the Ontonagon River near the junction of U.S. Highway 2 and U.S. Highway 45. Watersmeet Township is home of the Lac Vieux Desert Indian Reservation, established by U.S. treaty in 1854. This strip of the Lake Superior Band of Chippewa Indians, a large and decentralized group of Anishinaabe bands, has occupied the territory since at least the seventeenth century.

Is Douglass guided into the interior of the U.P., not Wisconsin? At one point he indicates a plan to head toward the Ontonagon River—which he only would do if he was near it, thus within the boundary of Michigan. To be on a body of water somewhere across the line such as Wild Cat, a real lake mentioned in the book, would have necessitated portages over unlikely distances and numerous other lakes. The society acknowledges that fictional lakes, locations, and routes are a feature of the book. Yes, Manitowish is another real place mentioned, but it is derived from "Manitou," a common Anishinabek word that is used at several geographic points in Michigan.[19]

Another hint comes with the cover—which was significant enough to gain notice by Grand Valley. A solitary individual (apparently Native) paddles a canoe on a lake, with the background filled by three snow-covered mountain peaks. The Wisconsin lake country is almost invariably flat; the closest heights are the Porkies, which can provide a haven for snow any time after August—though in appearance they are markedly different from the shapes found on the cover.

Where is the subject destination? Perhaps nobody is meant to know. Is the title a play on the "no man is an island" line by Donne?[20] Perhaps. Is Moody the author? Perhaps nobody will ever know for certain. Did the author know the wilderness firsthand, or had he spun the tale out of imagination, maps, railroad timetables, and parallel experiences?

That is what Ms. McClelland believes, that Moody's mentor was George Foster Peabody, partner at the Trask company where his mentee began on Wall Street, and whose philanthropy funded the award for media excellence.[21] Peabody owned a home named "Abenia" on Lake George in upper New York, and the idea of a remote idyll attached to a story of romance may have seeded the plot outline in Moody's mind. Peabody married Trask's widow, for whom he had long pined. When *Nobody's Island* appeared,[22] its author clearly was taken with the idea of a woodland retreat on a freshwater shore where life can be most fully enjoyed.

Not many works of fiction are situated in the far western U.P. It is the most remote section of Michigan, farthest from the downstate population centers. New York City is closer than Ironwood to Detroit. It is home to the aptly named Sylvania Wilderness, an eighteen-thousand-acre (thirty-square-mile) part of the National Wilderness Preservation System managed by the U.S. Forest Service. Within its borders lie thirty-four lakes set against a backdrop of old-growth forests. It represents one of only a handful of such areas left in the Midwest.

Little is known of the region before the late 1800s, other than that the area was frequently used by clans of Ojibwa Native Americans, as evidenced by the few scattered artifacts that have been found there. In 1895, a Watersmeet lumberman, A. D. Johnston, purchased acreage on Clark Lake for harvesting but relented because of its natural beauty. With friends, he formed the Sylvania Club to build lodges for a resort where fishing, hunting, and hiking predominated. Johnston named his home "Trossachs," homage to the Trossachs Valley, Loch Lomond, and Loch Katrine in central west Scotland, the setting for Walter Scott's 1810 poem "The Lady of the Lake." The Forest Service acquired the area in 1967;[23] in 1987, it was designated as a federal wilderness when the Michigan Wilderness Act was passed by Congress and signed into law by President Reagan. The Friends of Sylvania have sought to preserve the non-motorized nature of the region, which "straddles the divide between the Lake Superior and the Mississippi River drainage systems, occupying some of the highest ground in the Midwest." Thus, "many of the lakes in the park are more than 1,700 feet (520 meters) above sea-level," and "these deep, clear lakes are primarily landlocked, fed by springs and local run-off." The water is "pristine and pure."[24] Not many lakes on the planet can be so described. Not many so remote have their own guidebook. "If your spirit needs renewing," it concludes, "come away to this special corner of the world."[25]

Perhaps Loch Katrine is one such pure waterway. It spurred Scott's imagination for his long poem, where protagonist James Fitz-James wanders to the shore of this lake and is rescued by a young motherless woman, Ellen Douglas, who rows to him in a skiff and takes him to an island lodge, where he is fed and given a place to sleep and recuperate. He dreams of Ellen, but it becomes nightmarish when her face becomes that of his enemy, James Douglas, and he realizes they are related. In *Nobody's Island*, John Douglass falls in love with the motherless Mary Harrison. She, and his nemesis, are also father and daughter.

As novelist Thomas Clayton Wolfe (1899–1938) wrote, "I think the roots of all creation in writing are fastened in autobiography and that it is in no way possible to escape or deny this fact."[26] How much of *The King of Nobody's Island* can be verified as autobiographical remains an unsettled matter. For those intrigued, the rare book is freely available online.[27] So are two memoirs, in which he recounted how the man who pioneered Wall Street statistical research came, after the premature death of his son, to find God.

Selected Works

The King of Nobody's Island (1909)

Charles Kirk Munroe

A Tale of Peninsulas

September 15, 1850–June 16, 1930
Wrote about the Copper Country

During the early months each year, the frequency of Michigan and Ontario license plates on I-75 below Valdosta signifies the annual trek to Florida of "snowbirds." Spring brings them back, their loyalty to the north country unaltered by mechanically dependable air conditioning. In the 1920s, a research team at General Motors developed a "safe" refrigerant, patented it, and sold it through the Frigidaire subsidiary. The sweltering South became tolerable, and Northerners flocked in ever increasing numbers to the Sun Belt, reshaping America's geographic profile. Public policies aided and abetted the migration and continue to do so.

Charles Kirk Munroe anticipated this transformation. Born in Wisconsin, with a youth spent in Massachusetts followed by New York City employment as reporter and editor, he wrote *The Florida Annual*, first printed in 1884 by Vaux and Company of 27 Rose Street, New York City. A guidebook for a state whose population approached three hundred thousand inhabitants, it featured an introduction by none other than Harriet Beecher Stowe, the author in 1852 of *Uncle Tom's Cabin*—the novel that Abraham Lincoln regarded as having launched the Civil War.[1] Munroe was two when his future sister-in-law's polemic began to exacerbate regional tensions. By contrast, his output focused on fiction for young males, appealing to their adventurous and romantic inclinations.

In 1898, as America engaged in a war in the tropics, Kirk Munroe (dropping his first name as author) published a novel set well north of the forty-fifth parallel in Michigan. When Harper's of New York City came out with *The Copper Princess: A Story of Lake Superior Mines*, the region known as the Copper Country was enjoying its boom. Houghton County's population nearly doubled between 1890 and 1900, as its mines and others on the Keweenaw Peninsula yielded their precious metals and sustained a flourishing local economy. The *Journal of Education* praised the novel as another of Munroe's "delightful stories," a book "full of exciting events."[2] The *Detroit Free Press* reviewed it favorably: "It is a stirring story of the Lake Superior mining country, told with spirit and dash" and richly deserving the approval of its admirers.[3]

After a near-fatal rail incident opens the story, the protagonist reveals his reason for coming, penniless and friendless, to Calumet: "I was told that this was the one section of the United States unaffected by hard times."[4] Tall shaft houses and smokestacks spreading across the countryside, joined by "a swarming population," signify the economic engine that drew the hopeful from England, Finland, Scotland, and around the globe. A "sea-fight" on Lake Superior aids the drama. The title on the two-hundred-plus pages referred both to a mine and a "maiden" of that name, enabling the obligatory love story—which had a happy ending. Not necessarily so the region.

In 2020, U.S. Census data continued to chart the Upper Peninsula population at around 300,000—relatively flat since 1950 after its peak of just over 330,000 in 1920. The State Demographer has reported uneven patterns of population change within Michigan, but the U.P. has declined by three percent between 2012 and 2022. The residents of the upper portion were much older than the state's population, on average. Area jobless rates were higher for young males than for other demographics.[5] The boom times of the Keweenaw are a relic, preserved in a historic park, while Florida now boasts of a year-round population exceeding twenty-one million.

The Copper Princess remains available online, or on occasion in used bookshops, and the Upper Peninsula retains its remoteness and lack of attention in most travel guides. Except: the longest federal trail in the United States, longer than its Appalachian or Great Western or Pacific Crest counterparts, traverses the entire U.P. from end to end. The North Country National Scenic Trail, approved by Congress on March 5, 1980, in Public Law 96–199, enters on County Road 505 at the Montreal River north of Ironwood, routes past Little Girls Point, through Porcupine Mountains State Park, Marquette, Munising, Grand Marais, the Pictured Rocks National Lakeshore, and Tahquamenon Falls State Park, and ends at St. Ignace, having crossed the wild and scenic Ontonagon River near historic Old Victoria, Voelker's Laughing Whitefish

River, and Hemingway's Big Two Hearted River.[6] Following paved two-lane roads over a number of miles, the largely off-road path skirts numerous waterfalls (the U.P. hosts all but one of Michigan's three hundred plus) and a lighthouse or two.

In late 2023, the National Park Service announced that the trail had been added as a "unit" to the inventory of national parks. This heightened status meant eligibility for important funding and promotion.

Visitation data for 2025 support an estimate of nearly seventeen million total recreation visits on the Appalachian National Scenic Trail.[7] By contrast, "hundreds of thousands of people" requested information from the North Country Trail Association, the official partner of the National Park Service, in order to approach the much longer hike.[8] Perhaps a book would bring more.

Selected Works

At War with Pontiac: or, The Totem of the Bear, a Tale of Redcoat and Redskin (1895)
The Copper Princess: A Story of Lake Superior Mines (1898)

William Angus Murdoch

You Give Me Fever

September 11, 1904–July 2, 1962

Wrote a classic on the Copper Country

Two overlooks at the top of the Brockway Mountain Drive present views that rank among the best on the planet. As the highest route above sea level between the two great American mountain ranges, its panoramic vistas in every direction are breathtaking. On the clearest day, Isle Royale is visible fifty miles out in Lake Superior, that vast inland sea. Those with keener insight can see much farther. The county road perches on a ridge formed by centuries-old volcanic action; the same geologic forces brought great veins of copper to where humans could excavate and profit from the mineral. The Drive is flanked by M-26 to its north and US-41 on the south, by Copper Harbor to the east and the "Copper Country" to the west.

In the middle of the Second World War, the MacMillan Company of New York published "the story of Michigan copper" by an unlikely author. William Angus Murdoch was born in 1904 and raised in Chicago. He had expected a career at his family's Chicago heating and plumbing company. "Seeking more glamour," he wrote tour booklets with a local travel bureau before the Depression "bankrupted travel,"[1] when he became editor for the monthly *Plumbers Trade Journal*. Eventually, he freelanced for HVAC trade papers. In 1933, he married a Louisville, Kentucky, native named Florence. Not long after, the couple went on road trip:

> Seven years ago my wife and I headed our Ford for that conventional midwestern tour—a drive around Lake Michigan. Call it chance or whim—at any rate we left the concrete and followed U.S. 41 to the tip of the Keweenaw Peninsula. There we stayed, enthralled with pine forests that parted to reveal

tumbled mine sites, with a country which neither fenced off, nor charged admission to, the attractions of its past.[2]

That summer we had only a few weeks to explore this forgotten Lake Superior area. Even so, we managed to lose ourselves in a pine-hidden desert of stamp sand, to discover a full-fledged ghost town and talk with a genuine hermit. We hurried back the next year—and for every summer thereafter. We'd been "taken" with the Copper Fever as badly as any old-time prospector. The more we learned about this fabulous country, the more there seemed left to explore. Our status changed from tourists to summer citizens, and then we were accepted into circles of yarn-spinning Keweenawans. Perfunctory travel diaries expanded into fat notebooks, for it wasn't many summers before I decided that some day I would write the story of Michigan copper. Winter-bound city evenings at Chicago libraries resulted in a wealth of factual material. Library indexes showed that neither facts nor fancies had ever been gathered together in popular form.[3]

Boom Copper opens with a geographic lesson about US-41: its traffic-choked termination in Miami as the Tamiami Trail amid high-rises and high heat garners media attention for "its bathing beauties, palm trees, and gilded oddments." Overlooked is its "northern terminus which is, in its own rugged way, highly photogenic. Certainly, its romantic and improbable history more than makes up for any shortage of glamour-girls." It does not only run downhill southward. When it enters the upper state, it comes into "an endless forest of Christmas-tree green." Passing through ever-shrinking communities, the "black-top continues northward—one hundred, two hundred miles—finally winding its way through the twin towns of Houghton and Hancock spread out on opposite shores of Portage Lake."[4] The author revealed the extent of his infatuation:

> You might expect Forty-one to pull up here on the brink of Lake Superior; but it still has fifty-six miles of wilderness to go—swooping around the roller-coaster curves of Brockway Mountain to dissolve in sand on the very brim of the greatest body of fresh water in the world.[5]

One periodical termed *Boom Copper* the Bible of Copper Country social history.[6] Another reviewer called it "a popular, not always accurate history."[7] One newspaper reporter's review, headlined "Copper Country

Gets Its Historian," called it "a bang-up job."[8] An anthology regarded it as a "quirky, non-scholarly history."[9] The *New York Times* review was positive.[10] The *Journal of Economic History* panned it.[11] Murdoch—dropping the first name to emphasize an ancestry where many Scots were involved—produced what some characterize as a "classic." His purpose had not been to write the definitive history but "as a purely informal review of the life and times of an almost forgotten" place; he invited "a more serious historian" to pay it attention. They have.[12] None has been more unlikely to have staying power.

When the Murdochs experienced it, Keweenaw County's population had fallen from its 1910 peak of 7,156 to the 3,000–4,000 range. In 2020, it was 2,046, Michigan's least populous county. With 540 square land miles, density has always been low. Some six hundred miles from Southeast Michigan population centers, Copper Harbor is more distant from Detroit than Des Moines. A Great Lakes circle tour is what drew Angus to discover an unknown country. In late 1836, "every-day people" realized that this faraway land "had great attractions" as part of a state possessed "of enchanting scenery."[13] When in need of nature's sustaining power, there is no better thing than to say, "I'd go to the Upper Peninsula."[14]

Perhaps more will come to discover a different, unique, and heart-straining "landscape, the place that takes nothing for granted" at the very pinnacle of Michigan.[15]

Selected Works

Boom Copper: The Story of the First U.S. Mining Boom (1943)

Jane Johnston Schoolcraft/ O-bah-bahm-wawa-ge-zhe-go-qua

Poet of Stars in the Sky

January 30, 1800–May 22, 1842
Born and lived most of her life and wrote at Sault Ste. Marie and Mackinac Island

The Upper Peninsula, of the two main land masses in Michigan, is the far country much less respected and appreciated. With but one fifty-mile stretch of interstate highway, accessible across a five-mile strait that once required ferrying, and with a smaller populace than Pittsburgh, the remote landscape is the butt of joking or, even worse, being left off the state map. In the case of the Great Lakes State, fully half of the land mass and significant parts of these lakes were omitted—as if to say, "consider it terra incognita." Public Act 147 of 2009 took effect on November 19. It passed after a television commercial promoting the state, sponsored by the Michigan Economic Development Corporation, showed a map of Michigan with the Upper Peninsula missing.

The (sometimes benign) neglect of the upper half of the thirty-sixth state may underlie the lack of recognition of one of its greatest, and certainly one of the earliest, wielders of the pen. This author was female, she did not actively seek publication of her work, and she was of Native American heritage. Her husband acquired greater fame, and the bias of mainstream historians is a chief reason for that fame. Had they been more circumspect and objective, these chroniclers would long ago have highlighted the talents and works of the first known Indian lyricist, the first female Indian writer, the first Indian poet, the first to write poems in a native dialect, and the first to translate traditional stories.

Her birth name was O-bah-bahm-wawa-ge-zhe-go-qua, a lyrical-sounding phrase that carried much meaning, as did her life, brief though it was. Born in the first year of the nineteenth century, she would close her life at the untimely age of forty-two, carrying to the grave a heart touched by grief. Of her four children, two did not survive beyond the age of three. Another would die at an age similar to her own at death. As if to presage the forced anglicization of Indians in boarding schools, she wrote in Ojibwe a lament about having to leave a child at a school far away.[1] Her marriage had its trying times, and her ethnicity gave excuse to the narrow-minded to treat her with less than due respect. It would take nearly two centuries for her English-derived married name—Jane Johnston Schoolcraft—to begin gaining due renown.[2]

That recognition is appropriate for all of the firsts but equally because of her subjects and style. As a child of the Upper Peninsula who spent her formative years and much of her married life along the St. Marys River, her love for native country is a hallmark of her writing. Born to an Irish fur trader and an Ojibwe daughter of a tribal leader, encountering British and French influences in the people of the North, she drew from both cultures to write poetry in both languages. One work is set on the grounds of her U.P. home:

Amid the still retreat of Elmwood's shade,
    I count the long hours and counting mourn,
My heart with anxious fears is oft dismay'd,
    And unobserved, I spend those hours forlorn.
    Oft as I glance my eyes around,
    Fond memory brings him near,
To him I feel forever bound,
To me, he's more than dear.[3]

This piece remained unpublished until 2007. Others made it into print thanks to marriage. In 1823, Jane wed Henry Rowe Schoolcraft, the New York–born Indian agent for the U.S. government in that portion of the territory. In fact, their relationship owed itself to his appointment to the position in 1822 and move from Southeast Michigan to the international straits. During the winter of 1826–1827, Henry published sixteen issues of a manuscript periodical, *The Literary Voyager*—in Ojibwe, *The Muzzeniegun*—which included some of his wife's writings. The *Voyager*, the first ever Michigan magazine, stating its place of publication as Sault Ste. Marie, served chiefly as an outlet for Mr. Schoolcraft's studies of native culture, a knowledge set he achieved thanks to Mrs. Schoolcraft and her family and friends. It was widely distributed throughout the Lake Superior region, in Detroit, and in the eastern part of the country.

The Soo, as it is popularly called, had for centuries been a center of Native American activity and culture. Some Ojibwe lived there year-round; many others rendezvoused along the rapids during the summer fishing season to catch the whitefish that inhabited the great lake to the west. Europeans made first contact there in the early seventeenth century, and it became a fur trading hub. By 1800, when one million dollars of furs transited the site, it was home to a multi-cultural community of native, French, English, and American peoples. Henry Schoolcraft "knew very little about the red man and his ways" when he arrived in summer 1822. It was the "remarkable" Johnston family who paved the way for his epic studies and writings about the Ojibwe. Both parents' literary interests also informed their children's education, producing in Jane a young woman of great knowledge and intellect.

According to one prominent Michigan historian, Jane was her father's favorite. He frequently took her on business trips and, in 1809, back to Ireland and England. She was "attractive and talented" and after the marriage became regarded "as the 'northern Pocahontas.'" As charming as that myth-laden character was, Jane's personality drew visitors from far and wide who sought a relationship with one of graciousness, wit, and intelligence.[4] Schoolcraft moved into the Johnston home when he arrived in 1822, and within three months he and Jane were "exchanging notes of a sentimental character." He was soon "thoroughly enamored" of her, and part of the attraction was her intellect, a match for his.[5] Their relationship progressed until marriage on October 12, 1823.

The couple lived at the Soo in a Federal-style building with a two-story center flanked by one-story wings, one of which housed the agency office. In 1826, construction began with the design at the hands of Obed Wait, architect of the territorial Capitol in Detroit. Completed a year later, at which point the Schoolcrafts moved from next door, the structure was an imposing one-hundred-foot-long office, administrative, and residential structure. Its location high on the bank of the St. Marys River gave it access and visibility as vessels made their way across the rapids. The house consisted of fifteen rooms and an elegant interior. The grounds featured "clusters of elms, maples, mountain ash, and other shade trees" as well as "roses in perfection, hyacinths, lilacs, pinks, sweet William, violets, bachelor buttons, marigolds" and other heritage blooms.[6]

It also featured a kitchen garden.[7] When the agency moved to Mackinac Island in 1833, the building was leased to the American Fur Company.

Next door to Elmwood was the house in which Jane's parents originally lived. John Johnston constructed a home on the site shortly after settling here in 1793 and then rebuilt it after it was burned in 1815.[8] Far from rustic, it featured a library of "a thousand well-bound and well-selected volumes." It appears that her father's in-home collection formed the basis for her literary inventory, supplemented by several other sources.[9] Here it was that Henry and Jane were wed. It remains one of the oldest structures on the Great Lakes. John Johnston settled on the American shore, rather than elsewhere, for two reasons: "he was struck by the wild beauty of Lake Superior," and he was smitten with love for the youngest daughter of a native chief.[10]

Henry and Jane traveled between the Soo, Detroit, New York, and Washington on a periodic basis. On certain occasions when Henry attended the Territorial Council meetings in Detroit, the family went along. The couple also experienced numerous separations during the husband's trips on business. After the birth of her last child, Jane's health deteriorated. In the winter of 1835–1836, she suffered from pertussis. In 1837, she suffered from swelling in her legs and feet. In 1838, the couple traveled to New York in search of a respite from her maladies, but it may be that the use of laudanum, a common prescription in that era, caused her more harm than good. The resulting emotional strain also did nothing to strengthen her.[11]

Because of Henry's lack of employment in Michigan and Jane's physical condition, the couple decided in 1841 to relocate to New York City. Jane sailed from Detroit to Mackinac Island in May; they left in August. Jane would never see her home country again. In April 1842, Henry journeyed to England in pursuit of literary success. Jane decided not to try the three-week voyage and instead traveled to Ontario for a visit with a sister. The children were sent to Albany for school. On the evening of May 22, the sister "found her insensible, if not already dead." Jane was 42.[12]

It is not clear whether the widower visited his wife's grave in Canada or who might have handled the funeral arrangements, though her gravestone was inscribed with some wistfulness. Henry eulogized his deceased spouse in a letter to their children: "When I first saw her in 1820, her refinement, taste, propriety of manners, purity & delicacy of language, & correctness of sentiment were such as few females in any rank or station possess." He spoke of her literary output: "Her taste in literature was chaste. She wrote many pretty pieces."[13]

Characterizing them as "pretty" leaves a degree of confusion about Henry's assessment. It suggests a certain level of condescension; conversely, it could be read as a complimentary judgment, as opposed to a term such as "banal." Regardless, it seems an understated view when a poem like "Resignation" is considered:

How hard to teach the heart, oppress with grief,
Amid gay, worldly scenes, to find relief;
And the long cherish'd bliss we had in view,
To banish from the mind where first it grew!
But Faith, in time, can sweetly soothe the soul,
And Resignation hold a mild control;
The mind may then resume a proper tone,
And calmly think on hopes forever flown.

Her poetry dealt with loss. One work entitled "To My Ever Beloved and Lamented Son William Henry" dealt with it candidly:

Where is that voice attuned to love,
That bid me say "my darling dove"?
But oh! that soul has flown above.
Sweet Willy.

Whither has fled the rose's hue?
The lilly's whiteness blending grew,
Upon thy cheek—so fair to view.
My Willy.

The clouds in darkness seemed to low'r,
The storm has past with awful pow'r,
And nipt my tender, beauteous flow'r!
Sweet Willy.

But soon my spirit will be free,
And I my lovely son shall see,
For God, I know, did this decree.
My Willy.

Unlike other works in *Voyager*, this was attributed to "Jane Schoolcraft" and dated March 23, 1827.

In the third issue, her husband paid tribute to the Ojibwe contributions she was making: "In the foregoing story, we recognize the pen of a female correspondent, to whom we have before been indebted. A descendant herself, by European parentage, and of the race whose manners and customs, she depicts, in these legends, they derive additional interest from her familiar knowledge of the Indian legendary mind, and the position she occupies between the European and aboriginal races."[14] Their relationship clearly was one of equals, marked by genuine affection and mutual respect.

No less a contemporary than Charles C. Trowbridge, one of Detroit's leading citizens, found Jane's talents worthy of praise:

> The lines composed by Mrs. Schoolcraft . . . struck me with such peculiar force, as well in regard to the pathos of style as the singular felicity of expression, that I have taken the liberty to submit them for perusal to the Governor and one or two of our other mutual friends. The Governor has advised me to publish them.

The governor—Lewis Cass—was no easy critic.

Yet another requiem for her three-year-old son could only begin with and flow in a setting like upper Michigan:

> May the winds softly blow
> O'er thy lone place of rest
> And the white drifting snow
> Repose light on thy breast.
> . . .
> And my sighs shall increase,
> The soft murmurs of spring,
> As in thy requiem low,
> I so pensively sing.

Besides her own poetry in English, Jane translated Ojibwe stories. Those pieces arose from oral tradition, frequently told around family gatherings during the long northern winters. They were rooted in the forests, the lakes, and the skies of that country.[15] As a métis,[16] her life spanned cultural and language differences. She could hold her own in Anglo circles, but she also loved her native heritage. Her assistance to Henry proved invaluable, helping in his research, acting as interpreter, proofing his use of the Ojibwe language, and furnishing much native material for the *Voyager*.[17] It is not too much to say that Jane was "the primary influence on Schoolcraft's literary career," not the other way around.[18]

The very first issue of the periodical begins with an article entitled "Chippewas." It extols the distinguished nature of the tribe and points out the native inflexion of the word as "Od-jib-wa." No doubt such an understanding is a prime example of many insights derived from Jane and her family. Pen names of "Rose" and "Leelinau" provided cover for Jane's contributions.[19]

When Henry Wadsworth Longfellow's legendary poem "Song of Hiawatha" is compared to some of Jane's writings, the similarities in style are not to be missed. That was the trope of the day. Without her literary work and incorporation by her husband into his writing, Longfellow's would not have been possible. Her influence extended to his other poetry, including his famous "Evangeline."

Jane's childhood and young married home country in Great Lakes country proved to be a strong influence in her writing. The stories she recorded "often take place on or near a great lake, evoking the visually, ecologically, and culturally central role of water and of Lake Superior in the daily life of Schoolcraft's personal, familial, and Ojibwe world."[20]

The original site of Elmwood was at East Portage Avenue. It was designated a Michigan State Historic Site in 1956 and listed on the National Register of Historic Places in 1974.[21] The Johnston House received parallel designations in 1958 and 1970. Both are now found at the Soo Historic Sites location north of Johnston Avenue along East Water Street, having been relocated around 1900 during construction of a hydroelectric facility. Though the Soo Locks and the International Bridge to Canada are featured predominantly in tourism materials, neither is of the vintage or the value to Michigan's heritage as are these two structures.

Jane was buried in Saint John's Anglican Church Graveyard, Ancaster, Hamilton Municipality, Ontario, Canada, not far from the west end of Lake Ontario. Her grave is a lonely one, its inscription barely legible.[22] Fortunately, the treasure trove of her writings has been rediscovered, and they have been pressed into ink for evermore.

The connection of the Ojibwe people to the land outlasts each generation. As recently as 2020, Ontario Power Generation, a Canadian energy company, planned to locate a nuclear waste repository near Lake Huron. The idea went down in flames when the Saugeen Ojibway Nation members cast 85 percent of their votes in opposition. The company announced it would no longer pursue the site and would seek an alternative. In addition to concern for the land and lakes, the Ojibwe's love of community was an essential component of Jane's life and a formative ingredient in her writing. Her references to the land, homeland, or native land are legion. Whether gathered with her native relatives or in a woman's reading group at the government facilities, she rotated through circles that nurtured love for humanity and the environment. Indeed, many of her poems express an abiding spiritual faith in Nature's God.

In March 1823, she wrote a prophetic poem about how the great natural resources of Michigan would be plundered by those—whether for mineral, lumber, or other riches—who lacked a native love for and humility about Providence's provision. How in her youth a calm and tranquil setting, marked by music, literary artifacts, and community provided a blissful life, but then:

> How changed, since full of strife and fear,
> The world hath sent its votaries here.
> The tree cut down—the cot removed,
> The cot the simple Indian love,
> The busy strife of young and old
> To gain one sordid bit of gold
> By trade's o'er done plethoric moil,
> And lawsuits, meetings, courts and toil.[23]

A contemporary wrote an assessment of her mindset about the Ojibwe:

> While in conversation with her, new ideas of the Indian character suggest themselves; new sources of information are opened to me, such as are granted to few, and such as I gratefully appreciate. She is proud of her Indian origin; she takes an enthusiastic and enlightened interest in the welfare of her people, and in their conversion to Christianity, being herself most unaffectedly pious.

She taught her children, and spoke to them, in the native dialect.[24]

O-bah-bahm-wawa-ge-zhe-go-qua, Woman of the Sound that the Stars Make Rushing Through the Sky—Jane Johnston Schoolcraft—should be celebrated.[25] Born under American rule in the Michigan territory, a writer in her own right, she began to create at age fifteen before her famous husband came into her life. The innumerable "Schoolcraft" and Hiawatha designations all over central North America, meant to commemorate Henry, should properly be understood to encompass Jane as well. For her greatness should be the pride of two great nations—America and Ojibwe—and the pride of her native state, both for her precedence and for her attachment and writing about this Great Lakes State, extolling "the grandeur of Superior's show," the "pillared rocks and castle pomps" of places such as the Pictured Rocks, the view from Little Presque Isle near Marquette, the sound of the "bright silver rays" reflecting on the "dark deep stream" of the St. Marys River, and of how "the air is pure" in Pure Michigan.[26]

Addendum: Inscription on Jane Schoolcraft's Gravestone

JANE,
Wife of
HENRY R. SCHOOLCRAFT, ESQ.,
Born at St. Mary's Falls, Jan. 31st, 1800.
She died at Dundas, May 22nd, 1842,
In the arms of her sister, during a visit at the home
of the Rector of this church, while her husband was absent
in England, and her children at a distant school.
She was the eldest daughter of
John Johnston, Esq., and Susan, daughter of Waubojeeg,
a celebrated War Chief and civil ruler of the Ojibewa Tribe.
Carefully educated and of polished manners and
conversation, she was early fitted to adorn society, yet
of retiring and modest deportment. Early im—bued with
the principles of true piety, she patiently
submitted to the illness which for several years marked her
decline, and was inspired through seasons of
bodily and mental depression with the lively hope of
a blessed immortality.[27]

Part Two

Absolutely Everything (Almost) to Know about Michigan and Books

Bookshops

A wonderful feature of twenty-first-century life is to order a book you simply must have and then arrange, with little fuss, to have it shipped right to your door. Still, nothing compares to entering a good bookshop, sauntering down the aisles, perusing titles, perhaps sipping a beverage while idling and musing, and leaving with a book that wouldn't have been on any wish list. Bookshops—the brick-and-mortar kind—are invaluable building blocks in the health of our society. They provide "people, conversation, books to be held and happened upon, floors that creak, atmosphere."[1]

We confess: it's happened more than once that we've stopped in at one of these places to find our books being sold and eagerly volunteered to sign them, hoping that little bonus might provide value to the patron and the purveyor.

Having personally visited many of the independent booksellers listed next, we can report how much they are worthy of patronage. Many serve as community gathering spaces, sponsors of emerging authors, and educational resources through both inventory and programs. Shopping at these small businesses—no matter the size of their locales, and quite a number are in small towns—aids the community, the environment, and the local economy. A plus: if also a coffee or tea shop, three of the greatest pleasures in life—reading and buying a good book and sipping a warm (during most seasons) and delicious beverage—are combined.

The listing is arranged alphabetically (with one region handled specially) and is accurate as of spring 2026. Stores within libraries, schools, or chains are not included.[2]

Adventure Ink, 108 E. Main St., Milan 48160
Alcott's Attic, Detroit (pop-up locations)
aMaizing BookBee, 120 E. Main St., Flushing 48433
Anne-Marie's Bookstore, 1780 W. Columbia Ave., Battle Creek 49015
Another Look Books, 22263 Goddard Rd., Taylor 48180

Argos Comics & Used Book Shop, 1405 Robinson Rd. SE, Grand Rapids 49506
A Squared Books, 10344 Marshall Rd., South Lyon 48178
Baker Book House, 2768 E. Paris Ave., Grand Rapids 49546
Balcony Row Books, 109 S. Saginaw St., Holly 48442
Ballyhoo Books & Brews, 111 W. Superior St., Alma 48801
Barrett's Books, 111 W. Grand River Ave., Williamston 48895
Bay Books, 220 N. St. Joseph St., Suttons Bay 49682
Bella's Book Nook & Cafe, 8010 Miller Rd., Swartz Creek 48473
Beloved Books, 208 N. Bridge St., Linden 48451 (inside the 1908 Hall building)
Bestsellers Books & Coffee, 360 S. Jefferson St., Mason 48854
Bettie's Pages, 11635 Fulton St. E., #500, Lowell 49331
Between the Covers, 106 E. Main St., Harbor Springs 49740
Blue Vase Books, 2048 J. Maddy Parkway, Interlochen 49643
The Bluestocking Bookshop, 12330 James St., Holland 49424
Book Beat, 26010 Greenfield, Oak Park 48237
The Book Cellar, 8 N. 7th St., Grand Haven 49417
The Book Exchange of Jackson, 142 N. Mechanic St., Jackson 49201
Book Haven, 6 E. Chicago St., Quincy 49082
Book Love Bar, 110 W. Michigan Ave., Ypsilanti 48197
The Book Mark, 201 S. Rath Ave., Ludington 49431
Book Nook & Java Shop, 8744 Ferry St., Montague 49437
The Book Nook of Saugatuck, 242 Butler St., Saugatuck 49453
The Book Pile, 77 E. Division St., Sparta 49345
Book Suey, 10345 Joseph Campau Ave., Hamtramck 48212
Booked Up, 4518 W. Main St., Kalamazoo 49006
The Bookman, 715 Washington St., Grand Haven 49417
Bookmarks, 126 Townsend St., Midland 48640
Books & Mortar, 966 Cherry St. SE, Grand Rapids 49506
Books on the Ave, 35622 W. Michigan Ave., Wayne 48184
The Bookstore, 330 Main St., Frankfort 49635
Booksweet, 1729 Plymouth Rd., Ann Arbor 48105
Bound for Books, 7570 E. 34 Rd., Suite A, Cadillac 49601
Bromley's Books, 813 N. Third St., Marquette 49855
Brooks Books, 1805 Ford Ave., Wyandotte 48192
Buy the Book, 2894 S. Huron Rd., Kawkawlin, 48631
Calliope Bookshelf, 66870 Van Dyke Rd., Washington 48095
Canterbury Book Store, 908 Ludington St, Escanaba 49829

Cellar Bird Books, 415 Bridge St. NW, Suite B, Grand Rapids 49504
Charlin's Book Nook, 925 S. Main St., Frankenmuth 48734
Classic Book Shop, 32336 Woodward Ave., Royal Oak 48073
Comma Bookstore & Social Hub, 132 W. 2nd St., Flint 48502
Coreander's Children's Bookshoppe, 15118 Kercheval Ave., Grosse Pointe Park 48230
The Cottage Book Shop, 5989 S. Lake St., Glen Arbor 49636
Cottage Used Books, 8331 S. State Rd., Goodrich 48438
Courageous Books, 8063 Main St., Suite 1, Dexter 48130
Coy's Comics & Books, 3100 Enterprise Dr., Saginaw 48603
Crazy Wisdom Bookstore, 114 S. Main St., Ann Arbor 48104
D&K Books, 18004 E. Thirteen Mile Rd., Roseville 48066
David's Books, 112 W. Michigan Ave., Ypsilanti 48197
Dawn Treader Book Shop, 514 E. Liberty, Ann Arbor 48104
Detroit Specials Used Books, 8275 John R St., Detroit 48202
Diggers Books, Movies & Music, 410 N. 4th Ave. Ann Arbor 48104
Dog Ears Books, 106 Waukazoo St., Northport 49670
Dust & Blush, 116 S. Lake St., Boyne City 49712
Editorial Penuel, 2054 Junction Ave., Detroit 48209 (Spanish-speaking)
Elephant Ear Books, 449 S. Harvey St., Plymouth 48170
Epilogue Books, 10 E. Bridge St. NE, Rockford 49341
Falling Rock Café & Bookstore, 104 E. Munising Ave., Munising 49862
Fenton's Open Book, 105 W. Shiawassee Ave., Fenton 48430
Fine Print Bookshop, 109 E. Michigan Ave., Saline 48176
First Edition Too Bookstore, W4487 Worth Rd. Moran 49760
Flourish Books & Plants, 17649 US-12, New Buffalo 49117
Flying Bear Books & Creperie, 79 W. State Rd., Newaygo 49337
Flyleaf, 92 Kercheval Ave., Grosse Pointe Farms 48236
The Folded Leaf, 414 E. Eighth St., Traverse City 49686
Forever Books, 312 State St., St Joseph 49085
Gilbert and Ivy, 100 S. Main St., Vicksburg 49097
Glendora Bookshop, 110 E. Front St., Buchanan, 49107
Golden Hour Bookshop, 200 W. Main St., Lowell 49331
Grandpa's Barn, 340 Fourth St. Copper Harbor 49918
Great Matter Books, 2456 Plainfield Ave. NE, Grand Rapids 49505
Green Brain Comics, 13936 Michigan Ave., Dearborn 48126
Hello Books, 330 Kalamazoo St. # 2, South Haven 49090

Hidden Nook Booksellers, 207 E. Michigan Ave., Grayling 49738

Hoot & Honey Bookstore, 368 River St., Manistee 49660

Horizon Books, 243 E. Front St., Traverse City 49684; 115 S. Mitchell St., Cadillac 49601

Inkwell Archives, 120 E. Main St., Middleville 49333

An Inkwell Spent, Historic Canterbury Village, 2357 Joslyn Ct., Lake Orion 48306

Inner Light Bookstore, 26050 Crocker Blvd., Harrison Township 48045

Inscribe Books, 6421 Sashabaw Rd., Clarkston 48346

Island Books and Crafts, 101 E. Portage Ave., Sault Ste. Marie 49783

Island Bookstore, 7372 Main St., Mackinac Island 49757

Jason's Books & Coffee, 1590 44th St. SW, Wyoming 49509

Jellybean's Used Books and Entertainment, 2256 E. Main St., Owosso 48867

John K. King Used & Rare Books, 901 W. Lafayette Blvd., Detroit 48226;[3] John K. King's Books North, 22524 Woodward Ave., Ferndale 48220

Kazoo Books, 2413 Parkview Ave., Kalamazoo 49008

Kitab Café and Bookstore, 2727 Holbrook Ave., Hamtramck 48212; 422 W. Willis St., Detroit 48201

Landmark Books, 800 Cottageview Dr., Suite 45, Traverse City 49684

Leelanau Books, 109 N. Main St., Leland 49654

The Literary Hideaway, 8166 Macomb St., Grosse Ile 48138

Literati Bookstore, 124 E. Washington, Ann Arbor 48104

Lola Lee's Coffee & Books, 350 84th St. SW, Suite 900, Byron Center 49315

Love & Other Books, 251 E. Nine Mile Rd., Ferndale 48220

Lowry's Books and More, 118 W. Chicago Rd., Sturgis 49091; 22 N. Main St., Three Rivers 49093

McLean & Eakin Booksellers, 307 E. Lake St., Petoskey 49770; The Archives: Used Books by McLean & Eakin, 325 E Lake St., Petoskey 49770

Midland Street Books, 809 E. Midland St., Bay City 48706

Mon Coeur Books, 42823 Ford Rd., Canton 48187

Motte & Bailey Booksellers, 212 N. 4th Ave., Ann Arbor 48104

My Library Shelf Bookstore, 5474 N. Coleman Rd., Coleman 48618

Nacho Mama's Bookshop, 4681 Washington St., Hamilton 49419

New Story Community Books, 114 W. Michigan Ave., Marshall 49068

The Next Chapter Book Mart, 710 Chicago Dr., Suite 250, Holland 49423

Next Chapter Books, 16555 E. Warren Ave., Detroit 48224

North Wind Books, 437 Quincy St., Hancock 49930

Novel Book and Sandwich Shop, 307 S. Main St., Rochester 48307
Orchard House Books and Café, 1042 Michigan St. NE, Grand Rapids 49503
Pages & Grapes, 1760 44th St. SW, Suite 6, Wyoming 49519
Pages & Peonies, 2751 Alpine Ave. NW, Suite 3, Grand Rapids 49544
Pages Bookshop, 19560 Grand River Ave., Detroit 48223
Paper Trail Books, 414 S. Washington Ave., Royal Oak 48067
Plumfield Books, 574 Ada Dr. SE, Ada 49301
Quincy Book Haven, 6 E. Chicago St., Quincy 49082
R&B Used Books, 12830 S. Saginaw St., Suite F, Grand Blanc 48439
Read It Again Books, 39733 Grand River Ave., Novi 48375
Read My Lips, 768 N. Old Woodward Ave., Birmingham 48009; 131 W. Washington St., Suite B, Marquette 49855
Reader's World, 194 S. River Ave., Holland 49423
Red Fox Inn Bookstore, 5081 Boyne City Rd., Boyne City (Horton Bay) 49712
Redux Books, 1349 Lake Dr. S.E., Grand Rapids 49506
RJ's Books, 5947 Highland Rd., Waterford Township 48327
Road Less Traveled Books, 33300 Thomas St., Farmington 48336
Rolling Rabbit Books, 2495 84th St. SW, Byron Center 49315
Schuler Books, 2513 Jackson Ave., Ann Arbor 48103; 2660 28th St. SE, Grand Rapids 49512; 1982 Grand River Ave., Okemos 48864; 7260 Orchard Lake Rd., West Bloomfield 48322
Serendipity Books, 119 S. Main St., Chelsea 48118
Shaw's Books, 14932 Kercheval Ave., Grosse Pointe Park 48215
Sidetrack Bookshop, 325 S. Washington Ave., Royal Oak 48067; The Caboose: Sidetrack Bookshop for Kids, 220 W. Fourth Ave., Royal Oak 48067
Sleepy Dog Books, 120 E. Broadway St., Mount Pleasant 48858
Snowbound Books, 118 N. Third St., Marquette 49855
Stirling Books & Brew, 119 N. Superior St., Albion 49224
Sunflower Books and Coffee, 528 Quincy St., Hancock 49930
Third Mind Books, 118 E. Washington St., Ann Arbor 48104
this is a bookstore & Bookbug, 3019 Oakland Dr., Kalamazoo 49008
Til Death Books, 46695 Van Dyke Ave., Shelby Township 48317
Toadvine Books, 2783 Coolidge Highway, Berkley 48072
Too Little Time Books, 1305 Gratiot Blvd. #3, Marysville 48040
Totem Books, 620 W. Court St., Flint 48503
Tropetastic Books and Gifts, 112 W. Maumee St., Adrian 49221

Turn the Page Books, 9009 Davison Rd., Davison 48423
27th Letter Books, 3546 Michigan Ave., Detroit 48216
2 Dandelions Bookshop, 428 W. Main St., Brighton 48116
Vault of Midnight, 219 S. Main St., Ann Arbor 48104; 2857 E. Grand Blvd., Detroit 48202; 95A Monroe Center St. NW, Grand Rapids, 49503
Vesper Books and Wine, 5001 Grand River Ave., Detroit 48208
Water Brothers Books, 31208 Five Mile Rd., Livonia 48154
The Well Read Raccoon Books & Curiosities, 314 Shelden Ave., Houghton 49931
West Side Book Shop, 113 W. Liberty, Ann Arbor 48104
Whistler's Daughter Books, 703 Livernois St., Ferndale 48220
The Wild Wood Books & Music, 102 W. State St., Hastings 49058
The Windowsill Used & New Books, 107 S. James St., Ludington 49431
Words on Pages Bookshop, 200 E. Michigan Ave., Paw Paw 49079
Zoey's Treasures, 27822 John R Rd., Madison Heights 48071

African American owned:

Black Stone Bookstore and Cultural Center, 214 W. Michigan Ave., Ypsilanti 48197
Detroit Book City, 24361 Greenfield Rd. Ste. 305, Southfield 48075
Howard Family Bookstore, 13803 Puritan St., Detroit 48235
Nandi's Knowledge Café, 71 Oakman Blvd., Highland Park 48203
Source Booksellers, 4240 Cass Ave. # 105, Detroit 48201
We Are LIT, 87 Monroe Center NW, Grand Rapids 49503

There is the occasional odd bird that does not fit this category—nor is it a traditional library. One such shop is Café 1923 (2287 Holbrook Ave., Hamtramck 48212), a place for coffee and light food with a library section where the patron can peruse a book (and perhaps borrow it, with a promise to return it).

We have not included online outlets or most "pop-up" shops for the reason that they are of their own species—we do not in any way denigrate their value, for included among their number are small, family-owned, and friendly neighborhood booksellers. We've also not included stores focusing on the student trade.

Further note: though Michigan does not have its own trade association, two that exist for the purpose of advocating the interests of indie bookshops cover our fair state in whole or in part. They are

- Great Lakes Independent Booksellers Association, https://www.gliba.org
- Midwest Independent Booksellers Association, https://www.midwestbooksellers.org

The latter's coverage is of Upper Peninsula members.

Now, for a fervent wish, that Michigan might take a page from across the Atlantic. The Welsh market town of Hay-on-Wye in the county of Powys, situated along the border with England, has become known as "the town of books." It holds this distinction by virtue of identity as "the National Book Town of Wales," the location for the annual Hay Literary Festival, and home to more than a dozen bookshops. Its population does not exceed two thousand. Per capita, then, it may be the global leader in bookselling. It has two companions on the isle: Sedbergh is the national book town of England, and Wigtown is the national book town of Scotland.

In the State of New York, southwest of Albany, lies the town of Hobart in Delaware County. Its population is smaller than Hay—some four hundred residents—but it is equally a destination for book lovers. Its nickname of "Book Village of the Catskills" is not false advertising: Main Street features eight shops within easy walking distance.

Ann Arbor comes close to being such an attraction. Within a several-block area of its downtown—bordered by Catherine, Ashley, Liberty, and State Streets—can be found six shops in the earlier list that primarily sell books and other printed material.

Then there is the Lansing area:[4]

- A Novel Concept, 222 S. Washington Square, Lansing 48933
- Bestsellers Books and Coffee Co., 360 S. Jefferson St., Mason 48854
- Curious Book Shop, 307 E. Grand River Ave., East Lansing 48823
- Deadtime Stories, Books & Gifts, 1132 S. Washington Ave., Lansing 48910
- Everybody Reads Bookstore, 2019 E. Michigan Ave., Lansing 48912
- Hooked, 3142 E. Michigan Ave., Lansing 48912

- Summit Comics and Games, 216 S. Washington Square, Lansing 48933
- The Robin Books, 1105 S. Washington Ave., Lansing 48910

Before leaving this section, a lament: gone are Borders' original (and copycat versions) shop in Ann Arbor, Jocundry's in East Lansing, and Gordon's Bookstore on Griswold across from Capitol Park in Detroit. We have memories of our father driving us to Gordon's on Sundays, his purpose being to acquire the hefty *New York Times*, ours to have him acquire for us a *Classics Illustrated* comic book, a paperback, or some other work that would capture our imagination. They're gone—but impossible to forget, easy to cherish.

We offer a final word about books and those who encourage reading. Known for cherries and sweeping blue waters, the Traverse City region added the banner of the National Writers Series in 2010. As a year-round book festival, it has drawn more than three hundred noted authors for informal appearances before more than one hundred thousand patrons at local venues such as the historic City Opera House, Dennos Museum Center, and various outdoor sites. Events are also available online. A "Raising Writers" program seeks to encourage young readers and writers via writing workshops and scholarships for area high school students. The National Writers Series is a cultural gem in Northern Michigan.

Libraries

Personal favorites of ours, the libraries listed next make their appearance because of location, architecture, or another distinguishing feature that makes each memorable on a personal visit. Michigan is blessed with a vast multitude of public libraries (some four hundred, with many communities having more than one location) and world-class university-affiliated library institutions well worth patronizing. Public support carried them into existence and sustains them—whether via a Carnegie grant or some other means. A 1989 district library law provided the means for communities to create a local authority that can undergird the operation of these cultural magnets, removing them from the vagaries of other governmental arrangements. The vital importance of a library to a community, no matter the size or scope, is demonstrated overwhelmingly by their presence in many of Michigan's smaller communities.

An event in the fall of 2022 that made news around the world powerfully demonstrated the fondness of Michiganders for their local library. On Saturday, October 8, an estimated four hundred volunteers came together to form a human chain, passing each and every volume from the inadequate quarters in a fire station a quarter mile to the new Superior Township branch at 1900 Harris Road. The new Ypsilanti District Library facility dwarfs the cramped confines of the fire building. Drone photographs were featured in numerous media outlets.

Many Michigan library structures are of architectural, as well as literary, significance. Some remain, though repurposed, as with the Calumet Public Library now serving as a resource facility for the Keweenaw National Historic Park.

Our list of particular favorites:

Ann Arbor District Library, Pittsfield Branch, 2359 Oak Valley Dr., Ann Arbor 48103: Reminiscent of a vintage agricultural structure in a prairie and wetland setting and thus environmentally friendly, it is located southwest of the city.

Bacon Memorial District Library, 45 Vinewood St., Wyandotte 48192: In a red sandstone house built before 1900, on both State and federal historic registries, this library has multiple fireplaces and other interesting architecture.

Beaver Island District Library, 26400 Donegal Bay Rd., Beaver Island 49782: Not imposing, but as the library farthest from mainland Michigan, it is worth visiting.

Belleville Area District Library, 167 4th St., Belleville 48111: On February 29, 2020, a two-story, thirty-thousand-square-foot building opened to the public to better serve its patrons and the people of western Wayne County. It is an attractive building with a first-floor presentation space that invites attendance at book talks and other educational events.

Bloomfield Township Public Library, 1099 Lone Pine Road, Bloomfield Township 48302: Built in 1964, funded by millage in 1966, the community asset opened its current pavilion-featured facility in 1969 (since expanded) adjacent to busy Telegraph Road but with greenery dominating the site and main entrance.

Charlevoix Public Library, 220 Clinton St., Charlevoix 49720: Located in a dramatically renovated and expanded 1927 middle school, this facility is beautifully designed and just a block or so from the town's main street.

Darcy Library of Beulah, 7238 Commercial St., Beulah 49617: Within a stone's throw of Crystal Lake in its own little park, this sweet little building is named for a therapy dog who spent a score of years providing comfort to friends and strangers.

Detroit, Main Branch, 5201 Woodward Ave., Detroit 48202: This library was built in an Italian Renaissance style by Cass Gilbert, the architect who designed the U.S. Supreme Court building.

Dexter District Library, 3255 Alpine, Dexter 48130: Adjacency to the rails that once carried Michigan Central trains and to a "border-to-border" walking trail with the natural area onto which the reading area looks makes this a memorable haven.

Elk Rapids District Library, 300 Isle of Pines Dr., Elk Rapids 49629: The only library on an island with its own footbridge to the downtown and occupying a historic house dating to the 1860s, the size of the facility is greatly outweighed by its quaintness overlooking East Grand Traverse

Bay. It is listed on the State Register (1979) and denoted by a Michigan Historical Marker.

Ellis Library and Reference Center, 3700 S. Custer Rd., Monroe 48161: Nestled on the bank of the environmentally renewed River Raisin, the historical resources of this facility are equally inspirational, and its staff ranks among the most helpful to patron and painter of word pictures.

Gaines Station Library, 103 W. Walker St., Gaines 48436: This 1880s yellow brick rail station with exposed rafters houses the local library along the tracks of the Detroit, Grand Haven and Milwaukee Railway, an emblem of community engagement and proud preservation ethic.

Goodrich Library, 10237 Hegel Rd, Goodrich 48438: With roots back to an 1870s ladies' association, this library is now housed in the former 1897 town hall at the main junction in town.

Grand Rapids Public Library, 111 Library St. NE, Grand Rapids 49503: A classic Beaux Arts building has been adjoined to a modern structure, combining to make an appropriate site for literature in the state's second city.

Henika District Library, 149 S. Main St., Wayland 49348 (Allegan County): Opened in 1900 because of a key bequest by local philanthropist Julia Robinson Henika, this diminutive farm stone structure features bay windows and other charming attributes.

Hoyt Public Library, 505 Janes Ave., Saginaw 48607: The Romanesque architecture of this massive structure, far from intimidating, provides a sense of fascination that draws the patron inside.[1]

Interlochen Public Library, 9411 Tenth Street, Interlochen 49643: Hailed as a modern version of a northern Michigan cabin, its expanses filled with light and its entryway and roof supports made of natural wood, this facility is an appropriate feature of the world-renowned cultural institution.

Ishpeming Carnegie Library, 317 N. Main Street, Ishpeming 49849: Another Michigan Historic Site because of its history and architecture, built on a sandstone foundation, its entry porch features a pediment supported by Ionic columns and adorned with decorative carved stones with a front façade pierced by one-over-one fixed sash and pilasters.

J. M. Longyear Research Library, Marquette Regional History Center, 145 W. Spring Street, Marquette 49855: Chock full of books (including the rare variety), one of the finest private historical research libraries specializing in the history of the Lake Superior region.

Leland Township Library, 203 E. Cedar St., Leland 49654: Perched on a bend in the river before it rushes over a dam into Lake Michigan, this small but perfectly sited library is next to Fishtown.

Mackinac Island Public Library, 903 Huron St., Mackinac Island 49757: A sea glass–colored exterior with a tile-surrounded fireplace and rockers out the back on the island shore with the Mackinac Bridge, straits, lake freighters, and ferry boats, this site may be the most picturesque of all the state's libraries.

Milford Public Library, 330 Family Dr., Milford 48381: On a wooded ravine near water, this beautiful building holds impressive collections within an open and uplifting space.

Munising Public Library, 810 M-28, Munising 49862: Part of the public school system, the building housing the library is on the shore of South Bay west of the downtown, the same waterway on which the Pictured Rocks are found to the northeast.

Patmos Library, 2445 Riley St, Jamestown (Township) 49427: Located on the site of an interurban railway station that operated between Grand Rapids and the lakeshore in the early 1900s, the facility opened in 1999 and was designed to look like a turn of the century train station.

Peter White Public Library, 217 N. Front St., Marquette 49855: Built in 1895 and made possible by community philanthropists, this magnificent Beaux Arts classical building of white limestone features an interior of white marble and weathered oak, stained glass windows, and a skylight.

Ontonagon Library, 311 N. Steel St., Ontonagon 49953: With an entire county population of less than six thousand—not including bears, wolves, or fish—one has to be amazed at the five libraries here in the main township and in Ewen, Rockland, Trout Creek, and White Pine.

Plymouth District Library, 223 E. Main St., Plymouth 48170: Jack's hometown library is a commodious community center with a strong book and periodical collection in a charming downtown across from an iconic ice cream stand; it celebrated its one hundredth anniversary in 2023.

Alice and Jack Wirt Public Library, 500 Center Ave., Bay City 48708: Completed in 2005, the modern structure serves as the central library for the county's system.

Carnegie Libraries

According to the seminal modern study of the subject, Michigan was the beneficiary of fifty-three community grants for sixty-one of these facilities, placing it tenth among all jurisdictions. A "Carnegie library" is a building funded in significant part by Andrew Carnegie, American industrialist, during the period 1901–1918, through a grant to a community that met certain conditions: a demonstrated need for a public library, a building site, and a commitment to support services and facility maintenance with annual taxes equal to 10 percent of the grant. Nine of the sixty-one were in Detroit. Northern Michigan is home to sixteen, with seven in the Upper Peninsula. The list that follows includes date of application/grant/completion, location, historic designation(s), and current situation. An asterisk denotes continuing use as a library. The Society of Architectural Historians (SAH) has inventoried forty-odd; its designation is noted.

- Adrian (1904), Lenawee County, 110 E. Church Street, Michigan Historic Site (1976), National Register of Historic Places (1977), Lenawee County Historical Society Museum (SAH)
- Albion (1903),* Calhoun County, 501 S. Superior Street, public (district) library
- Allegan (1913),* Allegan County, 331 Hubbard Street, public (district) library
- Ann Arbor (1903), Washtenaw County, south side of E. Huron Street between State and N. Thayer Streets, demolished but façade (with "Public Library" carved above entrance) incorporated into north side of North Quadrangle Residential and Academic Complex; historical marker sponsored by Ladies' Library Association is affixed
- Armada (1913),* Macomb County, 73930 Church Street, free public library
- Bay City (1916), Bay County, 708 Center Avenue, commercial building
- Boyne City (1916),* Charlevoix County, 201 E. Main Street (entrance on S. Park Street), public (district) library
- Bronson (1910),* Branch County, 207 N. Matteson Street, public (district) library, State historical marker
- Cadillac (1903), Wexford County, Beech at N. Shelby Street, Michigan

Historic Site (1980), National Register of Historic Places (2007), Wexford County Historical Society Museum, State historical marker

- Cassopolis (1908),* Cass County, 145 N. Broadway Street, local history branch of public (district) library
- Charlevoix (1910), Charlevoix County, 107 State Street, on the grounds of the current location at 220 Church Street is the cornerstone with a time capsule embedded into the memorial
- Charlotte (1902), Eaton County, 200 N. Cochran Avenue (M-50), commercial building
- Cheboygan (1908), Cheboygan County, 400 W. Elm Street, most recently community center
- Detroit (1901), nine sites originally, remaining structures are Main, 5201 Woodward Avenue (M-1); Bowen Branch, 3648 W. Vernor Highway; Conely Branch, 4600 Martin Street; Duffield Branch, 2507 W. Grand Boulevard; former Ginsburg branch building on Brewster Street, south of Wilkins, west of Chrysler (I-75) service drive; former Utley branch building, 8726 Woodward Avenue (M-1), the administration building for the Detroit Wayne Integrated Health Network[2]
- Dowagiac (1903),* Cass County, 211 Commercial Street, public (district) library
- East Jordan (1915), Charlevoix County, 301 Main Street, arts center
- Escanaba (1902), Delta County, 201 S. 7th Street, Michigan Historic Site (1976), National Register of Historic Places (1977), privately owned
- Houghton (1908), Houghton County, 105 Huron Street, Michigan Historic Site (1976), partner heritage site of Keweenaw National Historical Park, museum
- Howell (1902),* Livingston County, 314 W. Grand River Avenue, Michigan Historic Site (1977), Carnegie district library, State historical marker (SAH)
- Hudson (1903),* Lenawee County, 205 S. Market Street, Carnegie district library (SAH)
- Iron Mountain (1901), Dickinson County, 300 E. Ludington Street, Michigan Historic Site (1977), museum, State historical marker
- Ironwood (1900),* Gogebic County, 235 E. Aurora Street, National Register of Historic Places (2011), Carnegie library
- Ishpeming (1901),* Marquette County, 317 Main Street, Michigan Historic Site (1980), Carnegie public library

- Jackson (1901),* Jackson County, 244 W. Michigan Avenue, Michigan Historic Site (1979), National Register of Historic Places (1980), district library (SAH)
- Lansing (1902), Ingham County, 214 W. Shiawassee Street, Michigan Historic Site (2011), community college, State historical marker
- Lapeer (1917),* Lapeer County, 921 W. Nepessing Street, Michigan Historic Site (1999), district library, State historical marker
- Ludington (1903),* Mason County, 217 E. Ludington Avenue (US-10), district library
- Mancelona (1916),* Antrim County, 202 W. State Street, township library
- Manistee (1902),* Manistee County, 95 Maple Street, Michigan Historic Site (1995), county library, State historical marker
- Marlette (1918),* Sanilac County, 3116 Main Street (M-53), Michigan Historic Site (1979), district library, State historical marker
- Mendon (1905),* St. Joseph County, 314 W. Main Street (M-60), township library
- Mount Clemens (1902), Macomb County, 125 Macomb Place, Michigan Historic Site (1978), art center, State historical marker
- Newaygo (1913),* Newaygo County, 44 State Road (M-37 and M-82), area district library
- Niles (1903), Berrien County, 321 E. Main Street, privately owned
- Owosso (1913),* Shiawassee County, 502 W. Main Street (M-21), district library
- Paw Paw (1917), Van Buren County, 129 S. Kalamazoo Street (M-40), Michigan Historic Site (2002), community center, State historical marker
- Petoskey (1907), Emmet County, 451 E. Mitchell Street, Michigan Hemingway Society marker, community center
- Port Huron (1902), St. Clair County, 1115 6th Street, Michigan Historic Site (2006), museum, State historical marker (SAH)
- Portland (1905),* Ionia County, 334 Kent Street, district library
- Sault Ste. Marie (1901), Chippewa County, 315 Armory Place, school district office
- South Haven (1904), Van Buren County, 600 Phoenix Street, art center
- Sparta (1916),* Kent County, 80 N. Union Street, Carnegie township library

- St. Joseph (1902), Berrien County, Main and Elm Streets, commercial building (SAH)
- Stambaugh (1914), Iron County, 601 Garfield Avenue, school district office
- Tecumseh (1903), Lenawee County, 304 W. Chicago Boulevard, commercial building
- Three Rivers (1902), St. Joseph County, 107 N. Main Street, Michigan Historic Site (1982), art center, State historical marker (SAH)
- Traverse City (1902), Grand Traverse County, 322 6th Street, art center

The following is a list of the demolished sites:

- Benton Harbor (1902), Berrien County, E Wall Street and 6th Street
- Charlevoix (1907), Charlevoix County, 107 State Street
- Flint (1902), Genesee County, Clifford Street and E. Kearsley Street
- Grand Haven (1903), Ottawa County, 15 N. 3rd Street
- Midland (1917), Midland County, Townsend Street near Larkin Street
- Sturgis (1907), St. Joseph County, Chicago Road (US-12) at North Street
- Wyandotte (1911), Wayne County, 3139 Biddle Avenue

One that qualifies for the category of "demolished by neglect" is the formerly magnificent McGregor Public Library at 12244 Woodward Avenue in Highland Park. As described in another chapter herein, this enclave city has fallen on hard times, its population dramatically reduced to around nine thousand in 2020 from the peak of over forty-five thousand a century prior. According to the city's website, the library's origins lie in the generosity of Katherine Whitney and Tracy W. McGregor, who donated a building and land in 1918 for the construction of a new library. When dedicated on March 5, 1926, the classic Beaux Arts design soon received an award from the American Institute of Architects. With forty thousand square feet of largely open-plan interior space, it proved years ahead of its contemporaries. The entry doors were alone remarkable. In addition to library usage, the building housed collections and a local history museum. It closed in 2002.

Another demolition, deliberately so, did its work in 1965 in Painesdale. The Sarah Sargent Paine Memorial Library, dedicated to the mother of the president of Copper Range Consolidated Company, was constructed in 1902–1903. It was located on Goodell Street by the high school (which remains). Main-floor shelves housed books in the languages of immigrants, and a children's room featured curved windows, window seats, a large fireplace, and children's books.

Other Library Structures on the National Register

- Bay City (1884), Bay County, 100 E. Midland Street, Historical Sage Library branch of Bay County Library System, listed in 1979, Michigan Historic Site (1979), State historical marker (SAH)
- Belding (1918), Ionia County, 301 E. Main Street, Alvah N. Belding Memorial Library, listed in 1993, State historical marker (SAH)
- Ionia (1903), Ionia County, 126 E. Main Street, Hall-Fowler Memorial Library, listed in 1971 (SAH)
- Kalamazoo, 333 S. Park Street, the Ladies' Library Association building, constructed in 1878, was listed in the National Register in 1970. The structure also bears a State historical marker commemorating the association as the first women's club in Michigan and the third in the United States. It was listed on the Michigan Register of Historic Sites in 1961.
- Lexington (1859), Sanilac County, 7239 Huron Avenue (M-90), Charles H. Moore Library, in such use since 1903 (originally a law office), one of two sites within the district library, listed in 1985
- Linden (circa 1850), Genesee County, 201 N. Main Street, the library has been located in the historic Linden gristmill since 1961, listed in 1972, State historical marker
- Onaway (1908), Presque Isle County, 20774 State Street (M-68) between Beech and Maple, branch of Presque Isle District Library in historic courthouse since 2001, listed in 1980

Also note that the Grosse Pointe Central Library (SAH) at 10 Kercheval Avenue in Grosse Pointe Farms, constructed in 1953, was listed on the National Register in 2021 as one of the first major public commissions in the United States of architect Marcel Breuer.

Other Libraries on the State Register

- Algonac (1849), St. Clair County, 1240 St. Clair River Drive, home of Clay Township Library, 1949–1997, now the Algonac Clay Historical Museum, listed in 1970, State historical marker
- Almont (1918), Lapeer County, 213 W. St. Clair Street, Henry Stephens Memorial Library, listed in 1991, State historical marker
- Colon (1914, SAH), St. Joseph County, 128 S. Blackstone Avenue (M-86), Colon Township Library, listed in 1986
- Columbiaville (1893), Lapeer County, 4422 1st Street south of Pine Street, listed in 1987, a State historical marker states that after this depot of the Detroit-Bay City Railroad Company closed in 1964, among its uses was as a library
- Quincy (1910), Branch County, 11 N. Main Street, branch of Branch District Library, listed in 1988, State historical marker
- Richland (1910), Kalamazoo County, 8951 Park Street, listed in 1987, Richland Community Library, State historical marker
- Traverse City (1909), Grand Traverse County, 216 Cass Street, Ladies Library Building, listed in 2018, State historical marker

Other Libraries of Particular Historic Distinction

The Branch County District Library's facilities also include one in Coldwater at 10 East Chicago Street. Known as the Edwin A. Clarke Library (SAH), It is one of the oldest Michigan libraries still functioning in its original building. With a heritage dating to 1870, including a Ladies' Library Association that helped modify State law to permit women to serve on local library boards, the associated 1886 cross gable–roofed, corner-towered, brick Queen Anne building is listed on both the National and State Registers. A recent refurbishment was coupled with a historically sensitive structure addition.

Hillsdale's community library enjoys a rich history. In 1879, local women formed a library association to provide "good literature among the people of Hillsdale."[3] The collection of nearly three thousand volumes became the first inventory of the Mitchell Public Library in July 1908; it was named for the family who donated the Second Empire house to the city. The structure included a marble fireplace, ornate ceilings, beautiful woodwork, and Pewabic tiles from the famous Detroit manufacturer. In 2003, a new structure was opened next door to house the public library, and this building became home to the Mitchell Research Center, a local and family history resource run by county historical society volunteers, at 22 North Manning Street.

The Canton Township Library occupies a primary location as part of the community's public services complex. Located appropriately facing Canton Center Road across from the municipal building and east of Heritage Park, the facility serves the township's nearly one hundred thousand residents and proclaims itself the busiest single-branch library in the state.

In Decatur, the Webster Memorial Library is today a branch of the Van Buren District Library system. Located at the corner of North Phelps and West St. Mary's Streets, it first opened in 1960 thanks to the philanthropy of Norman and Rose Webster. The town's tradition of a free public library dates to 1848 with the founding of a literary organization.

Perhaps no other library location combines two of Michigan's best attributes than that in Harbor Springs. The 1908 brick structure at South Spring Street and East Main now has a fudge emporium at its corner of the intersection where the post office once was. Its origin in 1894 was as a free reading room, founded by the Harbor Springs Christian Association. It truly is a community library, created and sustained by donations and good will of the town's residents.

Oak Park's library is a department of that city's government. Opened in 1958 based on a favorable bond issue vote in 1954, the structure doubled in size with expansion and renovation completed in 1968. Further renovations were accomplished in 2011.

In Wyandotte, the Bacon Memorial District Library occupies a historic house and adjacent structure at 45 Vinewood Street, corner of Biddle Street, continuing since 1943 as the site of the city's public library. The Ford-Bacon house dates from 1897, was listed as a Michigan Historic Site in 1987, and was on the National Register in 1997.

In Chelsea, the McKune Memorial Library has since 1959 occupied the 1860 mansion of the town's founder, Elisha Congdon, located at 221 S. Main Street. In 2008, the *Library Journal* announced that the facility was named "The Best Small Library in America."[4]

In Menominee, the Spies Library (SAH) has been in operation since 1905 at 940 1st Street. The facility is named for the donors, Augustus and Gertrude Spies, who supplied the funds to hire Chicago architecture firm Patton and

Miller, which designed many Carnegie libraries and other magnificent structures such as the Peter White Library in Marquette. This library's location on the waterfront of Green Bay makes it one of the most beautiful of all such Michigan institutions.

In Negaunee, the city hall constructed in 1915 has housed the municipal library since dedication. The library itself has existed since 1890. According to architectural information, the two-story structure is a highly eclectic, even flamboyant design, occupying a full block with a ninety-four-foot-high clock tower. Alternate courses of white pressed brick and grayish-white limestone with terra-cotta detailing form its walls.

In Calumet, the 1898 rock, brick, and sandstone library building (SAH) originated by the Calumet and Hecla mining conglomerate still stands as part of the Keweenaw National Historical Park at 25947 Red Jacket Road.

In Vermontville (Eaton County), the 1989 Opera House at 219 S. Main Street once housed the town library begun in 1948. Today it occupies a different historic structure at 120 E. First Street.

Ray Township Public Library is located in the heart of Ray Township, Macomb County, surrounded by the beautiful Ray Township Park and Wolcott Mill Metropark. Established as a Library in 1983, the building served as the historic one-room schoolhouse, the Mill School, from 1863 to 1953. In 1983, the simple Greek Revival–style school became the Ray Township Library.

In Saginaw, the Hoyt Public Library opened to the public on November 1, 1890, in a Richardson Romanesque–style building constructed of Bay Port limestone from Michigan's Thumb region as well as red sandstone elements and featuring a turret on the southwest corner. Located at 505 Janes Street, it includes additions from the 1920s and 1960s. Becoming part of a district library system in 1994, the landmark structure is one of Michigan's crown jewel libraries. Listed on the State Register in 1998, a Michigan historical marker was dedicated in 2000.

The first library in Fenton was named the A. J. Phillips Library and was dedicated in January 1906 at 310 S. Leroy Street. Since 1987, the library has been located in the nearby 1938 former U.S. Post Office building. The former library building now houses the A. J. Phillips Museum and Historical Society.

The Manchester District Library was voted into existence in 2000, supplanting the township library, which was one of the oldest in the state. According to the Michigan Historical Marker in front of the James A. Lynch House (circa 1867) at 202 West Main, the founding occurred in 1838 in the year following entry into the Union. Since 2002, the library has been located at 912 City Road (M-52) on the right bank of the River Raisin in a Henry Ford Village Industry structure that opened in 1940. Previously, the Premium Grist Mill operated here. The mill pond still exists, as does much of the equipment from the Ford factory.

The Superior District Library is special in a different way as the largest geographical district in the state. Multiple locations are spread across over 150 miles, in the communities of Brevort, Curtis, DeTour, Drummond Island, Engadine, Les Cheneaux, Pickford, Rudyard (Mollie R. Kahl Community Library), and Sault Ste. Marie (Bayliss Public Library). The population these facilities serve amounts to forty-three thousand souls.

But Superior is far from the tiniest library ambit. That honor, in terms of the three most diminutive, goes to

- Carp Lake Township Library, serving 722 patrons in Ontonagon County
- Beaver Island District Library, serving 657 patrons in Charlevoix County
- Whitefish Township Library, serving 575 patrons in Chippewa County

Honorable mention is awarded to Mackinac Island. Ostensibly, its patronage extends to 492 persons—but the influx of hordes of tourists each seasonal day easily multiplies the population actually served.

University Libraries

Within the Peninsular State are a number of excellent libraries at the collegiate level accessible by the public. Among these we would include:

- Bentley Historical Library, 1150 Beal Ave., Ann Arbor 48109
- Clarke Historical Library, 1200 S. Franklin St., Mount Pleasant 48859
- Hatcher Graduate Library, 913 S. University Ave., Ann Arbor 48109
- Lawrence Tech Library, 21000 W. 10 Mile Rd., Southfield 48075

Within certain of these and other Michigan libraries, great collectors of books donated their accumulated treasures to the public. Among them are counted:

- Clarence Monroe Burton (1853–1932), author, book collector, historiographer lawyer, and librarian whose personal library formed the foundation for the Burton Historical Collection at the main branch of the Detroit Public Library (SAH)
- William L. Clements (1861–1934), book collector, and manufacturer whose donation of collected Americana forms the basis for the Clements Library at UM (SAH)

Martha W. Griffiths Michigan Rare Book Room within the Library of Michigan in Lansing has six main areas of focus, consisting of collections in natural history, law, angling, travel and exploration, Native Americans, and Michigana.

No college library is more surprising than the Burrage in the tiny Eaton County town of Olivet. Designed in the Richardsonian Romanesque-style by a New York architect, the burly structure features two cylindrical towers, arches, block styling, and other classic medieval aspects. Inside are coffered ceilings and a massive stone fireplace and iron supports. The Main Street entrance has been moved to College Street, reflecting the change from a tourist to user orientation.

The Olivet College library experienced a golden literary era coincident with the Depression years. Notable visitors included Sherwood Anderson, Wysten Hugh Auden, Caroline Ferguson Gordon, Katherine Anne Porter, Carl Sandburg, Gertrude Stein, Alice Babette Toklas, and Ford Madox Ford. They spent weeks inculcating a love for words on the campus in the 1930s. The next scheduled writer in residence after Ford was Thomas Wolfe, but he died in 1938. All were drawn here by Joseph Hillyer Brewer, former principal in the New York publishing house of Brewer, Warren and Co. after life as a Paris expatriate in the 1920s and stint as business manager and writer for a literary magazine.

F. M. Ford's final effort, an 878-page tome ambitiously titled *The March of Literature*, warmly credited President Brewer (and Dean Robert Greenlees Ramsay):

> [H]ad you not provided me with a room in your admirable library, I should never have been able to finish this book—or not in ten years. But my spiritual obligation to you is no less deep. We have been working together for some time now, I under your presidency and deanship, in the attempt to restore

to the youth of this state a lost art—that of reading . . . and in the hope that that art may spread from this state in ever widening practice to the ends of the earth.[5]

Born in Michigan in 1898, Brewer came from a well-known family of industrialists in Grand Rapids. After graduation from Central High School in 1916, he began his college education at Dartmouth College but joined the Army during his sophomore year and became a second lieutenant. Obtaining his bachelor of arts at Dartmouth in 1920, he earned a master's from Oxford University in English language and literature.

In 1934, Brewer was invited to Olivet College. He resigned in 1944 and returned to New York where he received a library science degree from Columbia University and took a job as associate librarian and acting director for Queens College. He held that position until 1989; he died the next year. The grave in the Oakhill Cemetery in Grand Rapids is marked in Roman numerals, all caps, giving birth date as "October—IX—MDCCCXCVIII" and death date as "February—XXV—MCMXC."

Brewer's final Olivet address was delivered on Founder's Day on February 24, 1944. Titled "The Reconstruction of American Education," the oration spoke of how "it takes an impractical idealist . . . to undertake anything new and untried." The speech did not linger "in sentiment's pleasure groves" or blind adherence to tradition: "in themselves they are valueless unless they are constantly employed in ways suitable to the present." The efforts "of pressure groups" to push their special agendas was alarming; educators needed to respond. Brewer advocated inducting the student "into a whole culture, not a partial, not a lop-sided one." Olivet had kept its traditions alive; the writer-in-residence program had been "pioneering" in the best sense of the word. After all, the college from its beginning had offered equal coeducational learning opportunities consistent with a morality that rejected national and racial disunity and embraced an immutable ethic of loving one's neighbor.[6]

The campus of Michigan State University contains a collection of historic buildings dating from the nineteenth century. Among them is Linton Hall (SAH), the institution's original library, built in 1881. Above the entryway is etched "Library-Museum," memento of the original purpose for what later became the administration building, the office of the president, and offices for the Graduate School and the College of Arts and Letters.

Native American Libraries

Then, very important, are the tribal libraries. They include

- Little Traverse Bay Bands of Odawa Indians Cultural Library in Harbor Springs
- Nah Tah Wahsh Public School Library at the Hannahville Indian School in Wilson
- Ojibwa Community Library in Baraga
- Saginaw Chippewa Tribal Libraries in Mount Pleasant

Indeed, perhaps what should be counted as the first "book" is an Indigenous creation. At the Sanilac Petroglyphs Historic State Park just east of M-53 near Cass City, Michigan's largest known collection of early Native American teachings carved in stone are conserved. They are called *ezhibiigaadek asin*, "knowledge written on stone," in the Anishinaabemowin language. The property was deeded to the State of Michigan by the Michigan Archaeological Society in 1971, and it is co-managed by the State of Michigan and the Saginaw Chippewa Tribe. Between 1965 and 1967, the society raised private funds to purchase 240 acres of property surrounding the Petroglyphs. It is a sacred site for Native Americans and should be held as such by all Michiganders.

Sanilac is a small, rural community and home to a project entitled "Decolonizing Libraries to Foster Community Well-Being." A grant from the Institute of Museum and Library Services facilitated replacement of the Dewey Decimal and Library of Congress Classification systems in favor of an Indigenous approach.

Library of Michigan

Before leaving the subject of bibliotheca, the story of the "State Library" deserves consideration. It dates from 1828 when a territorial library, containing laws and government documents for use by the territorial council, was created. In February 1837, a month after Michigan became a state, Governor Stevens T. Mason appointed Oren Marsh as Michigan's first State librarian. Its facilities were in the Capitol building in Detroit's Capitol Park on Griswold at State until after the capital moved to Lansing.[7]

History was made in 1869 when Harriet Augusta (Edgerton) Tenney became State librarian, the first female to hold the position (and said to be the first female State officer in Michigan). She held the position until 1891, expanding the collection dramatically, managing its relocation on more than one occasion, increasing its appropriations support, and seeking to place the library on a footing equal to that of other states. She was succeeded by Margaret Emma (Custer) Calhoun, widow of Lieutenant James Calhoun and sister of the late General George A. Custer.

In 1893, a female and the first native Michigander was appointed to the position. Mary Clare (Wilson) Spencer served until her death in 1923 at age eighty-one. Under her visionary leadership, the State Library became a treasured resource for all residents. She initiated a policy whereby local libraries could "associate" with, and obtain books for patrons from, the Lansing stacks. In 1895, with her support, the Legislature appropriated funds for a traveling library system and became the second state, after New York, to implement the program. In May, the first set of fifty books was sent to North Star Township in rural Gratiot County. Shipped in oak cases, these sets included serious literature and fiction, seeking to cultivate readers who appreciated fine writing. Within a decade, over seven hundred traveling libraries were in operation with over seventy thousand volumes in circulation. These advancements helped change the State Library from one accessible only to legislators and other officials into a people's book collection.

In 1988, the Michigan Library moved to a new building on West Kalamazoo Street. In 2001, it achieved Cabinet-level status as part of the new Michigan Department of History, Arts and Libraries created by Public Act 63 (House Bill 4941). In July 2009, after only eight years of this status, the governor abolished the department and folded the library into the Department of Education.

Genesis of Three Bibliophiles

Michiganders are a diverse people. As persons of Finnish descent, we cannot omit a truly unique community for which literary matters were vital. Although most would connect emigrants from Finland to the Upper Peninsula, the lower mitten is home to a long-standing community that draws its origin to the land north of the 60th latitude known as Suomi. In 1894, two individuals of Finnish heritage moved to Maple Grove Township in Manistee County for the purpose of founding a settlement. They chose a site where the Pere Marquette line between Grand Rapids and Traverse City and the Manistee and North-Eastern (M&NE) rail lines met. They initially named it Manistee Crossing. It was platted, a post office was opened, and a town started to emerge. In 1900, when the county population crested at almost twenty-eight thousand inhabitants, the name was changed to Kaleva to invoke the nineteenth-century epic Finnish poem known as "Kalevala." Its classic version consists of 22,795 verses comprising fifty folk stories. In 1901, the Finnish Publishing Company moved to Kaleva from Brooklyn, New York, and the original building "still stands," says the Michigan Historical Marker. According to a January 1902 report, the publishing firm had recently moved from Brooklyn and published a bi-weekly paper entitled *Siirtolainen* ("emigrant" or "immigrant"), as well as books, pamphlets, and a variety of blank books for commercial purposes. The publishing company building does still stand as of fall 2022, home of the Art Gallery on the southeast corner of Wuoksi and Aura streets on the diagonal from the marker.

According to the Michigan Historical Marker erected in 1978, the Finns who populated the village "took pride in their cultural heritage, founded a lending library, and instilled in their children a love for music, books and God and country."[8] The marker is located at the northwest corner of the intersection of Wuoksi Avenue and Aura Street next to the post office. The Kaleva branch of the Manistee County Library System is located at 14618 Walta Street at the north end of the village. The old rail depot a few blocks away now serves as a museum. One can muse upon the 1909 *Near to Nature's Heart in a Corner of Michigan*, a "little book intended to give the reader some slight idea of the charms of the country along the line" of the M&NE. That country was "enchanted," a "beauty-spot," "God's country," where you would be "lulled to sound, sweet sleep, by a woodland wind chattering softly in the tree-tops" above "miles and miles of forest greenery" such that those who stopped off could "fill your cup of satisfaction to the brim." One can hardly imagine how, in 1915, almost two hundred thousand passengers rode the line and passed through Kaleva.[9]

The same civic faith in books and shared learning—captured in Kaleva's marker, its branch library, and the rail line's lyrical invitation—echoes on a smaller, more personal scale in the school libraries where many writers first discover the quiet power of a room full of stories. The little library at Will Rogers Elementary School on Fenton Avenue in Redford Township was an endless delight to one young and earnest reader. The school opened in 1956 just prior to his attending kindergarten, its mid-century modern features reminding him of the Kenner girder and panel building toy set he enjoyed at home. The boy found a second home in a room full of books that could be taken out at no charge, even the same one repeatedly.

The Snow Branch Library in Dearborn was a field of dreams in the 1960s for a lad raised to read. Set on busy Telegraph Road, the roar of whose traffic was irrelevant to the boy, the library seemed as big inside as Tiger Stadium but crammed with infinite volumes he wanted to explore. Each book represented an adventure, a promise of escape and wisdom born of vicarious experience. The limit on books that could be checked out on one visit was four—and that was the number he faithfully took home each time.

The new library that opened at Haigh School in fourth grade for one of your authors was a revelation. It replaced an older cramped 1950s version of a library. The new library—the most luxurious set of rooms in the school—with its beautiful carpeting, sleek modern furniture, and spacious setting, situated at the very heart of the school, was meant as a signal to the students about the central place of books in the life of an educated person. He can remember no happier times from his boyhood than when he was free to explore the shelves of this well-appointed library, to seek a book that would expand his life and take him to realms yet unexplored.

Areas of Outstanding Natural Beauty

It seems only fitting and proper that a guidebook on the writing dens of Michigan's authors under the pen of one of Michigan's natural and freshwater resource advocates should feature the most iconic and astonishing places—and these peninsulas have so many—near each. Such a list ought to be seasonal: fall's brilliancy is a feature making the long weeks after summer a favorite for many. Here, then, is our attempt at listing one for each of the principal locations for some of those writers, in alphabetical/geographical order, with pithy explanation.

Big Bay—John Voelker

In the town of that name is the Lumberjack Tavern that featured so prominently in *Anatomy of a Murder*. It's still a tourist attraction near the shores of Lake Independence and the bay, a true indication of the lasting power of good writing since an hour's round-trip drive is required from Marquette and the friendly confines of US-41. Other attractions are worth investigating—some of human origin—but relying on a different route for one of the legs over County Roads like 510 and AAA takes one to the Thomas Rock Scenic Overlook, Yellow Dog River and waterfall, a 1928 tower looking out over the Huron Mountains (and Michigan's tallest peak, Mt. Arvon), with the aptly named McCormick Wilderness to the south. The area at the mouth of the Huron River is one of the most naturally scenic shorelines on the peninsula. The North Country Trail skirts the southern edge.

Black River—Liberty Hyde Bailey

Not far from the house museum enshrining Hyde's legacy, terminating below the barn-red South Haven Lighthouse, this organic-hued waterway forks into smaller streams that trickle past orchards, tree lots, and prairie fens, a demonstration of the natural and cultivated beauty of the southwestern Lower Peninsula.

Bow in the Clouds Natural Area—Bessie Ray Hoover

Within the northeast corner of the Kalamazoo city limits, about five miles from Hoover's place on South Rose, is this nature preserve deriving its name from the Bible—the book of Genesis 9:13—where God set a "bow in the clouds" as the sign of a covenant relationship with humanity and the earth. Designed as a means for people to encounter something of the holy in the natural world, it is now cared for by the Southwest Michigan Land Conservancy. Sixty wild acres are accessed via trails and a boardwalk traversing a pristine stream, spring-fed wetland, sedge meadow, cattail marsh, wet meadow, shrub-carr, and swamp forest. It can be found north of Gull Road (M-43) along Nazareth Road.

Crystal Lake—Charles Bruce Catton, Sara Gwendolyn Frostic

Both authors made the south shore of this clear body of water their home base, near to the hopeful town of Benzonia—a name intended to convey the pure air breathable by all living things. The Betsie River flows past Frostic's studio, now a National Historic Site, reachable via the River Road, otherwise known as M-115, into the lake of the same name and an iconic Lake Michigan lighthouse. Road signs convey much, here as anywhere, with M-22 at its midway point between Manistee and the Leelanau Peninsula.

De Tour Township—John Tobin Nevill

At the extreme eastern tip of the upper state is the turning point for the shipping channel connecting Lake Huron and the St. Mary's River, across from expansive Drummond Island, with the DeTour Reef Light nearby. Nevill moved here from Detroit, compelled by the landscape.

Detroit River International Wildlife Refuge—George Matthew Adams, Donald Joseph Goines, Edgar Albert Guest, Dudley Felker Randall, Orlando Bolivar Willcox

Before it became the Motor City, Motown, the Motor Capital of the World—and prior iterations as seed and sewing machine manufacturing center—the environs along the strait across from Canada were devoid of concrete, skyscrapers, and grit, instead festooned with natural assets that made it a perfect habitat for permanent and migratory wildlife. Like pearls in a strand, units of North America's only international refuge dot the Michigan shoreline from Mud and Grassy Islands to Humbug Marsh and into Monroe County. All five authors benefitted from the river's proximity.

East Lansing—Liberty Hyde Bailey, Ray Stannard Baker, Emma Shore Thornton, Glendon Swarthout

The W. J. Beal Botanical Garden, Lewis Landscape Arboretum, and Horticulture Gardens on the campus of Michigan State University consist of numerous beautifully diverse acres representative of the natural plant environment that sets Michigan apart. These four authors plied the school's paths along the Red Cedar River.

Grand River—William McKendree Carleton, Holling Clancy Holling, Della Thompson Lutes, Maritta Wolff, Constance Maybury Rourke

The longest Michigan river commences in Hillsdale County near the state's southern boundary and terminates at Grand Haven on Lake Michigan. It gave its name to Grand Rapids, a paralleling street in Lansing, a main street in Detroit, and at other locations. In Jackson County, it is but a creek that helps drain the fertile soils of the former prairie that remained during the lives of these writers.

Grand Traverse Region—Harold Titus, Eugene Ruggles, James Beardsley Hendryx

The cherry orchards that have historically dominated the region still provide its identity. Nestled along shorelines with rolling hills and vistas that provide inspirational looks at fresh water's spiritual refreshment, the region continues to draw visitors, new residents, and writers such as these three.

Galien River watershed (Harbert, Chikaming Township)—Carl Sandburg

The Galien River watershed commingles along the white-sand beaches of Southwest Michigan that the poet once walked. Paralleling its route via the Red Arrow Highway, Kruger, Lakeside, Elm Valley, and Three Oaks roads to Indian Trail leads into an interior replete with farm fields, vineyards, vistas, and beech-maple forested land.

Huron River (Ann Arbor)—Robert Frost, Robert Hayden, Jane Kenyon, Ross Macdonald, Arthur Miller, Allan John Braitwaite Seager

As if hugging the metropolis that is Southeastern Michigan, this river originates in Oakland County, gains strength in Livingston County, makes a sharp turn toward Lake Erie in Washtenaw County, traverses Wayne County, and finally terminates in Monroe County—as if designed for this very purpose. Its beauty is obvious in the centers of Dexter, Ann Arbor, Ypsilanti, Belleville, Flat Rock, and Rockwood, as it provides tranquil and boisterous capabilities via walking paths, kayaking, canoeing, fishing, and bicycling. A favorite stretch for a fall drive begins where M-14 meets West Huron River Drive on the outskirts of downtown Ann Arbor, for the two-lane road parallels the waterway, crossing back and over, providing prime viewing of the forested, rocky route. More than university experiences have drawn writers such as these five.

Lake Superior—Carroll Watson Rankin

Practically any location along the over-nine-hundred-mile Michigan shoreline of this immense freshwater lake is worth a visit, with breathtaking vistas, massive dunes, rocky escarpments, sandy beaches, and radiant nighttime skies that feature the Aurora Borealis in all its magnificence. It has never lost its influence on the experiences of residents, as Rankin exemplified.

Muskegon River—Russell Amos Kirk, Julia Ann Moore

The peaceful river winds a rural way for over two hundred miles through seven counties, from Houghton Lake until reaching the lake and town on Lake Michigan to which it lends its name. It is accessible by motor vehicle at a number of places (Big Rapids, Croton, Evart, Hersey, and Newaygo). A tributary, Clam River, is also worth exploring. The main river, city, and lake draw original identity from the Indigenous peoples who pinned "Masquignon" for its marshy character. From its cutover spaces both profound (Kirk) and popular (Moore) literature sprang.

Pigeon River Country—Ernest Hemingway

Dubbed "The Big Wild" when it was assembled in the 1920s and 1930s by conservationist P. S. Lovejoy, the Pigeon River Country is a state of mind as well as a place in the natural world of the northern Lower Peninsula. As the Michigan Department of Natural Resources notes, at 107,600 acres, Pigeon River Country is "the largest block of contiguous undeveloped land in Michigan's Lower Peninsula—12 miles wide and 20 miles long—half the size of New York City." It is also the place where Ernest Hemingway fished, calling it "wild as the devil." An elk herd of more than one thousand animals, growing from seven Rocky Mountain elk imported in 1918 to replace the extirpated original Michigan population, attracts tourists and hunters alike.

Saginaw Bay watershed—Theodore Huebner Roethke

The largest watershed in Michigan, occupying 5.5 million acres in twenty-two of Michigan's eighty-three counties, Saginaw Bay's lands and feeder streams provide fertile soil for agriculture and countless wetlands that support fish and wildlife. The vast watershed is a favorite for many duck hunters. One of the wetlands in the watershed provided the soil wealth for the Roethke family nursery.

Shiawassee River—James Oliver Curwood

The Shiawassee is a sub-watershed of the Saginaw Bay watershed and offers excellent small-mouth bass fishing; great birding, kayaking, and canoeing; and mature forests that line 80 percent of the water trail's banks. Already seriously polluted in the early 1900s, the decline of the river spurred a lament from author Curwood, whose castle overlooked a bend of the river in Owosso. PCB contamination added to the river's woes in the 1960s and 1970s, but recent cleanup efforts offer hope of a long-term river recovery.

St. Clair Flats—Mary Frances Doner

Some twenty-five thousand acres comprise the world's largest freshwater coastal marsh in the delta of the St. Clair River. The flats provide critical habitat for migratory waterfowl, wading birds, sport and forage fish, muskrats, and other aquatic life. Doner was captivated and wrote about wintertime along this "Blue River. Under that ice it flowed—endomed yet living, breathing; a core of beauty."[1]

St. Joseph River—Ringgold Wilmer Lardner

One of Michigan's longest rivers, the St. Joseph drops over five hundred feet on its zigzag course toward Lake Michigan. Despite intensive agriculture use in several reaches, the watershed maintains generally good water quality. Indigenous peoples have resided in the watershed for thousands of years. A sixty-seven-mile Water Trail from Niles to the mouth of the St. Joseph provides exercise for canoeists and kayakers. Many segments of the river seem far removed from the fast pace of daily life that Lardner satirized.

Straits of Mackinac—Frances Margaret Fox

Linking Lakes Michigan and Huron, the 3.5-mile-long straits provide magnificent views but also serve as the graveyard for more than twenty-two vessels. Today, the straits are busy channels of commerce for modern freighters. Spanning the straits is the more than five-mile-long Mackinac Bridge, opened in 1957. To the east is, according to Fox, "the most beautiful island in all North America."[2] The straits boast an abundance of fish, and their flanks harbor several threatened plant species. Wilderness and Straits State Parks provide camping sites from which to enjoy the cooling summer breezes of the straits.

Upper Peninsula—Nevill, Rankin, Voelker

It's in a category all its own, this ten-million-acre world with its "Fisherman's Pond," whose location Voelker never disclosed. In 2025, a national publication named it number one among the ten best U.S. destinations for fall foliage—a distinction earned since 2018. With millions of acres of forest abutting the shores of three Great Lakes, "changing leaves are the main event" viewable over "10 fall color routes that cover a total of nearly 1,500 miles."[3] Those drives include

- 107th Engineers Memorial Highway, Silver City to Lake of the Clouds
- M-26 along the shores of Lake Roland and past Copper Country State Forest
- Adams Trail, H-58 from Munising to Grand Marais
- Black River National Forest Scenic Byway near Bessemer
- Brockway Mountain Drive on the Keweenaw Peninsula
- Copper Country Trail National Scenic Byway, also on the Keweenaw
- Curtis/Curly Lewis Memorial Highway from near Paradise to Sault Ste. Marie
- Iron County Heritage Trail between Crystal Falls and Iron River
- M-28 from Marquette to Munising
- Marshland Wildlife Drive near Seney
- U.S. 2 Top of the Lake Scenic Byway from St. Ignace to Manistique
- Western Shoreline Drive from Eagle Harbor to Silver City
- Whitefish Bay National Forest Scenic Byway

According to the Upper Peninsula Travel and Recreation Association's promotional website,[4] the U.P.—with 27 percent of Michigan's land base and 3 percent of its population—holds these features:

- 85 percent of its 16,538 square miles are forested
- 4,300 inland lakes
- 12,000 miles of streams
- 1,700 miles of shoreline on three Great Lakes
- All but two of Michigan's more than 200 waterfalls

A word about that last item: no matter the month, waterfalls present enjoyment. In winter, when largely frozen, they exhibit a stark beauty that contrasts with the free flow during spring. In fall, fringed by colors, or in summer, with the generous variety of greens abounding, they also merit a visit.

It is within the friendly confines of this land mass that one may most easily and frequently view the northern lights. In May 2024, however, the aurora borealis became visible on more than one night in areas beyond Michigan's southern border. For those in Michigan's region farthest from the North Pole, being able to look up into the night sky on their street, in their neighborhood, or out a few miles on a country road proved another great aspect to living in the Great Lakes State.

Combatting light pollution and inspiring non-aurora patronage of the sky, Michigan recently has become home to "dark" parks where the beauty of nature can be experienced in a very special way. A growing number of such sites exist as of the middle of 2024, restoring to the modern generations an experience commonplace up until the late 1800s. In the 1990s, the state became the first in the nation to designate a public land tract for this express purpose.

Beaver Island State Wildlife Research Area International Dark Sky Sanctuary: on Beaver Island in Lake Michigan, within Charlevoix County, encompassing 9,195.5 acres within the Wildlife Research Area and an additional 230 acres at Miller's Marsh; designated in 2024.

Headlands International Dark Sky Park: in Emmett County, containing approximately 550 acres of pristine woodlands and more than two miles of undeveloped Lake Michigan shoreline; designated in 2011, among the first ten International Dark Sky Parks in the world.

Keweenaw Dark Sky Park: located at the tip of the Keweenaw Peninsula and surrounded by Lake Superior on three sides, the park is headquartered at the Keweenaw Mountain Lodge; designated in 2022.

Lake Hudson State Recreation Area: a public recreation area located in southwestern Lenawee County, the park was established in 1979 encompassing nearly 2,800 acres. It is recognized as the first dark sky preserve in the Michigan park system; designated as such in 1993.

Dr. T. K. Lawless Park: in Cass County, including inland lakes and streams, received its name from physician Dr. Theodore Kenneth Lawless, MD, who posthumously deeded 850 acres to the county in 1971; designated in 2019.

Negwegon State Park: this rustic four-thousand-acre park features eight miles of Lake Huron lakeshore and is home to a designated dark sky preserve north of Black River in Alcona County.

Port Crescent State Park: just west of Port Austin on Michigan's Thumb in Huron County, the 640-acre park includes three miles of sandy Lake Huron shoreline, providing sunset viewing across Saginaw Bay, and features a dark sky preserve.

Rockport Recreation Area: on the border between Presque Isle and Alpena County, the more-than-four-thousand-acre park stretches along the Lake Huron shoreline and is home to a designated dark sky preserve.

Thompson's Harbor State Park: also in Presque Isle County along the Lake Huron shoreline, the five-thousand-acre park is also home to a designated dark sky preserve.

Wilderness State Park: Emmet County's second dark sky preserve is within the nearly thirteen thousand acres of this northwestern Lower Peninsula gem. With many miles of Lake Michigan shoreline and, as its name connotes, much wild and untamed space, the site stretches to the lighthouse at Waugoshance Island. Its beaches serve as habitat for the federally endangered Piping Plover.

Historical Sites and Things

Michigan's rich history encompasses the written word in many forms. The first Capitol housed a library after its completion in 1828. An 1851 report by the Smithsonian Institution listed public libraries in Albion at the Wesleyan College (700 volumes) and at the University of Michigan in Ann Arbor (5,000), the State Library in Lansing (4,400), the Monroe Public Library (1,500), the Central College in Spring Arbor (1,600), and two in Detroit—the St. Philips College (3,000) and Young Men's Society (1,815). It also reported nearly 3,300 volumes in seventy-four school district libraries and 43,926 volumes held in three hundred township libraries.[1] This heritage expanded over succeeding decades.

Ladies' Literary Clubs

In the era before suffrage, women bonded together to foster reading and knowledge of good literature through clubs, societies, and associations where they could govern and staff and become patrons. In some Michigan communities, women were prime movers in launching a public library, which would be open to female and youth patrons as well as males. A few of the women's organizations continue to exist. The sites of all, gone or not, deserve no longer to be "a forgotten part of Michigan history."[2]

Ladies Literary Clubs were found all the way from Allegan County to Hart to Lexington to Pontiac to Rochester to Stanton to Zeeland. When the governor helped dedicate the new facility of the Ladies' Library Association of Flint in June 1868, he praised the group as the first of its kind organized in the state.[3] Only eight years later, twenty-six clubs were recorded from Adrian to Ypsilanti.[4] State history signage marks sites in Dryden, Grand Rapids, Henika, Nashville, Traverse City, and Ypsilanti.[5]

Bronson (Branch County)

The Carnegie library on N. Matteson Street has its roots in the work of the Ladies' Library Association in the early 1880s. Bronson Township took responsibility for library operation in 1888, leading to the Carnegie grant in the early 1900s.

Cadillac (Wexford County)

The structure at 127 Beech Street, a block east of Business US-131, now the Wexford County Historical Society Museum, had its origins with a local women's group known as the Penelopean Society. In the late 1800s, members of the society purchased a number of books and launched a society library. In April 1897, a meeting in the Cummer Opera House resulted in forming an association to promote and maintain a public library. Although the name adopted was the Ladies' Library Association, over one-third of the stockholders were men. The purpose of the association was "the maintenance, enlargement and use of a library of such character as will conduce to advancement of its members socially, mentally and morally." Constructed with the support of an Andrew Carnegie grant, this Classical Revival–style building was completed in 1906.[6]

Dryden (Lapeer County)

Today, the sign on the building at 5480 Main Street says "Dryden Township Library." The Michigan Historical Marker on the face contains this text:

> The Ladies' Library Association was established in 1871 to provide reading material at a small cost to the community. In the beginning the association only allowed married women to be members and charged an annual fee of one dollar. The women of the association were also involved in charitable works, such as giving aid to Northern Michigan victims of fire in 1881. The association built this Italianate structure in 1885 for fifteen hundred dollars. The first floor contained the library, dining room and kitchen. The second floor hall, which includes a stage, continues to be used for plays and

community meetings. Dryden Township accepted the building in 1974 and made it the public library.

Farwell (Clare County)

In 1872, the Ladies' Library Association was organized in this town. Several years later, it received a donation of land for a library structure. People in the community contributed their labor and material as well as books to launch the facility. The building was completed in January 1883. It became the Surrey Township Library until a new facility was completed in 1975; soon after, it became the home of the local historical society. Located at 221 West Main Street, the narrow white frame structure with light aquamarine trim was listed on the State Register of Historic Sites in 1979.

Grand Rapids (Kent County)

The Ladies' Literary Club, also known as the Wednesday Literary Club, constructed a building in 1887 to serve as a social gathering point in Grand Rapids. The Ladies' Literary Association formally organized in 1870 and became the club in 1882. The Richardsonian Romanesque–style building still exists, located at 61 Sheldon Street SE, housing the Ryerson Library. It was listed on the National Register of Historic Places in 1971.

Hartford (Van Buren County)

Located at 15 Franklin Street a block south of Main, this Federal-style facility was originally the residence of Jennie Phelps Merriman and her husband George. After their deaths, the Hartford Ladies' Association was invited to move in and make it a permanent library facility after having occupied several locations after it first opened in 1895. In 1925, the Jennie Merriman Memorial Library opened to the public, commemorated by a plaque on the front of the building. It was the Hartford Public Library until August 2020 when sold to become a private residence. It was listed on the State Register of Historic Sites in 1980.

Henika (Allegan County)

The involvement of the local Ladies' Library Association in the community's literacy is commemorated by the Michigan Historical Marker at 149 S. Main Street in Wayland. The marker text places the structure within the Richardson Romanesque style, with the stonework sourced from a nearby farm field.

Holland (Ottawa County)

Inscribed above its main door, a stone edifice at 235 Central Avenue proclaims the structure as a home for the "Woman's Literary Club." The Woman's Literary Club was organized in 1898 by Anna Coatsworth Post, who called together the first Reading Circle. The club continues to exist as of 2021, and its Facebook page states, in part: "We are an association of women, organized in 1898, who value knowledge. We meet together to expand our knowledge as well as our horizons through literature, art, music, theater, and current topics."

Jonesville (Hillsdale County)

Ladies from two reading clubs organized the Jonesville Library on November 20, 1874, donated some fifty volumes, and called it the "Ladies' Library Association." The building at 310 Church Street, opened in 1899 with eighty-six patrons, still serves the community. Board members served as librarians and custodians without pay. Now a district library, it celebrated its sesquicentennial in 2024.

Kalamazoo (Kalamazoo County)

Located at 333 South Park Street, this 1879 structure was the first in the nation erected for use of a women's club as proclaimed by the title of the Michigan Historical Marker on site. The Ladies' Library Association, started in 1844 and organized in 1852, was the first in Michigan and the third in the United States. According to the marker text, Mrs. Lucinda H. Stone, known as the

"Mother of Women's Clubs," helped found this chapter. The front face contains an embedded stone identifying the structure as "Ladies' Library." It was listed on the State Register in 1961 and the National Register of Historic Places in 1970 (SAH).

Manistee (Manistee County)

Located at 95 Maple Street, the 1996 Michigan Historical Marker out front states:

> In 1885 a group of Manistee Ladies formed the Lakeside Club, whose primary goal was to create a library. In 1902 the club joined forces with the local literary society and successfully campaigned for a public library. The Andrew Carnegie Foundation funded the construction. The Manistee City Library opened in 1905. Designed by Port Huron architect George L. Harvey, the building, with its grand entrance pavilion, reflects Beaux Arts Classicism. The library is listed in the National Register of Historic Places.

Marlette (Sanilac County)

At 3116 Main Street is the Marlette District Library, whose website offers "We are proud to serve the Heart of the Thumb community! You will find our library to be friendly, cozy, and knowledgeable." This is where, according to the Michigan Historical Marker out front, "the Marlette Research Club, composed of women in the community," determined to build a public library in 1914. They succeeded in their campaign, and the building was constructed in 1921. Of classical design with a hipped roof, the elegantly simple structure symbolizes the end of the Carnegie grant project—it was the second to last in the nation to receive such support. Also displayed on its grounds is an 1859 artillery piece cast at the Tredegar Iron Works in Richmond, Virginia, that was deployed at Fortress Monroe on the James Peninsula on Chesapeake Bay. This artifact thus is connected to a great moment in the struggle for human freedom, for at this location in 1861, a Union General instituted a policy to refuse slaveholders' demands for the return of escaped enslaved persons—what became known during the Civil War as the "contraband" policy. The local chapter of the veterans' organization (Grand Army of the Republic) brought the cannon to the town in 1899.

Muskegon (Muskegon County)

The capstone above the wide doorway at 280 West Webster Avenue portrays a monogram with the letters "MWC." This insignia connotes its original identity as the Michigan Historical Marker validates:

> The Muskegon Woman's Club was founded in 1890, and dedicated to the intellectual 'improvement and development' of women. The Chicago firm of Weir and Perry designed this Neoclassical structure, built in 1902 with funds donated by Minnie Smith, the widow of Muskegon attorney Francis Smith. The club lobbied the city to hire the first policewoman, held performances, and worked with charitable groups such as the Red Cross and the Council of National Defense.

The marker's focus on the Illinois architects disappoints in terms of the literary legacy fostered here, but on the corner of the building, a metal sign giving the name of the organization with the image of a volume inscribed with "Books" completes the story.

Nashville (Barry County)

According to the Michigan Historical Marker on the structure at 327 North Main Street (M-66), which today bears a sign as the "Putnam Public Library," the history here is:

> Built in 1884–85, this red-bricked Italianate structure was the home of Charles W. and Agnes Putnam. Mr. Putnam was a hardware merchant and a banker; Mrs. Putnam taught music and was the first public school teacher in Nashville. Around the turn of the century, the Putnams hosted many elegant social events here. In 1921 they willed their home to Nashville for use as a public library. They established a ten-thousand-dollar trust fund to begin its operation. The Women's Literary Club launched the library in 1923.

Pontiac (Oakland County)

Hanna C. Farnham Stout was a founding member and first president of the local LLA, which opened a public facility in rented space downtown on Lawrence Street in the Gazette building in the 1880s. She died in 1892, age thirty-nine, and was buried in Oak Hill Cemetery. Her husband Byron, a State legislator and U.S. Congressman, died in 1896. Their bequests helped fund a new facility (named the State Memorial Library), which opened in 1898. Located at 45 Williams Street at West Lawrence, with signage from the MotorCities National Heritage Area, the hen-and-chicks-style building, made of brick and stone, continues its service as an arts center. It was listed on the State Register of Historic Sites in 1979.

Royal Oak (Oakland County)

"Organized 1902" says a sign on the property at 404 South Pleasant Street. The Michigan Historical Marker entitled "Royal Oak Woman's Club" states:

> Erected in 1839, this building was originally a small frame Baptist church. The village purchased it for a town hall in 1914 and used it for municipal purposes until 1923, when the Royal Oak Woman's Club acquired it. The club, founded in 1902 as a women's study group, has relocated the structure twice. In 1923 when the building was remodeled as a Tudor-style structure, a cobblestone fireplace was installed. This is the oldest building in the city of Royal Oak.

Schoolcraft (Kalamazoo County)

At 163 North Hayward Street, next to the post office remains a brick-gabled one-story structure constructed in 1896. It was listed on the State Register of Historic Sites in 1996. The Ladies' Library Association, founded in 1879, has been at this site since the building opened and remains in existence.

South Haven (Van Buren County)

At 652 Phoenix Street (Business I-196) sits a structure more than a century old. The Michigan Historical Marker on the Pearl Street side, entitled "Scott Club," says:

> This federated women's club, founded as a reading circle in 1883 and named for Sir Walter Scott, merged with the Literary and Antiquarian Societies to build a clubhouse in 1892. John Cornelius Randall designed the sandstone Queen Anne structure, built by local artisans and completed in 1893. Two stained glass windows created in Austria portray Sir Walter Scott and Henry Wadsworth Longfellow. This building has been in continuous use by the Scott Club as a cultural center providing fellowship for women of the area.

The site was listed in the State Register in 1980 and the marker placed in 1982.

Traverse City (Grand Traverse County)

According to the Michigan Historical Marker at 216 Cass Avenue, eight women organized the Ladies' Library Association in this community in 1869. In 1878, the association purchased its first building at 205 East Front Street. In 1909, the association sold that building and retained an architect and contractor to build this structure. The cornerstone and time capsule were put in place on July 23, 1909. The building was used as a library until 1949 and served the city until 1983. In 1986, it was renovated for commercial use.

Vicksburg (Kalamazoo County)

The address of the district library in this town is 215 South Michigan Avenue. Around the corner, at 120 West Maple Street, is the original Fanny M. Bair Library building. The Michigan Historical Marker reports that Ms. Bair "built this library and presented it to the Ladies' Library Association on November 21, 1902. Charles A. Fairchild of Kalamazoo designed the building with 'modern conveniences' like electric lighting and running water. The Ladies'

Library Association administered the library until ownership was transferred to the village of Vicksburg in 1948."

Ypsilanti (Washtenaw County)

The Ladies' Literary Club building at 218 North Washington Street was originally a private home, thus alternatively known as the William M. Davis House or the Arden H. Ballard House. The Ladies' Literary Club, founded in 1878, purchased the Greek Revival structure to use as their gathering location in 1913. It was listed on the National Register of Historic Places in 1972.

Although not necessarily the work of an association, a number of libraries trace their origins to the efforts of the community's females. The Mackinaw Area Public Library began in 1912 when a women's study group began to meet. A couple of years later, the group became the Mackinaw Woman's Club, and one year after that, a library was launched in the Clubhouse. The library, located at 528 W. Central Avenue in Mackinaw City with branches in Bliss and Pellston, celebrated its centennial in 2015.

State Markers

According to an online database, Michigan is home to six thousand historical markers—by which is meant a sign or monument of some sort that informs about a person, place, or event. Some are "official" Michigan markers; some are erected by local historical societies; some are sponsored by families, individuals, and other entities. Quite a number are related to writing, publishing, and books. A number have been cited in this text.

The Michigan Historic Marker program assumed official statewide status with the enactment of legislation in 1955, but its roots stretch back at least to 1917. A month after America entered World War I, Public Act 279 authorized Michigan county governments to appropriate up to $200 per annum "for the purpose of marking of historical places" and "for the erection of monuments or other memorials in commemoration of notable events." In 1931, the Michigan Historical Commission undertook and published a "preliminary survey" of markers erected around the state by "patriotic, state, and civic bodies, business organizations, clubs, and individuals." The commission recommended considering "accessibility" to "passersby" given "present-day arteries of travel." Book-related markers were included, such as the site of the first bookshop in Grand Rapids (dating to 1836), and for writers and their works, such as "Author Elizabeth Margaret Chandler 1807–1834" in Lenawee County and for the inspiration for "Anne" by Constance Fenimore Woolson on Mackinac Island.[7]

The concept that tourists would undertake travels to view such sites is, then, decades old. Soon after the 1955 act took effect, the commission published a guide to aid the traveler "driving through the state" over its "modern highways."[8] The most recent legislative changes to the State marker program in 2002 and 2017 expressly link heritage and travel with a stated official purpose to "enhance cultural tourism in this state by encouraging residents and visitors to investigate historic resources and this state's heritage sites." The 2017 legislation represented a recodification of the program along with honoring a champion of state history, John B. Swainson, forty-second governor. Markers, history, inspiration, writing, tourism, and state publications long have been and remain bundled.

Raggle-Taggle

This series of books endeavors to reveal the literary heritage of Michigan. The purpose of this section is to list some nationally or world-renowned authors who incidentally touched on Michigan in an interesting and perhaps lesser-known way and, therefore, perhaps do not justify a chapter. Plus one.

Gatsby, the Green Light, and Michigan

A piercing look into the American dream of wealth and false glory, F. Scott Fitzgerald's *The Great Gatsby* seems at first glance to be as far from the Upper Peninsula of Michigan as the novel's primary setting, the haunts of the rich on Long Island. But one scholar contends there is a direct geographic link between the two and between them and Gatsby's doomed longing for the embodiment of his romantic dreams, Daisy Buchanan.[1]

First-person narrator Nick Carraway, privy to Gatsby's life story of humble beginnings and later, fabulous wealth, reports that his friend spent time in early manhood as a clam-digger and salmon fisher on Lake Superior. Adrift in life (and known by his birth name, James Gatz), he finds his destiny when the self-made millionaire Dan Cody's yacht drops anchor in Little Girl Bay. This could be a renaming of Little Girls Point, on the far west end of Michigan's U.P.

The commencement of the Cody-Gatz relationship is immediate: "To young Gatz, resting on his oars and looking up at the railed deck, that yacht represented all the beauty and glamor in the world." Cody quickly takes a liking to the young Gatz, finding "that he was quick and extravagantly ambitious."[2] He takes the young man aboard, brings him to Duluth, and buys him a blue coat, six pairs of white duck trousers, and yachting cap. From there they make their way to the West Indies and the Barbary Coast. This launches Gatz (who has renamed himself Jay Gatsby) toward his ultimate destination in life, a member of the *noveau riche*, seeking to reclaim Daisy, who has married into old wealth.

The significance of Little Girl Bay is that it appears to be more than randomly selected for its evocative name, or perhaps Fitzgerald was unconsciously channeling its origins in a purported Native American tale. The story is *Leelinau, or The Lost Daughter*, said to have been told to Henry Schoolcraft by his Indigenous wife, Jane Schoolcraft, or Bamewawagezhikaquay.

The Lost Daughter spurns an arranged marriage with a member of her tribe in favor of a fairy lover. She occasionally appears as a moonlit figure on the shores of the bay, fleeing when observed by those who pass in the water, protected by her lover's green plumes.

The link is tightened by the birth name of Gatsby's object of longing, Daisy Buchanan, known before marriage as Daisy Fay, or fairy. Gatsby looks across the water from his West Egg mansion at a green light that signifies her and the culmination of his longings, which he finds empty when realized.

Whether the connection is genuine or not, Little Girls Point is. It is a favorite of agate hunters and picknickers. Its shores offer a majestic view of Superior and sometimes the faraway Apostle Islands and Porcupine Mountains, the representation of so many dreams.

James Fenimore Cooper's *Oak Openings*

Cooper's 1848 *Oak Openings* is more than the title of a novel—it is the name for a nearly vanished landscape that once occupied 7 percent of Michigan.

The immediate successor to Cooper's *Leatherstocking Tales*, *The Oak Openings; or, The Bee Hunter* concerns bee-hunter Benjamin Boden, whose nickname is Ben Buzz, and the encroachment of settlers on the ancestral homes of the Indigenous. Cooper describes the landscape:

> Although wooded, it was not as the American forest is wont to grow, with tall straight trees towering towards the light, but with intervals between the low oaks that were scattered profusely over the view, and with much of that air of negligence that one is apt to see in grounds, where art is made to assume the character of nature. The trees, with very few exceptions, were what is called the "burr oak," a small variety of a very extensive genus; and the spaces between them, always irregular, and often of singular beauty, have obtained

> the name of "openings;" the two terms combined giving their appellation to this particular species of native forest, under the name of "Oak Openings."
>
> These woods, so peculiar to certain districts of country, are not altogether without some variety, though possessing a general character of sameness. The trees were of very uniform size, being little taller than pear-trees, which they resemble a good deal in form; and having trunks that rarely attain two feet in diameter. . . . The grasses are supposed to be owing to the fires lighted periodically by the Indians in order to clear their hunting-grounds.[3]

Settlers described oak openings as park-like savannas of widely spaced mature oaks whose canopy covered approximately 10 to 60 percent of the savanna area. They found the oak openings particularly favorable. Towns, college parks, and cemeteries were established on former oak savannas. Oak openings lent themselves to agriculture, including crops, livestock, and timber harvest. The end of periodic natural burns and controlled burning by Indigenous people dramatically changed oak savannas to closed-canopy oak forests.

According to Michigan State University's Michigan Natural Features Inventory, oak openings have almost been eliminated and are known only from historical literature and data derived from severely disturbed sites.[4] Total Michigan oak openings have declined from an estimated nine hundred thousand acres to just three acres.

Herman Melville, the Great Lakes, and *Moby Dick*

The raging ocean is a virtual character in Herman Melville's 1851 classic, but within its covers, the author compares the power of the five inland seas to any salt waters:

> For in their interflowing aggregate, those grand fresh-water seas of ours,—Erie, and Ontario, and Huron, and Superior, and Michigan,—possess an ocean-like expansiveness, with many of the ocean's noblest traits; with many of its rimmed varieties of races and of climes. They contain round archipelagoes of romantic isles, even as the Polynesian waters do; in large part, are shored by two great contrasting nations, as the Atlantic is; they furnish long maritime approaches to our numerous territorial colonies from

> the East, dotted all round their banks; here and there are frowned upon by batteries, and by the goat-like craggy guns of lofty Mackinaw; they have heard the fleet thunderings of naval victories . . . for leagues and leagues are flanked by ancient and unentered forests, where the gaunt pines stand like serried lines of kings in Gothic genealogies; those same woods harboring wild Afric beasts of prey, and silken creatures whose exported furs give robes to Tartar Emperors; they mirror the paved capitals of Buffalo and Cleveland, as well as Winnebago villages; they float alike the full-rigged merchant ship, the armed cruiser of the State, the steamer, and the beech canoe; they are swept by Borean and dismasting blasts as direful as any that lash the salted wave; they know what shipwrecks are, for out of sight of land, however inland, they have drowned full many a midnight ship with all its shrieking crew.[5]

Melville's knowledge of the Great Lakes may have been based on more than hearsay. It is possible he voyaged in 1840 from New York to Chicago on the Great Lakes to reach what was then the Western frontier. But the evidence is ambiguous. It is known, however, that he spent a portion of the summer of 1840 in Galena, Illinois, visiting his uncle.

Melville visited Detroit at least once. In 1857–1858, to supplement his income, Melville joined the Midwest lecture circuit. He lectured on Roman statuary in Detroit in January 1858, observing that "among the higher emotions is a feeling for art, and this exists wherever there is beauty and grandeur."[6]

Of the River and the Trees

Yet another Hemingway item is appropriate with an August 2024 theatrical release based on his novel *Across the River and into the Trees*. The 1950 book may have been Hemingway's worst; it received almost universally negative reviews upon release. The movie may have done better during the 125th anniversary of his birth and the centennial year of perhaps his greatest short story.

A high school English teacher once said a little dismissively, "Everyone goes through a Hemingway phase." She was a big fan neither of Ernest Hemingway's macho bluster nor of his revolutionary—and easily satirized—writing style. She thought Hemingway's work was best enjoyed by adolescent males. Had she adequately considered, though, *Big Two-Hearted River*? Full of foreboding, the story concludes hopefully: "The river just showed through the trees. There were plenty of days coming when he could fish the swamp."

The story's river and the real-life river are different watercourses, the source of a misunderstanding that continues to this day. Hemingway was writing about the nearby Fox River but liked the Two-Hearted name and appropriated it for his story. The real Two-Hearted River is worthy of its own literature.[7] Clean and cool, it flows largely unvexed to Lake Superior in a little developed watershed.

The genesis of Hemingway's story is his state of mind and soul upon his return from the European front during World War I. He sustained serious wounds as an ambulance driver and recuperated for months in hospitals. Like many war veterans, he found his psychic wounds took longer to heal; they may never have done so.

In *Big Two-Hearted River*, after returning from war a hollowed-out man, Nick travels by train to Seney in the eastern Upper Peninsula, disembarks, and tramps through country recently ravaged by fire—not unlike the ruins of a battlefield. The close-up, small details of nature—a stream swirling with trout, a kingfisher, a grasshopper—capture his attention. As the hours pass, his spirit gradually renews. Detached from human company, Nick finds a growing contentment in a simple camp and hours of fishing. Hemingway's descriptive detail and rhythmic cadence render Nick's experience as if it were the reader's own.

The story was hailed as something utterly new and its influence lingers. "A century on, *Big Two-Hearted River* has helped shape language and literature in America and around the world," says author John Maclean, whose father Norman wrote his own paean to a river, *A River Runs Through It*. Which is why there are numerous centennial editions of the story in 2024.[8]

If there is any doubt of the influence of Northern Michigan landscapes in forming Hemingway's writing aesthetic, this deleted passage from *Big Two-Hearted River* dispels it:

> He wanted to write about country so it would be there like Cezanne had done it in painting. You had to do it from inside yourself. . . . He felt almost holy about it. It was deadly serious. You could do it if you would fight it out. If you'd lived right with your eyes. It was a thing you couldn't talk about. . . . He knew just how Cezanne would paint this stretch of river.[9]

In a 1919 letter to a friend, Hemingway described his attachment to Northern Michigan in words Nick Adams might have used:

> It is great northern air. Absolutely the best trout fishing in the country. No exaggeration. Fine country. Good color, good northern atmosphere, absolute freedom, no summer resort stuff and lots of paintable stuff. . . . It's a great place to laze around and swim and fish when you want to. And the best place in the world to do nothing. It is beautiful country Jim.[10]

As transformed as Northern Michigan and the world are one hundred years later, it's stunning that much of the beauty of the Two-Hearted and environs maintains its majesty.

The Lilac Path

By some accounts, the first mention of lilacs in Michigan is attributable to naturalist Henry David Thoreau. Seeking improvement from tuberculosis, Thoreau began a trip from Concord, Massachusetts, to Minnesota in May 1861. He traveled via the Great Lakes with a brief stop in Detroit, and he returned from Milwaukee and Sheboygan aboard the "propeller[ship] Edith." It put into "Carp River" (likely at Leland) on June 29, passed by the Manitou and Fox Islands, stopped at Beaver Island, and reached Mackinac Island at 2:00 a.m. on the 30th. He stayed four days at the Mackinaw House, walked much, and wrote copious notes about the flora. Among the plants listed was lilac.[11]

Others cite an account written on June 18, 1845, by "J.I.M.," a correspondent of the *Boston Post*. After a pleasurable stay that included accommodations at the Mission House, the reporter bade a reluctant goodbye:

> Adieu, beautiful island of Mackinac! . . . Farewell to your rocks and caves, your shady walks and stony beach, your clear air, sweetened by the lilac and apple trees but just in blossom—your delicious trout and white fish, and the kind hospitality of your people![12]

Was the aromatic blossom found there still earlier? Martha Stewart says so: "the common lilac has been part of the American landscape for centuries. Lilacs planted in 1650 on Michigan's Mackinac Island are some of the oldest known in the country."[13] Does Martha know? Apparently so; brought by French missionaries, "the oldest living lilacs on American soil are on Mackinac Island."[14]

The plant arrived in the United Kingdom from Europe—specifically, France. The British came to North America after the French; thus, it should not be surprising that the lilac found its way here in the stores of explorers, trappers, and traders from France. The earliest French settlement in Michigan was in 1668 at Sault Ste. Marie, according to some histories. In 1660, a trade mission from Quebec reached Lake Superior with Jesuit priest Rene Menard, who established St. Therese Mission in the Keweenaw Bay. The first Jesuit missionaries came to the Soo in 1641. Étienne Brûlé came earlier, landing at Bahweting (the Soo) in 1620. Perhaps plantings were made that early. J.I.M. mentioned that French was still the prevailing spoken word two centuries later. Thus Jane Schoolcraft could write of lilacs blooming in her dooryard at the Soo, and much later Jane Murfin of Quincy and Harriet Arnow near Ann Arbor were similarly inspired.

Aside from the profligacy of the syringa on the island near the Mighty Mac, other prime Great Lakes State locations exist. Sunny Fields is a private botanical park in Emmett Township in the Michigan Thumb. It is reputed to hold Michigan's largest collection of lilacs. Within the arboretum at Hidden Lake Gardens in Tipton is an area featuring lilacs. Fernwood Botanical Garden and Nature Preserve in Buchanan Township features a lilac collection.

According to the University of Michigan Herbarium, lilacs within the state may be found along roadsides, fencerows, clearings, fields, and shores.[15] Tradition holds that "the best lilac fragrance comes from the wild shrub of the roadsides and romance, *S. vulgaris*."[16]

Philip Levine employed it wistfully in one of his gritty poems. The setting is a rainy New York City night, Easter 1946:

> Was I expecting crocus and lilac
> to burst from the pavement and sweeten
> the air the way they did in Michigan once
> upon a time?[17]

Do we want to see and to hear and to smell the everyday bounty our predecessors saw and heard and enjoyed? Does the past serve as prologue, as promise-maker that tomorrow may be anticipated rather than dreaded?

Encountering the travails of today through the senses of the writers of Michigan can nurture hope and nourish joy. We only need to follow them down the lilac path.

In Tribute

Between the publication of this volume and its predecessors in the series, the books closed on the lives of several noted Michiganders of letters and heritage.

Philip Parker Mason, born April 1927 in Salem, Massachusetts, passed away on May 6, 2021, in Green Valley, Arizona. A veteran of U.S. Navy service during World War II, he received a master's degree in 1951 and PhD in 1956 from the University of Michigan. He worked at the Bentley Historical Library while a student. He pursued a career in history, focusing especially on his adopted home state of Michigan, and began serving as the archivist for the State of Michigan while pursuing his doctorate. In 1958, he became professor of history at Wayne State University and director of the University Archives. In 1990, he was promoted to distinguished professor of history. He retired from teaching in 2007. He was founding editor of the Great Lakes Book Series on local and regional history published by Wayne State University Press. The Mason family lived in Lansing, Pleasant Ridge, Dearborn, and Eagle Harbor.

Dr. Mason was founding director of the Walter P. Reuther Library at WSU. His contributions to the literature and published heritage of Michigan include numerous articles and a dozen books, including

- *Expedition to Lake Itasca: The Discovery of the Source of the Mississippi* (1958)
- *From Bull Run to Appomattox: Michigan's Role in the Civil War* (1961), with Paul J. Pentecost
- *Schoolcraft: The Literary Voyager or Muzzeniegun* (1962)
- *The Literary Voyager, or, Muzzeniegun* (1962), republished as *Schoolcraft's Ojibwa Lodge Stories: Life on the Lake Superior Frontier*
- *Detroit, Fort Lernoult, and the American Revolution* (1964)
- *Harper of Detroit: The Origin and Growth of a Great Metropolitan Hospital* (1964), with Frank B. Woodford
- *The Ambassador Bridge: A Monument to Progress* (1987)

- *Copper Country Journal: The Diary of Schoolmaster Henry Hobart, 1863–1864* (1991)
- *Rumrunning and the Roaring Twenties: Prohibition on the Michigan-Ontario Waterway* (1995)
- *Tracy W. McGregor: Humanitarian, Philanthropist, and Detroit Civic Leader* (2008)

Additionally, he authored numerous manuals to accompany filmstrips for the Michigan Historical Commission.

One of these studies looked at the life of Tracy William McGregor (April 14, 1869–May 6, 1936), along with that of spouse Katherine Whitney (January 18, 1873–June 7, 1954). Her father, David J. Whitney Jr., became one of the wealthiest Michiganders due to investments in lumber, transportation, and financial interests. He died in 1900, a year before his daughter wedded McGregor, and left behind an 1894 Romanesque Revival mansion that would become an elegant restaurant. The couple's benevolence extended to the homeless, recent immigrants, and other eleemosynary purposes. He founded a "Thursday Noon Group" of civic leaders who met and gave attention to the "social needs of the rising population, especially in the areas of city planning, sanitary housing, playgrounds for children, industrial education, child labor and workmen's compensation laws." In Part 4 of the biography, headed "Books, Libraries, and Education," Mason detailed how McGregor's interest in collecting books had come to occupy much of his waking hours. He visited local libraries and bookshops, purchasing hundreds of volumes. He loved to visit the University Club in Chicago because of its twenty-thousand-volume library, and he spent many hours at the Library of Congress and Folger Library in Washington, D.C. Because of this passion, he and his wife made possible the first public library for Highland Park by donating the land. With public support, including a bond issuance to fund construction, the beautiful facility with capacity for two hundred thousand volumes was dedicated in 1926.

McGregor served on the board of the William L. Clements Library at the University of Michigan. He created a plan to provide financial support for collecting rare Americana by U.S. college libraries. His own collection became a Library of American History at the University of Virginia. A conference center at Wayne State University had its dedication 1958, designed by and featuring classic characteristics of architect Minoru Yamasaki. Its reflecting pool was intended to memorialize Tracy McGregor's reflectiveness and love of beauty. The philanthropist's premature death at age sixty-seven, and his wife's in 1954, cut off further plans, leaving their legacy in the hands of trustees and executors. Above all, neither of them sought public recognition or expressed interest in a memorial to remind Michiganders of their charity. They preferred anonymity.[1] The McGregor Fund continues to invest in people. Their graves are in Woodlawn Cemetery in Detroit where a significant marble stone denotes their names and lives, together.

George Compton Weeks was born in 1932 in Traverse City and graduated from the community high school before obtaining his degree in Journalism from Michigan State University where he wrote for *The State News*. He was in the Army ROTC at MSU and served on active duty from 1955 to 1957 as a public information officer. He went to work for United Press International in Lansing in a more than decade-long stint that included writing a weekly "Michigan Outdoors" column, before joining the staff of Governor William G. Milliken as press secretary in 1969. In the 1970s, the Weeks family moved to Glen Haven and into a home on Lake Michigan near Sleeping Bear Point. In 1983, he returned to journalism at the *Detroit News*, where he wrote a political column and various stories on interesting issues. After retirement, he continued to write a weekly column on Michigan politics for the *Traverse City Record Eagle*. He died on November 30, 2018, at the age of eighty-six, in Traverse City with family by his side.

Weeks's interest in and knowledge of the environment and Michigan history were explored in several books. He authored *Stewards of the State: The Governors of Michigan*, *Sleeping Bear: Yesterday and Today*, *Sleeping Bear: Its Lore, Legends and First People*, and *Mem-ka-weh: Dawning of the Grand Traverse Band of Ottawa and Chippewa Indians*. The 1989 *Michigan: Visions of Our Past* included his chapter on "Leadership in a State of Change, 1945–1980s." He had been working on additional books on local and Michigan history at death. His historical collection (1881–2019) was donated to the Clarke Historical Library at Central Michigan University. Death notices and articles consistently referred to his strong love for Michigan and its heritage, especially regarding matters "Up North."

We also lament the untimely passing of Clifford Russell, a journalist whose love of Michigan history dovetailed with the underlying goal of this book to inspire the curious to get on the road in search of their heritage. His interest began as a child growing up in Conant Gardens in Detroit, grew while a high school athlete at the Roeper School, and ripened when he encountered the 1st Michigan Colored Volunteer Infantry Regiment State marker in Detroit. He began to look actively for the official green-and-gold signs and reached a point where he could point to having visited nearly 1,300 of the more than 1,700 markers across Michigan. He honeymooned in Marshall because of the number of markers there. "There's nothing like learning the history at the location where it happened," he was quoted as saying.

Russell worked for WWJ-950 AM in the mid-1980s until 1994, when he was appointed the first African American press secretary by Mayor Dennis Archer. He became the senior director of communications for the Detroit Tigers in 2002, the first African American to hold the position in Major League Baseball history. He was named to the Wayne State University athletic hall of fame for a sterling basketball career. His death at age sixty-one on February 19, 2018, was felt by many.

Key to Authors

The Roman numerals that follow refer to the volume in our three-part series in which the author's chapter is found:

I	*Ink Trails*
II	*Ink Trails II*
III	*Following Michigan's Ink Trails*

Southeast Michigan

George Matthew Adams [*I*]
Harriette Louisa (Simpson) Arnow [*III*]
Grace Lee Boggs [*III*]
Elizabeth Margaret Chandler [*III*]
Mary Frances Doner [*II*]
Godfrey Dell Eaton [*III*]
J. Oscar Frenette [*III*]
Robert Frost [*I*]
Donald Joseph Goines [*II*]
Edgar Albert Guest [*II*]
Robert Hayden [*III*}
Jane Kenyon [*I*]
Caroline Mathilda Stansbury (Kirkland) [*III*]
Elmore John Leonard Jr. [*III*]
Joan Agnes Theresa Sadie Brodel Leslie (Caldwell) [*III*]
Philip Levine [*III*]
Edmund G. Love [*III*]
Ross Macdonald [*III*]

Catherine Jane "Kittie" Cuthbertson McCoy [*III*]
Arthur Miller [*I*]
Milo Milton Quaife [*III*]
Dudley Felker Randall [*I*]
Gabriel Richard [*III*]
William Penn Adair Rogers [*III*]
Robert Anthony Snow [*III*]
David Augustus Straker [*III*]
Raoul Gustaf Wallenberg [*III*]
Orlando Bolivar Willcox [*II*]
Laura Ingalls Wilder [*III*]

Central/South Central Michigan

Ray Stannard Baker [*II*]
William McKendree Carleton [*I*]
James Oliver Curwood [*I*]
Marguerite de Angeli [*I*]
Lawton Thomas Hemans [*III*]
John Theodore Herrmann [*III*]
Holling Clancy Holling [*I*]
Anna M. Johnson [*III*]
Russell Amos Kirk [*II*]
Della Thompson Lutes [*II*]
Belle Kanaris Maniates [*III*]
James Milford Merrill [*III*]
Jane Bernice Macklem Murfin (Crisp) [*III*]
Clara Eleanor Dillingham (Pierson) [*III*]
Theodore Huebner Roethke [*I*]
Allan John Braitwaite Seager [*II*]
Glendon Swarthout [*II*]
Emma Shore Thornton [*II*]
Rose Hartwick Thorpe [*III*]
Maritta Wolff [*I*]

Southwest Michigan

Muhammad Ali [*III*]
Liberty Hyde Bailey [*I*]
Lyman Frank Baum [*III*]
Ben East [*III*]
Edna Ferber [*III*]
Bessie Ray Hoover [*III*]
Ringgold Wilmer Lardner [*I*]
Arnold Mulder [*II*]
Constance Maybury Rourke [*II*]
Carl Sandburg [*I*]
Isabella Van Wagenen/Sojourner Truth [*III*]

Northern Lower Michigan

David Salzer Broder [*III*]
Charles Bruce Catton [*I*]
Frances Margaret Fox [*II*]
Sara Gwendolyn Frostic [*I*]
Ernest Miller Hemingway [*II*]
James Beardsley Hendryx [*II*]
Johnston "Jack" Davis Kerkhoff [*III*]
Julia Ann Moore [*II*]
Eugene Ruggles [*I*]
Harold Titus [*II*]
Larry Woiwode [*III*]

Upper Peninsula

Charlotte Armstrong [*III*]
William Chalmers Covert [*III*]
Edward Everett Hale [*III*]
James Thomas Harrison [*III*]
Aldo Leopold [*III*]

John Bartlow Martin [*III*]
John Moody [*III*]
Charles Kirk Munroe [*III*]
William Angus Murdoch [*III*]
John Tobin Nevill [*II*]
Carroll Watson Rankin [*I*]
Jane Johnston Schoolcraft/*O-bah-bahm-wawa-ge-zhe-go-qua* [*III*]
John Donaldson Voelker [*I*]

Acknowledgments

We wish to thank our family and friends, who have supported us through this literary adventure and far beyond. In addition, the text contains references to additional sources that have been tremendously helpful to us in the drafting of this third volume in the series. Finally, we are deeply grateful to the entire team at Michigan State University Press, especially Director Elizabeth Demers, for belief in this work and their professional guidance in shaping the manuscript into its best possible published form.

Notes

INTRODUCTION

1. Louis Menand, "Are Bookstores Just a Waste of Space?," *New Yorker*, August 19, 2024. This article is a revealing historical survey that addresses "why does the world need bookstores?" in this internet-dependent era.

HARRIETTE LOUISA SIMPSON (ARNOW): WEEDKILLER'S DAUGHTER

1. In Henry Ford Hospital, according to Thomas L. Arnow, "On Being Harriette Arnow's Son," *Appalachian Journal* 32, no. 4 (Summer 2005): 460. Sister Marcella, born in Kentucky in 1941, graduated from the University of Michigan.
2. Interview with Harriette Arnow, April 1976, Interview G-0006, Southern Oral History Program Collection (#4007), Documenting the American South, https://docsouth.unc.edu/sohp/G-0006/G-0006.html; https://detroithistorical.org/learn/encyclopedia-of-detroit/arnow-harriette; Arnow, "On Being Harriette Arnow's Son," 463. 3220 Nixon Road is no longer farmland, replaced by residential developments.
3. In 1963, Ironton, Ohio, native Robert J. "Bobby" Bare won a Grammy for "Detroit City," written by Danny Dill (1924–2008) and Mel Tillis (1932–2017), with these lyrics: "Last night I went to sleep in Detroit City . . . Home folks think I'm big in Detroit City . . . But by day I make the cars and by night I make the bars."
4. Harriette Arnow, *The Dollmaker* (New York: Macmillan Co., 1954), 1, 137–143, 365–376. The 1914 building became derelict but was renovated and reopened in 2024.
5. Haeja K. Chung, ed., *Harriette Simpson Arnow: Critical Essays on Her Work* (East Lansing: Michigan State University Press, 1995), 251. This and the other quotes

are from a 1968 lecture. MSU Press has devoted considerable effort to Arnow scholarship.

6. Chung, *Harriette Simpson Arnow*, 251–254, 262.
7. Nancy Carol Joyner, "Harriette Simpson Arnow," *Appalachian Journal* 14, no. 1 (Fall 1986): 52, 55; see Glenda Hobbs, "A Portrait of the Artist as Mother: Harriette Arnow and 'The Dollmaker,'" Focus on Women Writers, special issue, *The Georgia Review* vol. 33, no. 4 (Winter 1979): 851, 862.
8. Sandra L. Ballard and Haeja K. Chung, eds., "Introduction," in *The Collected Short Stories of Harriette Simpson Arnow* (East Lansing: Michigan State University Press, 2005), xv, 209–225.

GRACE LEE BOGGS: DETROIT SPRING

1. Grace Lee Boggs, *Living for Change* (Minneapolis: University of Minnesota Press, 2016), 5.
2. Boggs, *Living for Change*, 27.
3. Boggs, *Living for Change*, 39.
4. Robert McFadden, "Grace Lee Boggs, Human Rights Advocate for 7 Decades, Dies at 100," *New York Times*, October 5, 2015, B18.
5. Grace Lee Boggs and Scott Kurashige, *The Next American Revolution: Sustainable Activism for the Twenty-First Century* (Los Angeles: University of California Press, 2011).
6. Rone Tempest, "The Odyssey of Grace and James Boggs: Famed Abroad as Workers in Detroit," *Detroit Free Press*, April 20, 1975, 39.
7. James and Grace Lee Boggs, *Revolution and Evolution in the Twenty-First Century* (New York: Monthly Review Press, 1974).
8. Boggs and Kurashige, *The Next American Revolution.*
9. Tempest, "The Odyssey of Grace and James Boggs," 42.
10. "Grace Lee Boggs," U.S. National Park Service, https://www.nps.gov/people/grace-lee-boggs.htm.
11. Boggs and Kurashige, *The Next American Revolution.*
12. Boggs and Kurashige, *The Next American Revolution.*
13. Boggs, *Living for Change*, 245.
14. "Detroit Summer: A Social Justice Focused Youth Collective," Detroit Summer, The James and Grace Lee Boggs Center, https://www.boggscenter.org/

detroitsummer.

15. "Bill Moyers Journal," Public Broadcasting Service, June 15, 2007, https://www.pbs.org/moyers/journal/06152007/transcript3.html, accessed October 9, 2025.
16. Jonathan Tilove, "At 91, She's Still a Revolutionary: Detroit Activist Grace Lee Boggs Is in More Demand than Ever Before," *Ann Arbor News*, May 20, 2007, A19.
17. "Quotes from Grace Lee Boggs (1915–2015) on Detroit, Rebellion and Revolutionary Strategy," Democracy Now!, October 5, 2015, https://www.democracynow.org/2015/10/5/legendary_activist_grace_lee_boggs_speaking.
18. Nancy Kaffer, "Champion of Detroit's Poor: Activist's Work Spanned an Era While Influencing Thousands," *Detroit Free Press*, October 6, 2015, 1.
19. "Statement by the President on the Passing of Grace Lee Boggs," The White House, Office of the President, October 5, 2015, https://obamawhitehouse.archives.gov/the-press-office/2015/10/05/statement-president-passing-grace-lee-boggs.

ELIZABETH MARGARET CHANDLER: VOICE OF LIBERATION

1. Virginia Law Burns, *Bold Women in Michigan History* (Missoula: Mountain Press Pub. Co., 2006), 23.
2. By the Lenawee County Historical Museum, 110 East Church Street, entitled The Antislavery—Underground Railroad Movement, 1830–1860, Lenawee County, MI.
3. Credited to "Emily," in *The Casket*, vol. 1 (Philadelphia: Atkinson and Alexander, 1826), 57–58.
4. Benjamin Lundy, *The Poetical Works of Elizabeth Margaret Chandler with a Memoir of Her Life and Character* (Philadelphia: Lemuel Howell, 1836), 12–13.
5. John I. Knapp and R. I. Bonner, *Illustrated History and Biographical Record of Lenawee County, Mich.* (Adrian: Times Printing Co., 1903), 15; Walter Romig, *Michigan Place Names: The History of the Founding and the Naming of More than Five Thousand Past and Present Michigan Communities* (Detroit: Wayne State University Press, 1986), 11.
6. Lundy, *The Poetical Works of Elizabeth Margaret Chandler*, 27–28.
7. Lundy, *The Poetical Works of Elizabeth Margaret Chandler*, 40; Carol E. Mull, *The Underground Railroad in Michigan* (Jefferson: McFarland and Co., 2010), 41.
8. Laura S. Haviland, *A Woman's Life-Work: Labors and Experiences of Laura S. Haviland* (Cincinnati: Walden and Stowe, 1882), 32, 494.
9. Kenneth E. Lewis, *West to Far Michigan: Settling the Lower Peninsula, 1815–1860*

(East Lansing: Michigan State University Press, 2002), 66–68.

10. Lundy, *The Poetical Works of Elizabeth Margaret Chandler*, 41.
11. Lundy, *The Poetical Works of Elizabeth Margaret Chandler*, 44, 116.
12. *William Lloyd Garrison, 1805–1879: The Story of His Life Told by His Children*, vol. 3, *1841–1860* (New York: Century Co., 1889), 392–393.
13. Lundy, *The Poetical Works of Elizabeth Margaret Chandler*, 70.

GODFREY DELL EATON: BRUTALLY BLUNT ICONOCLAST

1. *Plain Talk* 1, no. I, October 1927, 18–19.
2. Sibley was on the west side of Woodward between Adelaide and Winder streets, where Little Caesars Arena is now.
3. *1920 Michiganensian*, 389; *1921 Michiganensian*, 391; *1922 Michiganensian*, 181, 280 (photo of him with mustache reading in an armchair is found at the first cited page); *1923 Michiganensian*, 281.
4. *The Michigan Alumnus*, vol. 29 (Ann Arbor: Alumni Association of the University of Michigan, 1923, 1924, 1926), 966; *The Michigan Alumnus*, vol. 30 (Ann Arbor: Alumni Association of the University of Michigan, 1924), 318; *The Michigan Alumnus*, vol. 32 (Ann Arbor: Alumni Association of the University of Michigan, 1923, 1924, 1926), 561.
5. "Eaton Again Barred from U. of M. Campus," *Detroit Free Press*, April 27, 1925, 5.
6. *The American Mercury*, vol. 5, no. 17 (New York: Alfred A. Knopf, 1925), 124–125.
7. *New York Times Book Review*, February 15, 1925, 16.
8. James B. Stronks, *Modern Philology* 65, No. 4 (May 1968), 431.
9. Clayton S. Ellsworth, "Ceres and the American Men of Letters since 1929," *Agricultural History* 24, no. 4 (October 1950): 177.
10. *The Midland*, Vol. XI (Iowa City: John T. Frederick, 1925), 178–179; Clarence A. Andrews, *Michigan in Literature* (Detroit: Wayne State University Press, 1992), 136–137.
11. *McNaught's Monthly*, vol. 7, no. 1 (New York City: May 1926), 1, 23–24, 28, 31–32; *McNaught's Monthly*, vol. 5, No. 5 (New York City: January 1927), 152.
12. *The Michigan Alumnus*, vol. 36 (Ann Arbor: Alumni Association of the University of Michigan, 1930), 655.
13. *Detroit Free Press*, 5.

J. OSCAR FRENETTE: THE GREAT VOICE OF THE GOOD HISTORIAN

1. Robert B. Tuttle, *50 Years of Unique Radio* (Detroit: WJR, 1972), 16, https://worldradiohistory.com/Archive-Station-Albums/WJR-50-Years.pdf.
2. Letter of James H. Quello, Commissioner, Federal Communications Commission, March 16, 1988. It previously had been "Discover Detroit with Oscar Frenette" and "Sketches and Comments."
3. As "Mr. Michigan with another sketch from the gallery of life and things in the Great Lakes area," *Detroit Remember When—A Tribute to Dick Purtan*, Detroit Public TV, September 9, 2022.
4. John Gallagher, "WJR Personality's Strong Voice, Writing Turned Words into Images," *Detroit Free Press*, December 9, 1997, 115.
5. "The Fascination of History," Bentley Historical Library, University of Michigan.

ROBERT HAYDEN: THE FREEDOM TO RESPOND TO LIFE IN HIS OWN WAY

1. Judson Philips, Lawson Carter, and Robert Hayden, *How I Write/1* (New York: Harcourt Brace Jovanovich, 1972), 145.
2. Philips, Carter, and Hayden, *How I Write/1*, 149.
3. John Hatcher, *From the Auroral Darkness: The Life and Poetry of Robert Hayden* (London: George Ronald, 1984), 6.
4. Philips, Carter, and Hayden, *How I Write/1*, 142–143.
5. Carolyn Pajor, "Poet Hayden Remembered," *Michigan Daily*, February 22, 1990.
6. Philips, Carter, and Hayden, *How I Write/1*, 195; "Hayden—'Poet of Perfect Pitch,'" *Columbia (Missouri) Daily Tribune*, June 4, 1976.
7. Hatcher, *From the Auroral Darkness*, 10–12; "Hayden Studies Negro Past, Culture," *Michigan Daily*, August 15, 1943.
8. Hatcher, *From the Auroral Darkness*, 14.
9. Philips, Carter, and Hayden, *How I Write/1*, 140.
10. Philips, Carter, and Hayden, *How I Write/1*, 157.
11. Jo Thomas, "After a Lifetime of Quietly Crafting Words, Acclaim Comes to Robert Hayden," *Detroit Magazine*, September 12, 1976, 182.
12. Philips, Carter, and Hayden, *How I Write/1*, 165.
13. Philips, Carter, and Hayden, *How I Write/1*, 199.

14. Cal Samra, "Poet Wants Freedom to Respond to Life in His Own Way," *Ann Arbor News*, February 15, 1971.
15. Tom Stanton, "Detroit Abounds in the Work of a Famed Local Poet," *Detroit Free Press*, March 24, 2024.
16. Samra, "Poet Wants Freedom."
17. Thomas, "After a Lifetime," 184.
18. Laurence Goldstein, "Robert Hayden: A Poet Who Sang to Humanity," *Detroit Magazine*, April 20, 1980, 117.
19. Stanton, "Detroit Abounds."

CAROLINE MATHILDA STANSBURY (KIRKLAND): CAN YOU GO HOME AGAIN?

1. Bill Treichler, "The Kirkland's School in Geneva," in *The Crooked Lake Review* (February 1990).
2. Romig, *Michigan Place Names*, 442.
3. *Union Magazine of Literature and Art*, vol. 1, July–December (New York: Israel Post, 1847); *Union Magazine of Literature and Art*, vol. 2, January–June (New York: James L. DeGraw, 1848); *Union Magazine of Literature and Art*, vol. 2, July–December (New York: James L. DeGraw, 1848).
4. E.g., one by her sister-in-law, Marion Kirkland Reid, *Woman, Her Education and Influence* (New York: Fowlers and Wells, 1847).
5. Caroline Kirkland, *A New Home—Who'll Follow? Or, Glimpses of Western Life* (New York: C. S. Francis, 1855).
6. *A Forest Life* was published "by the author of 'A New Home'" in two volumes by C. S. Francis, New York City; *Western Clearings* was published under her own name by Wiley and Putnam, New York City.
7. Kirkland, *A New Home—Who'll Follow?*, 10, 13, 21.
8. Edgar Allan Poe, "The Literati of New York City—No. IV," in *Godey's Lady's Book* (Philadelphia: L.A. Godey & Co., 1846), 75–76.
9. John Nerber, "Introduction," in *A New Home—Life in the Clearings* (New York: G. P. Putnam's Sons, 1953), 3.
10. Writers' Program of the Work Projects Administration, *Michigan: A Guide to the Wolverine State* (New York: Oxford University Press, 1941), 145.
11. Ednah D. Cheney, ed., *Louisa May Alcott: Her Life, Letters, and Journals* (Boston: Roberts Brothers, 1892), 82.

12. E.g., Kenneth E. Lewis, *West to Far Michigan: Settling the Lower Peninsula, 1815–1860* (East Lansing: Michigan State University Press, 2002).
13. Denise Kay Jacobs, "East Meets Midwest in Caroline Kirkland's *Western Clearings*," in *MidAmerica XXVIII, The Yearbook of the Society for the Study of Midwestern Literature*, ed. David D. Anderson (East Lansing: Michigan State University Press, 2001), 87–97.
14. *Forest Life, by the Author of "A New Home"* (New York: James W. Judd and Co., 1842), 9. Our thanks to bibliophile Edward Surovell of Ann Arbor for bringing this author to our attention.

ELMORE JOHN LEONARD JR.: THE DICKENS OF DETROIT

1. Bruce McCall, "My Life in Cars," *New Yorker*, December 12, 2020.
2. 1940 U.S. Census, City of Highland Park, Michigan, E.D. No. 82–131, Sheet No. 8A.
3. *Arkansas Democrat-Gazette*, January 17, 2007.
4. "Elmore Leonard interviewed by Patrick McGilligan," *Film Comment*, March–April 1998, https://www.filmcomment.com/article/elmore-leonard-interview-patrick-mcgilligan/.
5. Appearing in *Short Stories for Men* ("the best in true adventures and exciting fiction"), August 1959.
6. Coincidentally, Newman acted in the 1962 adaptation of Hemingway's Nick Adams stories entitled *Hemingway's Adventures of a Young Man*, a 20th Century Fox CinemaScope release.
7. *Detroit Free Press*, May 26, 1974, 5-C.
8. A prime example is Hemingway's *To Have and Have Not* (1937); the 1944 Warner Brothers flick with Humphrey Bogart and Lauren Bacall has more affinity with *Casablanca* (1942) than with the novel.
9. All three published by Delacorte Press, New York.
10. The moniker was first applied by J. D. Reed in *Time* magazine, issue of May 28, 1994, not as "the" but as "a." Charles Dickens's use of serial publications contributed to his financial well-being; his father had been in debtors' prison.

1. The Donaldson and Meier complex of church, school, clergy house, and hall, dating from 1929, remained standing late in 2025. The church pipe organ was relocated to St. Patrick's in White Lake, Michigan.
2. *Detroit Free Press*, June 20, 1943, 4.
3. A. J. Baime, *The Arsenal of Democracy: FDR, Detroit, and an Epic Quest to Arm an America at War* (Boston: Houghton Mifflin Harcourt, 2014), 286.
4. Warner Brothers, 1942, selected by the Library of Congress for the National Film Registry.
5. *Detroit Free Press*, August 21, 1941, 17. The Vogue was located on Harper Avenue at Harvard Road in Detroit.
6. Joan Leslie, "Foreword," in, *Hollywood Canteen: Where the Greatest Generation Danced with the Most Beautiful Girls in the World*, by Lisa Mitchell and Bruce Torrence (Duncan: Bear Manor Media, 2012), 9; Sherrie Tucker, *Dance Floor Democracy: The Social Geography of Memory at the Hollywood Canteen* (Durham: Duke University Press, 2014), 7.
7. *Detroit Free Press*, October 21, 1933, 14; *Detroit Free Press*, October 27, 1933, 20. One booking was at the Blossom Heath Inn on Jefferson in St. Clair Shores. *Detroit Free Press*, March 16, 1946, 12; "My Sisters and I," in *Silver Screen* 11, no. 11 (September 1941): 36, 75–76; *Detroit Free Press*, September 12, 1937, 44.
8. With a cameo from Ronald Reagan and a role played by Clara Blandick, Auntie Em in *The Wizard of Oz*.
9. *Leonard Maltin's Movie Crazy* (Milwaukee: M Press, 2008), 140.
10. Front page news in her hometown: *Detroit Free Press*, March 18, 1950, 1; One became a professor at Kalamazoo College. "It was this family affair," she said; "It meant a lot of time, but it was a wonderful experience. So I got to know these students very well and was intimately involved in decision making about where they were going and what they were going to do." In addition to mentoring students, she established a writing center at the school. David Marshel, "CSUF Advisor and English Professor Understands Student Life Outside of Class," *Daily Titan*, November 1, 2017.
11. Titles from the *Washington Post*, *The Guardian*, the *New York Times*, and the *San Diego Union-Tribune*, respectively. "The Girl Next Door" is the chapter title on Leslie in Daniel Bubbeo, *The Women of Warner Brothers: The Lives and Careers of 15 Leading Ladies* (Jefferson: McFarland and Co., 2002), 141.
12. She did not make many personal appearances but did at the 2005 345th Bomber

Group Reunion, honoring "truly great men" who had fought for freedom. "My Leading Men" speech, Margaret Herrick Library, Academy of Motion Picture Arts and Sciences, Beverly Hills, California.

13. Also see Patricia Majher, *Great Girls in Michigan History* (Detroit: Wayne State University Press, 2015), 107–110; Vince Agul, "Joan Leslie: A Yankee Doodle Sweetheart," *Michigan History* (November 1, 2009); Thomas G. Aylesworth, *Hollywood Kids: Child Stars of the Silver Screen from 1903 to the Present* (New York: E. P. Dutton, 1987).

PHILIP LEVINE: BLUE-COLLAR BARD

1. Margalit Fox, "Philip Levine, a Poet of Grit, Sweat and Labor, Dies at 87," *New York Times*, February 15, 2015, 1.
2. Peter Kobs, "Soot-Covered Hopes, Dreams Laid Bare in Philip Levine's 'One for the Rose,'" *Clarion-Ledger*, August 15, 1982, 82.
3. Mark Stryker, "Poet Celebrated Soul of Working Class," *Detroit Free Press*, February 16, 2015, 1.
4. "Philip Levine in Conversation with Studs Terkel," June 4, 1987, Studs Terkel Radio Archive, https://studsterkel.wfmt.com/programs/philip-levine-conversation-studs-terkel.
5. Webster Schott, "Any Idea May Be Shaped into Poetry," *Kansas City Star*, December 2, 1963, 28.
6. Ivan Olson, "Fresnan's First Book Is a Sellout," *Fresno Bee*, July 21, 1963, 117.
7. Eddie Lopez, "Philip Levine Looks Back on a Rewarding, Continuing Career," *Fresno Bee*, July 3, 1983, 87.
8. "Segment: Philip Levine on America's Workers," Billmoyers.com.
9. Joyce Carol Oates, "A Cluster of Feelings: Wakoski and Levine," *American Poetry Review*, May/June 1973, 55.
10. Charles McGrath, "Voice of the Workingman to Be Poet Laureate," *New York Times*, August 9, 2001.
11. Andrew Goldman, "Philip Levine Still Knows How to Make Trouble," *New York Times Magazine*, November 4, 2011, 10.
12. Margalit Fox, "Philip Levine, a Poet of Grit. Sweat and Labor, Dies at 87," *New York Times*, February 15, 2015, A1.

EDMUND G. LOVE: WHIMSY AND WOE

1. An early town father named the burg Flushing after Flushing, Long Island, New York, where he had lived. The name of that village in turn was Anglicized from Vlissingen, its name during Dutch colonization.
2. Joan Cook, "Edmund G. Love, an Author, 78; Wrote 'Subways Are for Sleeping,'" *New York Times*, September 1, 1990, 25.
3. A. I. Malabre, book review, *Hartford Courant*, October 20, 1957, 104.
4. "Monday Club Hears Attack on Emily Post," *Binghamton Press and Sun-Bulletin*, February 3, 1959, 14.
5. Kevin Kelly, "Light-Hearted, Lively, Tuneful Are Subways," *Boston Globe*, November 29, 1961, 53.
6. Edmund Love, "Waiter! The Story of a Man Who Is Eating His Way Through 5,000 New York Restaurants in Alphabetical Order," *Saturday Evening Post*, May 23, 1964.
7. Reba Stevenson, "Tarts—Without Calories," *The Tennessean*, January 8, 1968, 40.
8. "Controversial Flushing Memoir Turns 50," MLive, August 28, 2015,https://www.mlive.com/news/flint/2015/08/edmund_g_loves_flushing_memoir.html.
9. Judd Arnett, "Small Town Memoirs," *Detroit Free Press*, September 1, 1965, 46.
10. Sidney Fields, "Forgives So Much: Only Human," *New York Daily News*, September 11, 1967, 43.
11. Edmund Love, letter to the sports editor, *Detroit Free Press*, January 18, 1980.

ROSS MACDONALD: THE TRANSFERENCE OF GUILT

1. Paul Nelson and Kevin Avery, *It's All One Case: The Illustrated Ross Macdonald Archives* (Seattle: Fantagraphics Books, 2016), 266.
2. Nelson and Avery, *It's All One Case*, 186.
3. Tom Nolan, *Ross Macdonald: A Biography* (New York: Scribner, 1999), 22–23.
4. Nelson and Avery, *It's All One Case*, 10.
5. Nolan, *Ross Macdonald*, 31–32.
6. Nolan, *Ross Macdonald*, 62.
7. Nolan, *Ross Macdonald*, 54–55; Nelson and Avery, *It's All One Case*, 52, 177.
8. Nolan, *Ross Macdonald*, 63.
9. Nelson and Avery, *It's All One Case*, 6.
10. Nolan, *Ross Macdonald*, 127.

11. Nelson and Avery, *It's All One Case*, 234.
12. Nolan, *Ross Macdonald*, 100.
13. Nelson and Avery, *It's All One Case*, 271–272.
14. "Millar Terms Mystery Stories Too Unrealistic," *Michigan Daily*, July 2, 1953.
15. Nelson and Avery, *It's All One Case*, 45.
16. Nelson and Avery, *It's All One Case*, 29–30, 82, 87.
17. Nelson and Avery, *It's All One Case*, 266, 269.
18. Martin Malina, "Thrillers: A Small, Pleasant Vice," *Montreal Star*, February 2, 1974.

CATHERINE JANE "KITTIE" CUTHBERTSON MCCOY: REAL MCCOYS

1. National Register of Historic Places Registration Form, received March 3, 2009. https://s3.amazonaws.com/NARAprodstorage/opastorage/live/28/3403/25340328/content/electronic-records/rg-079/NPS_MI/08001105.pdf. The Department of the Interior rejected this criterion; it was resubmitted and status granted for "Social History."
2. Kitty C. McCoy, *Buds and Blossoms* (Pontiac: Gazette Publishing House, 1886).
3. So scarce that perhaps only two copies remain, both at the Library of Michigan.
4. In Lillian Drake Avery, "Centenary of the Settlement of Oakland County," vol. 1 (Lansing, 1917), 74–75.
5. See Philip A. Greasley, ed., *Dictionary of Midwestern Literature*, vol. 1: *The Authors* (Bloomington: Indiana University Press, 2001), 208.

MILO MILTON QUAIFE: PROLIFIC CHRONICLER

1. *Detroit Free Press*, September 2, 1959, 3.
2. Joe L. Norris, ed., *Forty-six Years: The Published Writings of Milo M. Quaife, 1910–1955* (Detroit: Algonquin Club, 1956). Quaife helped found the club in 1934 as the Detroit History Club and served on its Publication Committee.
3. His article in November on "Detroit's Presidential Candidate," i.e., Lewis Cass, referred to his espousal of popular sovereignty vis-à-vis slavery as "deceptive phraseology."
4. Mark Beltaire, *Detroit Free Press*, September 5, 1959, 22. Beltaire was known as "the Town Crier."
5. *Life of Black Hawk: Ma-Ka-Tai-Me-She-Kia-Kiak* (Chicago: R. R. Donnelley and

Sons, 1916), x.

6. Republishing the *Journal of Thomas Verchères de Boucherville* and *The Capitulation* by an Ohio soldier originally printed during the War of 1812. Originally printed in New York by Sheldon and Co., 1874.
7. Books as Christmas gifts form the essence of Jólabókaflóðið, the "Yule book flood" tradition of Iceland, begun during World War II's paper shortage, in which books are exchanged and the evening spent reading and drinking hot chocolate.
8. One of the first true scholars of the Black Canadian past, according to Michele A. Johnson and Funké Aladejebi, eds., *Unsettling the Great White North: Black Canadian History* (Toronto: University of Toronto Press, 2022).
9. Milo M. Quaife, *Lake Michigan* (Indianapolis: Bobbs-Merrill Company, 1944), 284.
10. Milo M. Quaife, *The Kingdom of Saint James: A Narrative of the Mormons* (New Haven: Yale University Press, 1930). Michigan State University Press published a more complete version of Strang's diary in 1961, edited by Mark A. Strang.
11. *History News*, vol. 14, no. 11 (September 1959), 106. Trail: H-63, the roadway between St. Ignace and the Soo.
12. See Lauck, *The Good Country: A History of the American Midwest, 1800–1900* (Norman: University of Oklahoma Press, 2022.

GABRIEL RICHARD: MICHIGAN'S GUTENBERG

1. *Speramus Meliora* and *Resurget Cineribus*, meaning "We hope for better things" and "It will rise from the ashes."
2. He first appeared on December 8, 1823, after the session opened on December 1. *Annals of Congress*, 18th Congress, 1st Session, 803. His election was contested; the matter was referred to committee and never emerged; Douglas C. McMurtrie, *Early Printing in Michigan, with a Bibliography of the Issues of the Michigan Press, 1796–1850* (Chicago: John Calhoun Club, 1931), 33. This work credits Richard as "Owner and Patron of the Earliest Literary Press in Michigan.."
3. Paul J. Foik, *The Michigan Essay: Michigan's First Newspaper* (South Bend: University of Notre Dame, 1912), 4.
4. Leroy Barnett and Roger Rosentreter, *Michigan's Early Military Forces: A Roster and History of Troops Activated Prior to the Civil War* (Detroit: Wayne State University Press, 2003), 46–47.
5. Silas Farmer, *The History of Detroit and Michigan; or, The Metropolis Illustrated* (Detroit: Silas Farmer and Co., 1884), 670.

6. Farmer, *The History of Detroit and Michigan*, 694.
7. John C. Oswald, *Printing in the Americas* (New York: Gregg Publishing Co., 1937), 334.
8. McMurtrie, *Early Printing in Michigan*, 35–36, 82–83, 95. The prize for the second location for printing is held by Monroe, commencing in 1825. The publishing company became the official printer for the journals of the Territorial Legislature the following year. Ann Arbor became the third in 1829. Adrian became "a printing and publishing center of some importance" soon thereafter.
9. Farmer, *The History of Detroit and Michigan*, 694.
10. Kathryn MacKay, *200 Years of Detroit Booksellers: 1817 to 2007* (Detroit: Book Club of Detroit, 2010).

WILLIAM PENN ADAIR ROGERS: OUR NATION TURNS ITS LONELY EYES

1. *Detroit Free Press*, May 7, 1922, D9. The Capitol Theater opened in January 1922, designed by famed architect C. Howard Crane, seating 3,367. It now serves as the Detroit Opera House at 1526 Broadway Avenue.
2. Alice George, "Will Rogers Was One of a Kind," *Smithsonian Magazine*, August 5, 2020, https://www.smithsonianmag.com/smithsonian-institution/will-rogers-was-one-kind-180975472.
3. "Prohibition: 'From and After,'" *Time*, January 14, 1929, 12; "Mercy in Life," *Time*, January 27, 1930, 15.
4. *New York Times*, December 13, 1928, 26.
5. Column by Frank Daugherty, *United Press International*, August 17, 1935.
6. Others have existed, such as one in the Pontiac school system.
7. The title is not remembered; the subject matter related to pre–American Independence, perhaps the French and Indian War.
8. Charlie LeDuff, "Where There's a Will, There's the Truth," *The Detroit News*, September 13, 2023, 12A. Legendary *Detroit Free Press* columnist Judd Arnett wrote a similar item on January 27, 1980, 19.
9. James M. Smallwood, ed., *Will Rogers' Daily Telegrams*, vol. 2 (Stillwater: University of Oklahoma Press, 1978), 882.
10. P. J. O'Brien, Will Rogers, *Ambassador of Good Will, Prince of Wit and Wisdom* (Chicago: John C. Winston Co., 1935), 169–170. Rochelle Riley, retired from the *Detroit Free Press*, was a recipient of the Will Rogers Award of the National Society of Newspaper Columnists.

ROBERT ANTHONY SNOW: GENTLY FALLING

1. Nolan Finley, "Tony Snow Was a Family Man First," *Alexandria Times*, July 14, 2008.
2. A. L. Weeks, ed., *The Style Book of the Detroit News* (Detroit: Evening News Association, 1918), 1.
3. Tony Snow, "American Journalism and the Constitution," *Imprimis*, vol. 30, no. 12, December 2001.
4. Tony Snow, "Tough Schools Can Help Tough Kids," *Cincinnati Enquirer*, September 24, 1995, 48.

DAVID AUGUSTUS STRAKER: TO RAISE AND RECONCILE

1. Howard University Alumni Directory, 1870–1919 (Washington, D.C.: Howard University, 1919), 168; Union Alumni Association, Alumni Catalogue of Howard University with List of Incorporators, Trustees, and Other Employees, 1867–1896 (Washington, D.C.: Howard University Print, 1896), 26–27.
2. Carrie Sharlow, "Michigan Lawyers in History: David Augustus Straker," *Michigan Bar Journal* (January 2015): 42–43.
3. Proceedings of the National Convention of Colored Men, Held in the City of Syracuse, NY, October 4, 5, 6, and 7, 1864 (n.p., 1864), 8, 41, 44, 47.
4. Eric Gardner, "A Word Fitly Spoken: Edmonia Highgate, Frances Ellen Watkins Harper, and the 1864 Syracuse Convention," in *The Colored Conventions Movement: Black Organizing in the Nineteenth Century*, ed. P. Gabrielle Foreman et al. (Chapel Hill: University of North Carolina Press, 2021), 72.
5. *Detroit Free Press*, September 24, 1899, 4.
6. William J. Simmons, *Men of Mark: Eminent, Progressive and Rising* (Cleveland: Geo. M. Rewell Co., 1887), 53–54, 744ff.
7. G. F. Richings, *Evidences of Progress Among Colored People* (Philadelphia: Geo. S. Ferguson Co., 1904), 284–289.
8. 1900 U.S. Census, Wayne County, Michigan, E.D. No. 38, Supervisor's District No.116, 14. The location is east of the Masonic Temple.
9. D. Augustus Straker, *The New South Investigated* (Detroit: Ferguson Printing Co., 1888), iv, 17–18, 37, 40–44, 53. The book contained endorsements by Frederick Douglass, D. Bethune Duffield, and Sylvester Larned.

10. *Detroit Free Press*, July 13, 1907, 12.
11. Quotes and the facts of the case are from *Ferguson v. Gies*, 82 Mich 358 (1890). His client's printing house published the *New South* book.
12. Richings, *Evidences of Progress*, 289–290.
13. James P. Danky and Maureen E. Hady, eds., *African-American Newspapers and Periodicals: A National Bibliography* (Cambridge: Harvard University Press, 1999), 193.
14. Carrie Sharlow, "Michigan Lawyers in History: David Augustus Straker," *Michigan Bar Journal* (January 2015): 42–43.
15. From Detroit Historical Society website and online resources. Spelling, punctuation, underling, and inserts (< >) are as in the original, with but one paragraph inserted for additional emphasis. Catalog no. 2001.061.156.
16. D. Augustus Straker Bar Association History and Mission, https://strakerlaw.org/about.php.
17. Laura R. Ashlee, ed., *Traveling Through Time: A Guide to Michigan's Historical Markers* (Ann Arbor: University of Michigan Press, 2005), 460; "Fort Wayne Hotel," Historic Detroit, https://www.historicdetroit.org/buildings/hotel-fort-wayne; *Detroit News*, November 15, 2022. The area has been designated as the Cass Park Historic District.
18. Straker, *The New South Investigated*, 107, 229.

RAOUL GUSTAF WALLENBERG: TRULY "RUDY"

1. Bentley Historical Library, Emil Lorch Papers, 1891–2004.

LAURA INGALLS WILDER: LITTLE HOUSE IN THE TALLEST STORE

1. Caroline Fraser, *Prairie Fires: The American Dreams of Laura Ingalls Wilder* (New York: Henry Holt and Co., 2017), 393–394.
2. Burton Historical Collection, Detroit Public Library.
3. Caroline Fraser, ed., *Laura Ingalls Wilder: The Little House Books*, vol. 1 (New York: Library Classics of the United States, Inc., 2012), 585, 588.
4. John Hall Wheelock, ed., *Editor to Author: The Letters of Maxwell E. Perkins* (New York: Charles Scribner's Sons, 1950), 99.

5. *Detroit Free Press*, May 9, 1949, 7.
6. Burton Historical Collection.
7. Fraser, *Prairie Fires*, 508.

LAWTON THOMAS HEMANS: PURE MICHIGANDER

1. Silas Farmer, *The History of Detroit and Michigan* (Detroit: Silas Farmer & Co., 1884), 112.
2. Lawton T. Hemans, *History of Michigan, from Its Earliest Colonization to the Present Time* (New York: Harper and Brothers); Electa Maria Sheldon, *The Early History of Michigan, from the First Settlement to 1815* (New York: A. S. Barnes and Co., 1856).
3. Lawton T. Hemans, *Life and Times of Stevens Thomson Mason: The Boy Governor of Michigan* (Lansing: Hammond Pub. Co.; Lansing: Michigan Historical Commission, which issued a "Second Edition" in 1930).
4. Bruce Catton, *Michigan: A Bicentennial History* (W. W. Norton and Co., 1976).
5. *Detroit Free Press*, November 20, 1916, 3.

JOHN THEODORE HERRMANN: GENIUS IS NOT ENOUGH

1. Edward Dahlberg, *Alms for Oblivion* (Minneapolis: University of Minnesota Press, 1964), 54–55.

ANNA M. JOHNSON: HOPE DARING

1. Fact Sheet entitled "VA's Headstones and Markers," U.S. Department of Veterans Affairs, September 2007, 2.
2. Albert N. Marquis, ed., *Who's Who in America*, vol. 20 (Chicago: A. N. Marquis Co., 1938), 1346–1347. Hastings was named for the original landholder. Romig, *Michigan Place Names*, 257.
3. John W. Leonard, ed., *Woman's Who's Who in America* (New York: American Commonwealth Co., 1914), 433. The same address is given as her residence in the 1930 U.S. Census. That source also provides her middle initial.

4. Andrews, *Michigan in Literature*, 112, 234.
5. Willah Weldon, "Michigan Woman's Press Association," in *Women's Press Organizations, 1881–1999*, ed. Elizabeth V. Burt (Westport: Greenwood Press, 2000), 114–115, 118.
6. Andrews, *Michigan in Literature*, 112.
7. Hope Daring, *Madeline: The Island Girl* (New York: Eaton and Mains, 1906), 12–13. *An Abundant Harvest*, its sequel, is also set there.
8. Iona Fuller, *The Loon Feather* (New York: Harcourt Brace and Co., 1940) (copyright renewed 1968). *The Atlantic* review: "Beginning novelists take notice that this is a first novel and an exceptionally good one." May 1940. The *New York Times*: "has a delightful quality." February 25, 1940. It was the winner of the Hopwood Award for fiction.
9. Richard Matheson, *Bid Time Return* (New York: Viking Press, 1975); subsequently *Somewhere in Time* (New York: Tom Doherty Associates, 1998). The cinematic treatment was released in 1980 by Universal Pictures.
10. New York: Harper and Brothers. Woolson (related to James Fenimore Cooper) was a prolific writer. Her career essentially began with a short story collection, *Castle Nowhere: Lake-Country Sketches* (Boston: J. R. Osgood and Co., 1875), based on experiences on Mackinac Island and the Great Lakes. One of the stories was entitled "St. Clair Flats." See Victoria Brehm, ed., *Constance Fenimore Woolson's Nineteenth Century: Essays* (Detroit: Wayne State University Press, 2001). She is commemorated on the island's East Bluff with a bronze plaque erected in 1916.

BELLE KANARIS MANIATES: A STUDIOUSLY CHEERFUL WOMAN

1. She is not listed in the family household in the 1860 U.S. Census, appearing at age nine a decade later.
2. Andrews, *Michigan in Literature*, 204; *San Jose Mercury-News*, 92, no. 70, March 11, 1917.
3. *Lansing State Journal*, March 16, 1922, 11.
4. Bill Castenier, "Rediscovering Maniates: Chance Encounter Leads to Re-publishing of Lansing Author," *City Pulse*, May 31, 2017, https://www.lansingcitypulse.com/stories/rediscovering-maniates,2141.
5. *Arizona Daily Press*, April 10, 1906; *State Republican*, April 13, 1906, 4.

JAMES MILFORD MERRILL: FOR NICKELS AND DIMES

1. Edward T. LeBlanc Dime Novel Bibliography, made possible in part by the National Endowment for the Humanities (https://dimenovels.org), is a comprehensive online database of such works. See also "Dime Novels and Popular Literature," Falvey Library, Villanova University, https://digital.library.villanova.edu/Collection/vudl:24093/.
2. E.D. No. 202, Supervisor's District No. 2, 14.
3. Older brother Davis Merrill enlisted in company A, 10th Michigan Cavalry, August 26, 1863, at Bridgeton, for three years, age seventeen. Died in Knoxville, Tennessee, April 27, 1864. Gravestone in Bridgeton Township Cemetery, Newaygo County. The town was named for Ulysses S. Grant.
4. James M. Merrill, *Cloudwood; or, The Daughter of the Wilderness* (New York: Frank Starr and Co., 1871), 9, 97.
5. S. Emma E. Edmonds, *The Female Spy of the Union Army* (Boston: DeWolfe, Fiske and Co., 1864).
6. Almon Gilbert lived from 1833–April 20, 1919, according to gravestone in Oakhill Cemetery, Grand Rapids. His find-a-grave entry indicates he was "Cabinet Maker at Stow and Haight in 1880." The firm was a Grand Rapids furniture maker.
7. James Milford Merrill, *An American Sovereign* (Boston: C. M. Clark Publishing Company, 1909), 1.
8. Merrill, *An American Sovereign*, 132.
9. Merrill, *An American Sovereign*, 132, 212–213, 271–272, 288, 297. Another character is a blatant and "ignorant" racist. Judgments on slavery, however, are ahistorical.
10. Albert N. Marquis, ed., *Who's Who in America*, vol. 7 (Chicago: A. N. Marquis and Co., 1912), 1430.
11. *Chicago Ledger*, 45, no. 15, 17.
12. See Jeff Alexander, *The Muskegon: The Majesty and Tragedy of Michigan's Rarest River* (East Lansing: Michigan State University Press, 2006), a 2007 Michigan Notable Book. The phrase is said to have originated with Francesco "Petrarch" Petrarca.

JANE BERNICE MACKLEM MURFIN (CRISP): FROM QUINCY TOWN TO TINSELTOWN

1. Romig, *Michigan Place Names*, 463.

2. *Branch County Directory and Historical Record* (Ann Arbor: Courier Steam Printing House, 1871), 112.
3. "Macklem, Mrs. H. S., millinery, south side Chicago. Macklem, James, agent Wheeler & Wilson sewing machine" appears in *Branch County Directory and Historical Record*, 115. In 1883, James played a role in the fiftieth anniversary of the founding of Quincy: "made an exhibit of the New Home sewing machine, with Miss Grace at work upon one." *Collections of the Pioneer Society of the State of Michigan*, vol. 6 (Lansing: Wynkoop Hallenbeck Crawford Co., 1907), 227.
4. "Women's History Month—Morrill Hall," Archives @ MSU, https://msuarchives.wordpress.com/tag/morrill-hall/.
5. Lawrence Cosentino, "Walls Come Crumbling Down," *Lansing City Pulse*, November 3, 2010. The building was demolished in 2013.
6. *Directory of Faculty and Students of the Michigan Agricultural College* (1903–1904), 17.
7. *M.A.C. Record*, 9, no. 3, 2.
8. Sault Ste. Marie, Ward 2, Chippewa County, Michigan, E.D. 20, 12.
9. *GlücAuf*, published by Class of '05, M.A.C., 136–137 (unnumbered). She appears in the photo of members on the far right of the front row.
10. 1910 U.S. Census, Detroit, Wayne County, Michigan, E.D. 124, 9A.
11. *Dau's Blue Book for Detroit* (New York: Dau Pub. Co., 1911), 98. "The Fine Arts Society of Detroit was founded by leaders of the community in January 1906 to bring together professional and amateur lovers of the Arts. Members first met in their homes, then in local theaters such as the Arts and Crafts Theater and the Gem Theater." Fine Arts Society of Detroit website, https://fineartsdetroit.org.
12. *Social Register, Detroit, 1920*, vol. 34, no. 16 (New York: Social Register Association, November 1919), 87.
13. Summary of Returns Relative to Divorces, County of Wayne, State of Michigan, for the year 1918, with accompanying Schedule, submitted October 6, 1919, numbered page 230, available via ancestry.com. He became a Regent of the University of Michigan; its North Campus is located along Murfin Avenue, and the "Murfin Gate" joins the West Quadrangle and the Connector buildings on East Madison, Main Campus.
14. *Ladies Home Journal*, November 1917, vol. 34, 147.
15. *Detroit Times*, June 4, 1914, 2, "Last Edition."
16. Digitized at "Log of the North Shore Club," J. Rowe Heritage Consulting, https://www.wawahistory.com/uploads/3/8/6/3/3863300/the_north_shore_club_1910b.pdf.

17. February 7, 1917, 11.
18. *New York Tribune*, August 15, 1917, 9.
19. From the 1951 renewed copyrighted script by Jane Murfin, published by Samuel French in New York, 94, 107.
20. State of New York, Manhattan Borough, E.D. No. 1049, sheet 4B.
21. Burns Mantle, *The Green Book Magazine*, vol. 22, no. 3 (Chicago: Story Press Corporation, 1919), 54.
22. *Stockton Independent*, vol. 123, no. 111, November 19, 1922, 7.
23. Julie Buck, "Jane Murfin," in, *Women Film Pioneers Project*, ed. Jane Gaines, Radha Vatsal, and Monica Dall'Asta (New York: Columbia University Libraries, 2013), https://doi.org/10.7916/d8-wwsf-rc28. See Kathryn Fuller-Seeley and Jeremy Groskopf, "The Dogs Who Saved Hollywood," in *Cinematic Canines: Dogs and Their Work in the Fiction Film*, ed. Adrienne L. McLean (New Brunswick: Rutgers University Press, 2014), 54–77; J. Allen Boone, *Letters to Strongheart* (New York: Prentice-Hall Inc., 1939), vii (describing Murfin as "the distinguished writer of stage and screen plays").
24. *New York Times*, August 16, 1932, Radio Amusements, 20; *San Bernardino Sun*, vol. 38, August 17, 1932, 4. James Murfin also remarried.
25. *San Pedro News Pilot*, vol. 17, no. 159, September 7, 1944, 4; *San Pedro News Pilot*, vol. 17, no. 194, October 18, 1944, 5.
26. Amy L. Banks, "The Forgettable Ms. Murfin," in *When Women Wrote Hollywood*, ed. Rosanne Welch (Jefferson: McFarland and Co., 2018), 203. The cover features a photo of Murfin, rather than the twenty-three other female subjects.
27. *The Women was* co-written with Anita Loos after they took over from F. Scott Fitzgerald. Banks, "The Forgettable Ms. Murfin," 203. The film was selected in 2007 by the Library of Congress for preservation in the National Film Registry as being culturally, historically, or aesthetically significant. Movie posters for the film typically include her name in the credits; Murfin shares credit with Aldous Huxley, author of *Brave New World* in 1932, for *Northwest Passage* and *Pride and Prejudice*.
28. *San Bernardino Sun*, vol. 43, January 28, 1937, 3. That salary is equivalent to approximately $2 million today.
29. *Los Angeles Illustrated Daily News*, vol. 14, no. 24, September 30, 1936, 19.
30. Banks, "The Forgettable Ms. Murfin," 201–202.
31. Source: American Film Institute, which also credits her as director of *Flapper Wives* (1924).
32. *Los Angeles Illustrated Daily News*, vol. 8, no. 44, October 23, 1930, 21.
33. *American Film Institute Catalog*, https://catalog.afi.com/

Film/5929-THE-LIFE-OF-VERGIE-WINTERS?cxt=filmography.

34. Clare Booth Luce, *The Women* (New York: Dramatists Play Service, Inc., 1995).
35. *San Pedro News Pilot*, vol. 17, no. 177, September 28, 1944, 2.
36. *Los Angeles Daily News*, April 24, 1943, 23.
37. *San Bernardino Sun*, vol. 56, no. 319, August 28, 1950, 4.
38. *Santa Cruz Sentinel*, vol. 103, no. 41, February 18, 1959, 11.
39. *Los Angeles Times*, August 11, 1955, 4.
40. Section E, Lot #4348, Space 5, in the middle of the park. Jane Cowl was buried in Section E, Lot #4256, Space 4, a curb property. The graves are not adjacent, as might be expected in certain relationships. Banks, "The Forgettable Ms. Murfin," 200, 203. Appreciation to staff of the cemetery for the location information.
41. Buck, "Jane Murfin."

CLARA ELEANOR DILLINGHAM (PIERSON): AT HOME IN NATURE

1. "Autobiography," n.d., Clara E. D. Pierson Papers, Bentley Historical Library, University of Michigan. Many details of her life related in this chapter are found in her unpublished autobiography.
2. Meddlesome Mattie is a "naughty child" character in a poem authored by Ann Taylor and popularized for children's consumption by McGuffey Readers.
3. "Autobiography," chapter 4, p. 5.
4. "John W. S. and Clara Dillingham Pierson Home," Montcalm County, MIGENWeb, https://www.migenweb.org/montcalm/townships/douglass/stantonpiersonjohnwhome.html.
5. "Autobiography," chapter 17, p. 5.
6. "Autobiography," chapter 18, p. 3.
7. Clara Dillingham Pierson, *Among the Meadow People* (New York: E.P. Dutton and Company, 1899), 5.
8. Pierson, *Among the Meadow People*, 7.
9. Pierson, *Among the Meadow People*, 189.
10. Clara Dillingham Pierson, *Among the Forest People* (New York: E.P. Dutton and Company, 1900).
11. "Mrs. Pierson's Nature Studies," *Brooklyn Daily Eagle*, December 7, 1901, 22.
12. Kate Sanborn, "Mrs. Pierson's Nature Stories," *Brooklyn Daily Eagle*, December 7, 1901, 22.
13. "Among the Meadow People," *Buffalo Commercial*, April 12, 1902, 9.

14. "A Happy Barnyard," *New York Times*, October 1, 1904.
15. "Autobiography," chapter 23, p. 7.
16. "Plow Stories," *Minneapolis Tribune*, November 11, 1923, 72.
17. "Pierson Estate Filed," *Holland Sentinel*, December 4, 1952, 13.

ROSE HARTWICK THORPE: THE POEM HEARD 'ROUND THE WORLD

1. George Whartman James, *Rose Hartwick Thorpe and the Story of 'Curfew Shall Not Ring Tonight'* (Pasadena: Radiant Life Press, 1916).
2. According to Rose, the queen appointed a commission that the source material for the poem was grounded in fact and concluded that it was. "Mrs. Rose Thorpe, Poet, Is Dead at 89," *New York Times*, July 21, 1939.
3. Rose Hartwick Thorpe, *Ringing Ballads* (Boston: D. Lothrop Co., 1887), 17.
4. James, *Rose Hartwick Thorpe*, 17.
5. James, *Rose Hartwick Thorpe*, 5.
6. Critics were increasingly dismissive. In 1914, one expressed surprise that she was still living and branded the title of her latest volume, *The Poetical Works of Rose Hartwick Thorpe*, "grandiloquently termed," as her work was "scarcely poetry in any sense of the word." "Poets and others: Volumes of verse not all touched by inspiration," unsigned review, *New York Times*, March 23, 1913.

   A sample verse from "The Soldier's Reprieve":

   The President sat at his writing
   But the eyes were kind and mild
   That turned with a look of wonder
   On the little shy-faced child.

7. Lucy Maud Montgomery, *Anne of Green Gables* (Boston: L. C. Page and Co., 1908), 191.
8. "Forgotten History Brought to Light by 'Curfew Must Not Ring Tonight,'" *Kansas City Star*, July 25, 1939, 14.
9. George Whartman James, *Rose Hartwick Thorpe and the Story of 'Curfew Shall Not Ring Tonight* (Pasadena: Radiant Life Press, 1916), 21.

MUHAMMAD ALI: OF THE GOAT AND THE RIVER

1. Dale Brewer, "When Ali Was King," *The Herald-Palladium*, September 16, 2018, A3.
2. Brewer, "When Ali Was King," A3.
3. Maya Angelou, "On the Pulse of Morning" (poem presented at the inauguration of President Bill Clinton, Washington, D.C., January 20, 1993).
4. With daughter Hana Yasmeen Ali, *The Soul of a Butterfly: Reflections on Life's Journey* (New York: Simon and Schuster, 2004), 5, 152. She was born in Berrien General Hospital.

LYMAN FRANK BAUM: MACATAWA'S MAN

1. Mike Sonnenberg, *Lost in Michigan*, vol. 2, *History and Travel Stories from an Endless Road Trip* (Saginaw: Etaoin Publishing, 2018), 31–33.
2. Katharine M. Rogers, *L. Frank Baum, Creator of Oz* (New York: St. Martin's Press, 2002), 116, 175. They sold it in 1909. L. Frank Baum, *Father Goose: His Book* (Chicago: George M. Hill Company, 1899). W. W. Denslow, the illustrator of *Father Goose*, used royalties to acquire an island in the main harbor of Bermuda, now known as Bluck's, and wanted to be referred to as King Denslow I.
3. Angelica Shirley Carpenter and Jean Shirley, *L. Frank Baum: Royal Historian of Oz* (Minneapolis: Lerner Pub. Co., 1992), 53, 54. The now-demolished residence had three levels, a two-level stairway to the shore, bay windows, several spacious balcony porches, and a cupola.
4. Frank Joslyn Baum and Russell P. MacFall, *To Please a Child: A Biography of L. Frank Baum, Royal Historian of Oz* (Chicago: Reilly and Lee Co., 1961), 106–121, 134. Frank attended the Michigan Military School in Orchard Lake, Michigan (as did Edgar Rice Burroughs), enlisted in the U.S. Army, and served as an officer during World War II in the Philippines.
5. Rogers, *L. Frank Baum, Creator of Oz*, 85.
6. John Estes Cook [L. Frank Baum], *Tamawaca Folks: A Summer Comedy* (Tamawaca Press, 1907), 8.
7. William Bollman, *1899: L. Frank Baum's Oz-Inspiring Macatawa Park* (Bloomington, IN: Trafford Pub., 2013), 87–89. See also Donald L. van Reken, *Macatawa Park: A Chronicle* (Holland: n.p., 1991).
8. Carpenter and Shirley, *L. Frank Baum: Royal Historian of Oz*, 101.
9. Rebecca Loncraine, *The Real Wizard of Oz: The Life and Times of L. Frank Baum*

(New York: Gotham Books, 2009), 194, 205, 223.

10. John Fricke, *The Wonderful World of Oz: An Illustrated History of the American Classic* (Camden: Down East Books, 2013), 41.
11. Bollman, *1899*, 89.

BEN EAST: CONSERVATION CURMUDGEON

1. Frank Mainville, "Ben East Continues Writing, 8th Book Underway," *Lansing State Journal*, February 11, 1976, 39.
2. Mainville, "Ben East Continues Writing," 39.
3. "Ben East Goes to Outdoor Magazine," *Ironwood Daily Globe*, December 13, 1945, 10.
4. Frank Mainville, "Ben East: True Friend of Conservation," *Lansing State Journal*, December 12, 1973, 49.
5. "Newspaper Man Heads First Winter Expedition to Isle Royale in Cabin Monoplane," *Ironwood Times*, February 14, 1931, 4.
6. "Ben East Urges Action, Says Michigan Must Get Moving on Meeting Recreation Needs," *Traverse City Record-Eagle*, October 5, 1961, 1.
7. Ben East, "It All Started With a Fishing Trip," Friends of the Porkies, https://porkies.org/it-all-started-with-a-fishing-trip.
8. Dave Richey, "Crusader Journalist Ben East," Outdoor Writers Association of America, https://owaa.org/owaa-legends/crusader-journalist-ben-east.
9. G. Mennen Williams, "Governor's Weekly Letter," *The Bessemer Herald*, July 9, 1953, 6.
10. Richey, "Crusader Journalist Ben East."
11. "Ben East's Movies of Alaska Thrill 1200 Here," *St. Joseph Herald-Press*, February 7, 1942, 5.
12. Gordon Charles, "Outdoors with Gordie," *Traverse City Record-Eagle*, January 25, 1975, 22.

EDNA FERBER: A NOTE

1. Edna Ferber, *A Peculiar Treasure* (New York: Doubleday, Doran and Co., 1939), 19, title derived from Exodus 19:5.
2. Ferber, *A Peculiar Treasure*, 19–20.

3. Ferber, *A Peculiar Treasure*, 14, 22–23. The phrase appears on facing pages, drilling home the point, and reappears in her second memoir, *A Kind of Magic* (Garden City: Doubleday and Co., 1963), 68.
4. Ferber, *A Kind of Magic*, 277. Edna Ferber, *Come and Get It* (New York: Doubleday, Doran and Co., 1935).
5. Ferber, *A Peculiar Treasure*, 371–372.

BESSIE RAY HOOVER: WRITER TO THE VERY END

1. One might wonder whether her first name sabotaged serious consideration of her capabilities, but "Bessie" once was among the most popular female names.
2. E.g., Carol Smallwood, ed., *Michigan Authors*, 3rd ed. (Michigan Association of Media in Education, 1993), 173.
3. *Herald-Palladium*, October 20, 1922, 7.
4. The map dates from 1887. The house is south of 3917 and across from 3994.
5. William L. Hyde, *History of the One Hundred and Twelfth Regiment N.Y. Volunteers* (Fredonia: W. McKinstry and Co., 1866), 187.
6. Bessie Ray Hoover, "Wayside Ambrosia," *Everybody's Magazine*, vol. 15, July–December 1906, 554.
7. Anna Lorraine Guthrie, ed., *Readers' Guide to Periodical Literature*, vol. 2 (Minneapolis: H. W. Wilson Co., 1910), 1060; Anna Lorraine Guthrie, ed., *Readers' Guide to Periodical Literature*, vol. 3 (White Plains: H. W. Wilson Co., 1915), 1236.
8. Bessie Ray Hoover, "The Anniversary Present" and "Mr. Flickinger's Vacation," T*Harper's Monthly Magazine*, vol. 117, June–November 1908, ii, 155, 803.
9. *The Book Review Digest*, vol. 5 (Minneapolis: H. W. Wilson Co., 1909), 212.
10. *The Book Review Digest*, quoting *New York Times*.
11. *The Book Review Digest*, vol. 6 (Minneapolis: H. W. Wilson Co., 1910), 192. It contained, however, no other reviews.
12. Andrews, *Michigan in Literature*, 205.
13. October 9, 1930, 12.
14. Invaluable aid was provided for this chapter by Jill Rauh, Reference and Government Information, Benton Harbor Public Library.

ISABELLA VAN WAGENEN/SOJOURNER TRUTH: GREATEST BLACK WOMAN OF THE 1800S

1. Sojourner Truth, *Narrative of Sojourner Truth: A Northern Slave, Emancipated from Bodily Servitude by the State of New York, in 1828* (Boston: J. R. Yerrinton and Son, 1850), 1.
2. Margaret Washington, ed., *Narrative of Sojourner Truth* (New York: Vintage Books, 1993), 125. The 1884 version compiles correspondence addressed to her from numerous notable individuals of the prior third century, including Jonathan Walker. See Jack Dempsey, "The Man with the Branded Hand," *Michigan History*, January/February 2015.
3. Washington, *Narrative of Sojourner Truth*, ix–x.
4. Carleton Mabee and Susan Mabee Newhouse, *Sojourner Truth: Slave, Prophet, Legend* (New York: New York University Press, 1993), 95–96.
5. Romig, *Michigan Place Names*, 252.
6. As one example, in 1877–1878 she held meetings in thirty-six Michigan towns. Sojourner Truth, *Narrative of Sojourner Truth* (Battle Creek: Review and Herald, 1884), xii.
7. Now occupied by the Fort Custer Industrial Park.
8. Nell Irvin Painter, *Sojourner Truth: A Life, a Symbol* (New York: W. W. Norton and Co., 1997), 7.
9. Mabee and Newhouse, *Sojourner Truth*, 61.
10. Painter, *Sojourner Truth*, 7–8, 242, 248, 259.
11. Marcus Robinson, "Account of the Women's Rights Convention," *The Anti-slavery Bugle*, vol. 6, no. 41 (Salem: June 21, 1851), 160.
12. Robinson, "Account of the Women's Rights Convention," 160.
13. Sojourner Truth, *Narrative of Sojourner Truth* (Boston: n.p., 1875), v.
14. Washington, *Narrative of Sojourner Truth*, xii.
15. Battle Creek: Review and Herald Office, 1884, 184–185. Several similar circumstances were also related.
16. Washington, *Narrative of Sojourner Truth*, xii.
17. Truth, *Narrative* (1884), 208–209.
18. Washington, *Narrative of Sojourner Truth*, xiii.
19. Truth, *Narrative* (1884), 216. Chapter 5 in the Mabees' work addresses this issue, albeit with speculation.
20. Washington, *Narrative of Sojourner Truth*, xxxiii, with "orality" as her medium, xxvii.

21. Truth, *Narrative* (1884), 230, 239–240, 276–277.
22. *Portrait and Biographical Album of Calhoun County, Michigan* (Chicago: Chapman Bros., 1891), 990.
23. Truth, *Narrative* (1884), 126.

DAVID SALZER BRODER: COMMUNITY OVER CELEBRITY

1. David Salzer Broder, "A Sense of Community," in *The Beaver Island Columns* (Beaver Island: Big Rock BI Pub., 2012), 25. This book was compiled by his sons, who wrote the book's introduction, published as a local fundraiser.
2. Broder, *The Beaver Island Columns*, 38, 41, 51, 52, 58, 62, 66, 69, 82–83, 85, 91, 98, 10, 119.
3. David S. Broder, "Wall Street Woes Work Against McCain," *Columbus Dispatch*, September 18, 2008.
4. Broder, *The Beaver Island Columns*, 93, 120, 133–134.
5. Laura R. Ashlee, ed., *Traveling Through Time: A Guide to Michigan's Historical Markers* (Ann Arbor: University of Michigan Press, 2005), 267.

JOHNSTON "JACK" DAVIS KERKHOFF: HOME (BITTER) SWEET HOME

1. Jack Kerkhoff, *How Thin the Veil: A Memoir of 45 Days in the Traverse City State Hospital* (Traverse City: Mission Point Press, 2023).
2. The author's book was promoted in his hometown newspaper as a journalist's coverage "of his own crack-up and recovery." The same advertisement dubbed the book "perhaps the most vivid self-portrait of its kind ever written." *Traverse City Record-Eagle*, October 25, 1952, 2.
3. Kerkhoff, *How Thin the Veil*, 22.
4. Kerkhoff, *How Thin the Veil*.
5. Kerkhoff, *How Thin the Veil*, 3.
6. Johnston Kerkhoff, "Bruno's Alibis Failed to Convince Judges in Kidnapping," *Pittsburgh Sun-Telegraph*, February 19, 1936, 9.
7. "Paper to Publish Corrective Story on Old Dominion," *Richmond Times-Dispatch*, August 28, 1943, 4.
8. The title of the article in question was "I Rode with the Flint Vigilantes." "Reporter, Cited for Contempt, Released," *Grand Rapids Press*, February 10, 1937, 17.

9. Convicted in 1894 on falsified evidence of sharing secret military information with Germany, French Artillery officer Captain Alfred Dreyfus became a cause célèbres. In 1906 he was exonerated.
10. Unsigned review, *Arcadia Tribune*, July 15, 1932, 8.
11. Kerkhoff, *How Thin the Veil*, 126.
12. Kerkhoff, *How Thin the Veil*, 304.
13. During a 1954 visit to his daughter's residence, a local newspaper said that Kerkhoff was working on a book about the newspaper business, *Eye on the World*. It was never published. "Newspaperman Returns to New York Home," *Chula Vista Star-News*, August 12, 1954, 5.
14. "Body of Man Found in Tijuana Identified," *The Star-News National City and Chula Vista*, May 4, 1958, 1.
15. F. A. Behymer, "Grist for a Writer's Mill," *St. Louis Post Dispatch*, March 9, 1953, 16.

LARRY WOIWODE: MICHIGAN'S DAKOTA BARD

1. Penelope Green, "Larry Woiwode, Who Wrote of Family, Faith and Rural Life, Dies at 80," *New York Times*, May 15, 2022, 21.
2. Thomas Woiwode, personal communication, April 25, 2023.

CHARLOTTE ARMSTRONG: UNDERGROUND DISCOVERIES

1. Rusticus, "Books in the News: The Place Fairly Teems with Corpses," *Richmond News-Leader*, February 5, 1955, 8.
2. Charlotte Armstrong, *I Know a Fellow Who Was Six-feet High: The Life of Frank Hall Armstrong* (Norway: Jake Menghini Museum, 2022).
3. The actual death toll from Michigan mining accidents of all kinds may be much higher. One source documents more than 2,300 fatalities from 1869 to 1963. "Michigan Mine Accident Index," https://miningquiz.com/pdf/Fatalities/MI_Report_various.pdf.
4. "New Armstrong Mystery Is Published: Green Bayite's Sister Has Varied and Interesting Background," *Green Bay Press-Gazette*, April 15, 1959, 14.
5. These descriptions are of Thor, the thinly disguised city of Vulcan, in Armstrong's novel based on her early life, published under the pen name Jo Valentine. *The Trouble in Thor* (New York: Coward-McCann-Inc., 1953).

6. In contrast to Vulcan, Thor derives from Norse mythology as a god associated with thunderstorms and the protection of mankind.
7. Valentine, *The Trouble in Thor*, 4.
8. "New Armstrong Mystery Is Published."
9. "New Armstrong Mystery Is Published."
10. Jerry Lewi, "A Son's Remembrance," Charlotte Amrstrong, charlottearmstrong.org/about.
11. Lewi, "A Son's Remembrance."
12. Though a critic called it "a tender little play." Arthur Pollack, "The Happiest Days, a Kind-Hearted Play about a Couple of Youngsters in Love, Opens at the Vanderbilt," *Brooklyn Daily Eagle*, April 12, 1939, 11.
13. Rick Cypert, *The Virtue of Suspense: The Life and Works of Charlotte Armstrong* (Selinsgrove: Susquehanna University Press, 2008).
14. *Green Bay Press-Gazette*, February 21, 1946, 15.
15. "Hair-Rising," unsigned book review, *Lexington Herald-Leader*, January 13, 1946, 11.
16. Robert Weaver, "Charlotte Armstrong Literate and Witty," *Toronto Star*, May 25, 1963, 31.
17. Anthony Boucher, "Criminals at Large," *New York Times*, July 15, 1951, 73.
18. "New Armstrong Mystery Is Published."
19. Valentine, *The Trouble in Thor*, 27.
20. "Charlotte Armstrong, Author of Mystery Tales, Dies at 64," *New York Times*, July 20, 1969, 57.
21. "Charlotte Armstrong 'Tops,'" *The Daily News-Journal* (Murfreesboro, Tennessee),·August 9, 1970, 18.
22. Lewi, "A Son's Remembrance."

WILLIAM CHALMERS COVERT: IN THE CATHEDRAL OF CREATION

1. The "valley" is the region where the Saginaw River, formed by the confluence of the Tittabawassee and Shiawassee rivers, drains into Lake Huron.
2. William C. Covert, *Wild Woods and Waterways* (Philadelphia: Westminster Press, 1915), 15.
3. William C. Covert, *Glory of the Pines: A Tale of the Ontonagon* (Philadelphia: Westminster Press, 1914), vii–ix, 4, 13, 23, 42, 60, 89, 162, 166, 245.
4. Romig, *Michigan Place Names*, 417. The southwest Lower Peninsula town of Covert is named for him.

5. Kathryn Bishop Eckert, *Buildings of Michigan* (New York: Oxford University Press, 1993), 484.
6. Kathryn Bishop Eckert, *Buildings of Michigan* (Charlottesville: University of Virginia Press, 2012), 497.
7. Covert, *Wild Woods and Waterways*, 59, 224, 245.

EDWARD EVERETT HALE: SUPERIOR COUNTRY

1. Van Wyck Brooks, "Introduction," in *The First Book Edition of The Man Without a Country*, by Edward E. Hale (New York: Franklin Watts Inc., 1960), v. Illustrations were by Leonard Everett Fisher, born June 24, 1924, and alive at the time of initial drafting of this chapter.
2. *The Atlantic Monthly: A Magazine of Literature, Art, and Politics*, vol. 12 (Boston: Ticknor and Fields, 1863) [December, no. 74], 665–679.
3. Edward E. Hale, *The Man Without a Country* (Boston: S. J. Parkhill and Co., 1903), iv, v.
4. Hale, *The Man Without a Country* (1903), ix.
5. His successor was Edward Cummings, father of poet E. E. Cummings. Hale served in leadership of the American Antiquarian Society and became a member of the Academy of Arts and Sciences. Poet James Russell Lowell was a classmate and friend.
6. *The Trial [of] Hon. Clement L. Vallandigham, by a Military Commission* (Cincinnati: Rickey and Carroll, 1863), 11, 14, 21, 27, 259. U.S. District Judge Humphrey H. Leavitt denied the writ. Leavitt was a Democratic Party member, appointed to the court by President Andrew Jackson.
7. James L. Vallandigham, *A Life of Clement L. Vallandigham* (Baltimore: Turnbull Brothers, 1872), 326–329, 348. He lost by over one hundred thousand votes.
8. Edward Everett Hale, *The Works of Edward Everett Hale*, Library Edition, vol. 6 (Boston: Little, Brown & Co., 1900), 338; Hale, *The Man Without a Country* (1960),8.
9. "An Act to prohibit the importation of Slaves into any port or place within the jurisdiction of the United States, from and after the first day of January, in the year of our Lord one thousand eight hundred and eight." Richard Peters, ed., *Public Statutes at Large of the United States of America*, vol. 2 (Boston: Little and Brown, 1845), 426–430. Jefferson called for the measure in his December 1806 message to Congress, labeling the trade "violations of human rights which have been so long

continued on the unoffending inhabitants of Africa." "Complete State of the Union Addresses from 1790 to 2006," Project Gutenberg, https://www.gutenberg.org/files/5050/5050-h/5050-h.htm#y1806.

10. Hale, *The Man Without a Country* (1903), 73, 77–78.
11. Hale, *The Man Without a Country* (1903), 93.
12. Hale, *The Works of Edward Everett Hale*, 324.
13. Maria Campbell and James F. Clarke, *Revolutionary Services and Civil Life of General William Hull; Prepared from His Manuscripts* (New York: D. Appleton and Co., 1847), 33–38.
14. "Mr. Melville's Lecture," *Detroit Free Press*, June 24, 1898, 10.
15. Andrews, *Michigan in Literature*, 234; Boston: Roberts Bros., 1873.
16. Hale, *The Man Without a Country* (1960), v; the 1962 version improved upon the original 1949 edition. William B. Jones Jr., *Classics Illustrated: A Cultural History*, 2nd ed. (Jefferson: McFarland and Co., 2011), 74, 176, 325 (this compendium is a tour-de-force); see also William B. Jones Jr., "*Classics Illustrated* and the Evolving Art of Comic-Book Literary Adaptation," in *The Oxford Handbook of Adaptation Studies*, ed. Thomas Leitch (New York: Oxford University Press, 2017), 214–236.
17. Brianne Turczynski is also author of *Proper Mourning: A Legend's Tale* (Detroit: Vintage House Press, 2018), and *Detroit's Lost Poletown: The Little Neighborhood That Touched a Nation* (Charleston: The History Press, 2021).

JAMES THOMAS HARRISON: WORD WEAVER

1. Bill Castanier, "Remembering the MI Roots of Author, Poet Jim Harrison," WKAR Public Media, March 28, 2016, https://www.wkar.org/arts-culture/2016-03-28/remembering-the-mi-roots-of-author-poet-jim-harrison.
2. Daniel Wanschura, "The Woman who Helped Jim Harrison Write," Interlochen Public Radio, October 20, 2017, https://www.interlochenpublicradio.org/news/2017-10-20/the-woman-who-helped-jim-harrison-write.
3. Doug Peacock, "Doug Peacock Remembers Jim Harrison," Elk River Books, April 2, 2016, https://elkriverbooks.com/peacock-harrison.
4. Will Hearst, "She Helped Him 'Do Life,'" *Alta*, September 27, 2021, https://www.altaonline.com/books/poetry/a37419647/joyce-harrington-bahle-jim-harrison-will-hearst-q-a.
5. Joseph Bednarik, ed., *The Sumac Reader* (East Lansing: Michigan State University Press, 1997).

6. Other awards included the MSU College of Arts and Letters Distinguished Alumni Award, the MSU Distinguished Alumni Award, and membership in the American Academy of Arts and Letters.
7. Brautigan was author of *Trout Fishing in America* (San Francisco: Four Seasons Foundation, 1967).
8. Jimmy Buffett, "Jimmy Buffett Remembers Jim Harrison," Literary Hub, March 31, 2016, https://lithub.com/jimmy-buffett-remembers-jim-harrison/. Ford produced the mid-size Cortina largely overseas.
9. The Pickle Barrel House, corner of Lake and Randolph streets. The 1964 State historical marker for the town may hold the record for the most uses of the signage's place-name, eight (!), in the "same text both sides" format.
10. Harrison, *The Essential Poems*, 24.
11. Harrison, *The Essential Poems*, 213.
12. Harrison, *The Essential Poems*, 206.
13. Garrison Keillor, "A Hymn for Jim Harrison," *Chicago Tribune*, March 31, 2016, https://www.chicagotribune.com/entertainment/books/ct-prj-jim-harrison-garrison-keillor-20160331-story.html.

ALDO LEOPOLD: HABITAT FOR HUMILITY

1. "About Aldo," Aldo Leopold Festival, http://www.aldoleopoldfestival.org.
2. Curt Meine, *Aldo Leopold: His Life and Work* (Madison: University of Wisconsin Press, 1988).
3. Meine, *Aldo Leopold.*
4. "Aldo Leopold," Wisconsin Conservation Hall of Fame, https://wchf.org/aldo-leopold.
5. Aldo Leopold, *Game Management* (Madison: University of Wisconsin Press, 1986), i.
6. Aldo Leopold, *A Sand County Almanac and Sketches Here and There* (Oxford, UK: Oxford University Press, 1949).
7. Leopold, *A Sand County Almanac.*
8. The Aldo Leopold Archives, University of Wisconsin-Madison, https://search.library.wisc.edu/digital/AAldoLeopold.
9. The Huron Mountain Club is an enclave of over twenty thousand privately owned acres west of Big Bay in the Upper Peninsula. Henry Ford is an example of the prominent and wealthy who have been members.

10. Aldo Leopold, "Report on Huron Mountain Club," privately published, 1938, 1.
11. Aldo Leopold, "The Last Stand," Outdoor America, 1942, quoted in "Aldo Leopold and 'The Last Stand,'" Friends of the Porkies, https://porkies.org.
12. In 2025, the festival ran from May 28 to June 1.

JOHN BARTLOW MARTIN: MESMERIZED BY THE U.P.

1. John Bartlow Martin, *Call It North Country: A History of Upper Michigan* (New York: A. A. Knopf, 1944; repr., Detroit: Wayne State University Press, 1986).
2. John Bartlow Martin, *Call It North Country: The Story of Upper Michigan* (Detroit: Wayne State University Press, 1986), 23.
3. Martin, *Call It North Country*, 8.
4. "'Call It North Country' Tells History of U.P.," *Escanaba Daily Press*. May 6, 1944, 10.
5. "Writer John Bartlow Martin, Former Envoy, Journalism Prof," obituary, *Chicago Tribune*, January 5, 1987, 20.
6. Ray E. Boomhower, "John Bartlow Martin: Smith Lake Camp, Herman, MI," *The New Territory*, https://newterritorymag.com/literary-landscapes/john-bartlow-martin-herman-michigan.
7. John Bartlow Martin, "There Goes Upper Michigan," *Harper's Magazine*, December 1947, 559–561.
8. Martin, "There Goes Upper Michigan," 559.

JOHN MOODY: A RIDDLE WRAPPED IN A MYSTERY INSIDE AN ENIGMA

1. David Pearson, *Speaking Volumes: Books with Histories* (Oxford: Bodleian Library Publishing, 2022), 1.
2. The LOC is home to the Center for the Book, promoting books and libraries, literacy and reading, and poetry and literature since its founding in 1977.
3. *The Book Review Digest*, vol. 5 (Minneapolis: H. W. Wilson Co., 1909).
4. Thomas Gibson, *Simple Principles of Investment* (Garden City: Doubleday, Page and Co., 1919).
5. "Book Library," Index Fund Advisors, https://www.ifa.com/book-library.
6. Thomas Enright, *The King of Nobody's Island* (New York: Gibson Publishing Co., 1909), https://digitalcollections.library.gvsu.edu/document/26255.

7. Clarence Andrews, "A Bibliography of the Literature and Lore, Together With Historical Materials, of the Upper Peninsula of Michigan," *The Great Lakes Review* 3, no. 1 (Summer 1976), 37, 45.
8. Named for a store owner/postmaster and by the Native Americans, respectively. Romig, *Michigan Place Names*, 83, 584.
9. In another coincidental link, Gibson wrote on the subject of "scalping" in a "Special Letter" dated February 14, 1907: "There are many different methods and degrees of scalping. The word is supposed to express all the forms of trading between the 'Chaser of eighths' and the man who operates for a profit of several points." *Thomas Gibson's Market Letters for 1907* (New York: The Gibson Publishing Company, 1908), 10. The word is employed in a different, more dramatic way in *Nobody's Island*.
10. *Successful American*, vol. 7, no. 3, March 1903, 172–173.
11. "About Us," Moody's, http://www.moodys.com/moodys/cust/AboutMoodys/AboutMoodys.aspx?topic=history.
12. He died on February 16, 1958, age eighty-nine.
13. This from his first partial autobiography, *The Long Road Home*. Perhaps a hint of the reason for his cloaking of identity is the self-effacing statement on the first page: "Why should I, a man of no importance outside my little world, indulge in such insufferable conceit as to write a story about myself, and flaunt it before the public." He did so, ostensibly, because—like the *King* book—the story had a happy ending. He had discovered that the successful businessman was not to be envied because "they were mainly discontented, unhappy men." John Moody, *The Long Road Home* (New York: Macmillan Co., 1933), vii, viii, ix, 129, 148, 151.
14. Moody, *The Long Road Home*, 151.
15. Dave Dempsey, *Superior Shores: A Novel of Conservation* (pub. by author, 2010).
16. Moody, *The Long Road Home*, 59, 60–61.
17. Moody, *The Long Road Home*, 123, 39 ("History interested me most," 32), 91, 40–43, 215, 59–61, 96.
18. "Official Railroad Map of Wisconsin, 1900," Library of Congress, https://www.loc.gov/resource/g4121p.ct001917/?r=0.503,0.297,0.178,0.083,0; *A History of the Origin of the Place Names in Nine Northwestern States Connected with the Chicago & North Western and Chicago, St. Paul, Minneapolis & Omaha Railways* (Chicago: n.p., 1908), 136.
19. On the other hand, the protagonist is threatened: "If you are in the Manitowish Waters one week from to-day, you will never leave them alive" (Moody, *The Long Road Home*, 119). One must "go down to Manitowish" (128). "Brief pilgrimages"

are made to Manitowish, clearly the town, for supplies, but only every two or three weeks, suggesting a bit of a journey.

20. John Donne, "Meditation XVII," in *Devotions Upon Emergent Occasions* (1623).
21. Not many Michiganders are aware of the University of Notre Dame Environmental Research Center Land O' Lakes, the school's property on the border of Wisconsin and Michigan west of the town of that name. Occupying some seven thousand heavily wooded acres with roughly thirty lakes, the area's lush vegetation and placid waters invite visitors to leave daily anxieties behind to be enveloped in the serene, natural beauty as they study nature. Donated in the 1930s, most of the buildings are on the Michigan side.
22. A book of that shortened title by Beatrice Grimshaw appeared within a score of years: *Nobody's Island* (Garden City: Doubleday, Page Co., 1923).
23. In September 1967, First Lady Johnson officially dedicated the area in a ceremony at Clark Lake.
24. Friends of Sylvania, https://www.friendsofsylvania.org.
25. Bonnie Peacock, *Sylvania* (Waite Park: Park Press Inc., 1986), 44.
26. Robert D. Meade, "'You Can't Escape Autobiography': New Letters of Thomas Wolfe," *The Atlantic*, vol. 166, November 1940, 80.
27. Thomas Enright, *The King of Nobody's Island* (New York: Gibson Publishing Co., 1909), https://www.loc.gov/item/09019034/.

CHARLES KIRK MUNROE: A TALE OF PENINSULAS

1. Annie Fields, ed., *Life and Letters of Harriet Beecher Stowe* (Boston: Houghton Mifflin and Co., 1897), 269.
2. "Book Review: The Copper Princess," *Journal of Education* 48, no. 24 (December 22, 1898), 407.
3. *Detroit Free Press*, December 5, 1898, 7.
4. Kirk Munroe, *The Copper Princess: A Story of Lake Superior Mines* (New York: Harper & Brothers), 5.
5. "Michigan Center for Data and Analytics, Upper Peninsula Michigan Works! 2024 Annual Planning Information and Workforce Analysis Reports," Michigan Center for Data and Analytics, May 1, 2024, https://www.michigan.gov/mcda/-/media/Project/Websites/mcda/reports/2024/apiwar/PlanningReports2024_Upper_Peninsula. pdf?rev=c7d42607828842299c9c56c 19b752d42&hash=822764EE56809AB31055C1C6F2C287A2.

6. A new book explores the subject, really: Bob Otwell, *The Real Two Hearted: Life, Love, and Lore Along Michigan's Most Iconic River* (Traverse City: Mission Point Press, 2024).
7. "First Official Visitation Data Released for the World's Longest Hiking-Only Trail," Appalachian Trail Conservancy, March 13, 2026, https://appalachiantrail.org/news-stories/appalachian-trail-16-9-million-visits-2025/.
8. "2023 Annual Report," North Country Trail Association, 4, https://northcountrytrail.org/files/transparency/2023%20Annual%20Report.pdf.

WILLIAM ANGUS MURDOCH: YOU GIVE ME FEVER

1. The source for these two quotes is an unattributed typeset article (perhaps from the dust jacket) clipped and pasted inside front pages of the authors' family copy of Angus Murdoch, *Boom Copper: The Story of the First U.S. Mining Boom* (New York: MacMillan Company, 1943).
2. Murdoch, *Boom Copper*.
3. The source for this quote is an article pasted inside the authors' family copy of the book.
4. Murdoch, *Boom Copper*, 1.
5. Murdoch, *Boom Copper*.
6. *Detroit Free Press*, April 8, 1979, 123.
7. Clarence Andrews, "A Bibliography of the Literature and Lore, Together with Historical Materials, of the Upper Peninsula of Michigan," *The Great Lakes Review*, vol. 3, no. 1, Summer 1976, 37, 54.
8. Owen C. Deatrick, "Copper Country Gets Its Historian," *Detroit Free Press*, March 21, 1943, 57.
9. Erik Nordberg, "Selected Readings on Lake Superior Copper Mining," Michigan Technological University, August 24, 2005.
10. *New York Times*, April 4, 1943, Section BR, 26.
11. F. E. Richter, *Journal of Economic History* 4, no. 2 (November 1944): 226–228.
12. Murdoch, *Boom Copper*, 245. See, e.g., C. Harry Benedict, *Red Metal: The Calumet & Hecla Story* (Ann Arbor: University of Michigan Press, 1952); Mary Doria Russell, *The Women of the Copper Country: A Novel* (New York: Atria, 2019) (fictional history).
13. Bruce Catton, *Michigan: A Bicentennial History* (New York: W. W. Norton and Co., 1976), 58, 93.

14. Ernest Hemingway, "The Last Good Country," in *The Nick Adams Stories* (New York: Bantam Books, 1973), 80.
15. Linda Nemec Foster, "Copper Harbor: Early October," in *Poetry in Michigan/ Michigan in Poetry*, ed. William Olsen and Jack Ridl (Kalamazoo: Western Michigan University, 2013), 47.

JANE JOHNSTON SCHOOLCRAFT/O-BAH-BAHM-WAWA-GE-ZHE-GO-QUA: POET OF STARS IN THE SKY

1. Robert Dale Parker, ed., *The Sound the Stars Make Rushing Through the Sky: The Writings of Jane Johnston Schoolcraft* (Philadelphia: University of Pennsylvania Press, 2007), 2, 45, 141. Parker's approbation of her literary skill is significant as a professor of American literature and critical theory who wrote academic critiques of William Faulkner.
2. One twentieth-century study by a former Michigan governor and spouse noted her "literary interests" and how "physically, mentally and spiritually she was out of the ordinary." She was reported to be gentle and soft-spoken and "an unusually intelligent woman" with "a highly cultivated mind." Chase S. Osborn and Stellanova Osborn, *Schoolcraft-Longfellow-Hiawatha* (Lancaster: Jaques Cattell Press, 1942), 528, 530–532.
3. Parker, *The Sound the Stars Make*, 124.
4. Tammrah Stone-Gordon, *Woman of the Sound the Stars Make Rushing Through the Sky: A Literary Biography of Jane Johnston Schoolcraft* (East Lansing: Michigan State University, 1993, Master's Thesis), xviii, xxi, xxiii–xxiv, 26.
5. Stone-Gordon, *Woman of the Sound the Stars Make*, 32.
6. Richard G. Bremer, *Indian Agent and Wilderness Scholar: The Life of Henry Rowe Schoolcraft* (Mount Pleasant: Clarke Historical Library, 1987), 94, 96–97, 105.
7. Osborn and Osborn, *Schoolcraft-Longfellow-Hiawatha*, 515.
8. Laura R. Ashlee, ed., *Traveling Through Time: A Guide to Michigan's Historical Markers* (Ann Arbor: University of Michigan Press, 2005), 91.
9. Parker, *The Sound the Stars Make*, 13, 32–33.
10. Philip P. Mason, ed., *Schoolcraft: The Literary Voyager or Muzzeniegun* (East Lansing: Michigan State University Press, 1962), xxii.
11. Bremer, *Indian Agent and Wilderness Scholar*, 216–217. She used the drug on the advice of physicians, and it was not an uncommon prescription. Parker, *The Sound the Stars Make*, 42.

12. Bremer, *Indian Agent and Wilderness Scholar*, 229, 255.
13. He did visit Ontario in 1846. He would also remarry a South Carolina widow and slave owner; Henry advised her "of his acceptance of slavery," thus enabling the marriage. Bremer, *Indian Agent and Wilderness Scholar*, 256, 289.
14. Mason, *Schoolcraft*, 26–27, 157–158, 38–39.
15. Parker, *The Sound the Stars Make*, 35, 56, 132.
16. The term "métis" is French and refers to a person of mixed Indigenous and Euro-American ancestry.
17. Bremer, *Indian Agent and Wilderness Scholar*, xxiv–xxv.
18. Stone-Gordon, *Woman of the Sound the Stars Make*, 4.
19. Mason, *Schoolcraft*, 1, 5, 171 n. 39–40.
20. Parker, *The Sound the Stars Make*, 2, 56–58.
21. According to the Statement of Significance, the structure "is significant for its association with Henry Rowe Schoolcraft, noted explorer, author, and student of Native American culture." No mention was made of Jane.
22. See the addendum for the inscription on Jane Schoolcraft's Gravestone.
23. E.g., Parker, *The Sound the Stars Make*, 89, 92, 118, 120–121. "Plethoric" means excessive.
24. Osborn, *Schoolcraft-Longfellow-Hiawatha*, 532, 534.
25. Alternate nomenclature includes "Bamewawagezhikaquay" and "The Sound the Stars Make Rushing Through the Sky."
26. Parker, *The Sound the Stars Make*, 36, 48, 93–94, 105, 109, 147.
27. Osborn, *Schoolcraft-Longfellow-Hiawatha*, 537.

BOOKSHOPS

1. Evan Friss, *The Bookshop: A History of the American Bookstore* (New York: Penguin Books, 2024), 5.
2. Barnes & Noble locations are in Allen Park, Ann Arbor, Battle Creek, Flint, Fort Gratiot Township, Grand Rapids, Grandville, Green Oak Township, Holland, Lansing, Midland, Northville, Orion Township, Portage, Rochester Hills, Saginaw, Shelby Township, and Troy. Books-A-Million stores: Beverly Hills, Kalamazoo, and Traverse City.
3. In 2022, the four-story Detroit location, encompassing forty-five thousand square feet, ranked fifth largest on the list of North American private bookshops.
4. Gratitude to Yvette Collins of Lansing for the list.

LIBRARIES

1. Included in Kenneth Breisch, *American Libraries, 1730–1950* (New York: W. W. Norton and Co., 2017), 224. Also mentioned are the Peter White (Marquette), Ryerson (Grand Rapids), and Kalamazoo and Muskegon library facilities.
2. Heartwarming is the reopening of DPL branches closed by economic and pandemic causes. An announcement in early 2025 of a $3 million grant from the Downtown Development Authority promised reopening of the Skillman branch at 121 Gratiot Ave.
3. "About," Hillsdale Community Library, https://hillsdale-library.org/about/.
4. "History of the Library," Chelsea District Library, https://www.chelseadistrictlibrary.org/about-us/who-we-are/history-of-the-library/.
5. Subtitled from Confucius, *Day to Our Own* (New York: Dial Press, 1939), v–vii.
6. Gratitude to Grand Rapids History Center, Grand Rapids Public Library, for providing a copy.
7. Jack Dempsey, *Capitol Park: Historic Heart of Detroit* (Charleston: History Press, 2014), 36.
8. Laura R. Ashlee, ed., *Traveling Through Time: A Guide to Michigan's Historical Markers* (Ann Arbor: University of Michigan Press, 2005), 290.
9. Manistee & North-Eastern Railroad, *Near to Nature's Heart in a Corner of Michigan* (Toledo: B.F. Wade & Sons Co., 1909).

AREAS OF OUTSTANDING NATURAL BEAUTY

1. Mary Frances Doner, *Blue River* (Garden City: Doubleday & Co., 1946), 8.
2. Frances Margaret Fox, *Nancy Davenport* (New York: Rand McNally & Co., 1928), 160.
3. "10 Best Places to See Fall Colors in the United States," *USA Today* 10 Best, September 17, 2025, https://10best.usatoday.com/awards/best-destination-for-fall-colors/.
4. "Michigan's Upper Peninsula Named USA Today's Best Fall Foliage Destination," Upper Peninsula Travel and Recreation Association, https://www.uptravel.com/blog/post/usa-todays-best-fall-foliage-destination/.

HISTORICAL SITES AND THINGS

1. Charles C. Jewett, *Notices of Public Libraries in the United States of America* (Washington, D.C.: 1851), 184–185.
2. Mildred Louise Jackson, "'Do what you can': Creating an Institution, the Ladies' Library Associations in Michigan, 1852–1900" (PhD diss., Michigan State University, 1998), 1, https://doi.org/doi:10.25335/gw7t-rx61.
3. *Address Delivered by His Excellency, Gov. Henry H. Crapo, at the Dedication of the Library Building of the Ladies' Library Association of Flint, on June 30th, 1868* (Flint: Wolverine Citizen Steam Press, 1868), 7.
4. Mrs. A.F. Bixby and Mrs. A. Howell, *Historical Sketches of the Ladies' Library Associations of the State of Michigan* (Adrian: Times and Expositor Steam Print, 1876).
5. Laura R. Ashlee, ed., *Traveling Through Time: A Guide to Michigan's Historical Markers* (Ann Arbor: University of Michigan Press, 2005), 17, 27, 142, 228, 238–239, 442.
6. *Cadillac Evening News*, June 12, 1971, 47.
7. Percy H. Andrus, "Historical Markers and Memorials in Michigan," *Michigan History Magazine*, vol. 15, Spring 1931, 167–168, 171, 262, 277, 279.
8. Michigan Historical Commission, *Historic Michigan: A Guide to Michigan's Official State Markers* (Lansing: Michigan Historical Commission, 1958), 1.

RAGGLE-TAGGLE

1. Julie Kenyon, "'Little Girl Bay,' Frontier, and Folklore: Fitzgerald's Use of Regional History in *The Great Gatsby*," *The F. Scott Fitzgerald Review* 16, no. 1 (2018): 109–126.
2. F. Scott Fitzgerald, *The Great Gatsby* (New York: C. Scribner's Sons, 1925), 120.
3. James Fenimore Cooper, *The Oak Openings; or, the Bee-Hunter* (New York: Burgess, Stringer and Company, 1848), 10–11.
4. "Oak Openings," Michigan Natural Features Inventory, Michigan State University, https://mnfi.anr.msu.edu/communities/description/10691/oak-openings.
5. Herman Melville, *Moby Dick; or, The Whale* (New York: Harper and Brothers, 1851), 272.
6. *Detroit Free Press*, January 14, 1858, 1.
7. The Two-Hearted gets a full treatment in a book authored by Bob Otwell, *The Real*

Two Hearted: Life, Love, and Lore Along Michigan's Most Iconic River (Traverse City: Michigan Point Press, 2024).

8. John N. MacLean, "The Power of the Unsaid: John N. Maclean on Ernest Hemingway's *Big Two-Hearted River*," Literary Hub May 11, 2023, https://lithub.com/the-power-of-the-unsaid-john-n-maclean-on-ernest-hemingways-big-two-hearted-river/.
9. Ernest Hemingway, "Big Two-Hearted River," in *The Nick Adams Stories*, ed. Philip Young (New York: Bantam, 1973).
10. *The Letters of Ernest Hemingway, Volume I, 1907–1922*, ed. Sandra Spanier and Robert W. Trogdon (Cambridge: Cambridge University Press, 2011), 183.
11. Walter Harding, ed., *Thoreau's Minnesota Journey: Two Documents* (Geneseo: Thoreau Society Inc., 1962), 25.
12. *Boston Post*, June 28, 1845, 1.
13. Martha Stewart, "My Colorful and Fragrant Lilacs," *Martha: Up Close & Personal* (blog), May 4, 2024, https://www.themarthablog.com/2024/05/my-colorful-and-fragrant-lilacs.html.
14. Len Trankina, *Mackinac Island Memories* (Indianapolis: Travel Memories Press, 1999), 35.
15. "Syringa," University of Michigan Herbarium, https://michiganflora.net/genus/Syringa.
16. Jennifer Bennett, *Lilacs for the Garden* (Buffalo: Firefly Books Inc., 2002), 17, 57.
17. Philip Levine, *The Mercy: Poems* (New York: Alfred A. Knopf Inc., 1999), 41.

IN TRIBUTE

1. All cites are to Philip P. Mason, *Tracy W. McGregor* (Detroit: Wayne State University Press, 2008), 123, 169–174, 215, 218.